JOYCECHOYCE

A. Norman Jeffares was born in Dublin and now lives in Fife Ness in Scotland. He has held several professorships and published many books including *A History of Anglo-Irish Literature* (1982), *W. B. Yeats: A New Biography* (1988), *Yeats: The Love Poems* (1990) and *Jonathan Swift: The Selected Poems* (1992).

Brendan Kennelly was born in County Kerry and is now professor of Modern Literature at Trinity College, Dublin. He has published many books, including *Cromwell* (1987), *A Time for Voices: Selected Poems 1960-1990* (1990) and *The Book of Judas* (1991). His version of Euripides' *Medea* was published in 1991. He has edited the *Penguin Book of Irish Verse* (1970, 1990).

JOYCECHOYCE

THE POEMS IN VERSE AND PROSE
OF
JAMES JOYCE

edited by
A. NORMAN JEFFARES AND BRENDAN KENNELLY

KYLE CATHIE LIMITED

A. Norman Jeffares and Brendan Kennelly are hereby identified as editors of
this work in accordance with Section 77 of the Copyright, Designs and
Patents Act 1988

This collection first published 1992 by
Kyle Cathie Limited
3 Vincent Square, London SW1P 2LX

ISBN 1 85626 066 6 paperback

A Cataloguing in Publication record for this title
is available from the British Library

Typeset by DP Photosetting, Aylesbury, Bucks
Printed and bound in Great Britain by Biddles Ltd, Guildford, Surrey

CONTENTS

From *Dubliners*

From *Stephen Hero*

CONTENTS

From *A Portrait of the Artist as a Young Man*

From *Ulysses*

ACKNOWLEDGEMENTS

The Editors and Publishers wish to thank the following for permission to quote from copyright material.

The Society of Authors as literary representatives of the Estate of James Joyce to quote from *Finnegans Wake* and *Ulysses* in European countries where the texts remain in copyright.

Random Century Group for material from *Stephen Hero*.

Faber and Faber Ltd for letters taken from *Letters of James Joyce* edited by Stuart Gilbert and *Letters of James Joyce Volume Two* edited by Richard Ellmann.

FOREWORD

We believe that James Joyce's work which began in lyric poetry developed into superb comic epic. In this book we have included most of his verse (the whole of *Chamber Music* and *Pomes Penyeach* as well as other poems and some squibs from letters) and have selected from *Dubliners*, *Stephen Hero*, *A Portrait of the Artist as a Young Man*, *Ulysses* and *Finnegans Wake* passages (to which we have given titles to assist in their identification) which we regard as poems in verse or prose that illustrate the development of this great twentieth-century author's mind and art. Always the musician, Joyce moved towards a use of language as music, fulfilling Walter Pater's dictum that 'all art aspires to the condition of music'.

In 1903 another great Irish writer, W. B. Yeats, admired the poetic technique of the youthful Joyce, regarding it as 'much better than the technique of any young Dublin man I have met during my time'. When *Ulysses* was published in 1922 Yeats found in it 'our Irish cruelty also our kind of strength', considering the Martello Tower episode full of beauty, the work of 'a cruel playful mind like a great soft tiger cat'. From being regarded as a young Dublin man, Joyce was now seen by the older writer as representing Irish qualities. Yeats died in 1939, the year in which *Finnegans Wake* was published. He would surely have recognised its achievement of universality. That achievement is multifold: dreaming fantasy, dramatic dialogue, narrative variety and skill, imaginative richness, poetic technique and innovative invention. These skills inform and indeed irradiate Joyce's last book: it is the culmination of his work with words, the comic creation of an indomitable individual human spirit.

This choice of Joyce's poetry is intended for continuous reading; we have avoided academic comment and interpretation, believing Joyce should be read – preferably aloud – without interruption. Instead we offer a brief Afterword (p. 260) as a guide to the works in which his poetry appeared.

INTRODUCTION

By October 1904 when James Joyce made his final decision to leave
Ireland, taking Nora Barnacle with him, he had written the poems of
Chamber Music (1907), which he once described as a suite of songs.
Had he been a musician, he supposed, he would have set them to music
himself. Many others have done so, for the poems are reminiscent of
Elizabethan and Cavalier poetry in their lyric quality. They express
their traditional idealism with a refined elegance and technical skill,
reminding us not only of Ben Jonson but of Tom Moore in their
fluency. Moore wanted the music to which he sang his Irish melodies
to be printed with his words, and Joyce, like Moore, had a fine voice. It
is well to emphasise that Joyce grew up in a city with a strong and
popular musical life, that he is part of a long tradition of oral literature
and that his writing is at its best when read aloud.

In his first book of poems there emerges an impressive ability to
handle language with assurance and energy. Joyce was for ever
intellectually curious; he stocked his mind with traditional images and
ideas and then set this knowledge to serve his narrative imagination.
He was a storyteller *par excellence*. *Chamber Music* has a narrative
order (no matter that Joyce's original order of the poems was altered,
at his request, by his brother Stanislaus), but Joyce was soon to expand
beyond this: the lyric mode suited some of his purpose, but stripping
his ideas down to bare essentials was too restrictive for his reflective but
restless genius; ultimately he needed the epic form to accommodate his
overflowing inventiveness.

His Catholic education was traditional. Aristotle and Aquinas shaped
his thought processes, but within his classicism there worked the yeast
of Gaelic exuberance. His creative impulses were akin in their rich
complexity to those of the monks who wrote the text of the gospels in

the Book of Kells but could not refrain from the delight of decorating capitals and filling spaces with strange beasts and complex designs. *Stephen Hero*, which he began in Dublin in 1904, was to be an account not only of the frustrations Joyce experienced in his intellectual rebellion against the Catholicism in which he had been brought up and educated, but also of his attitudes to art and his aspirations as an artist. As in *Chamber Music*, he was stripping away, striving to get to the basic truths of experience.

In *Stephen Hero*, however, Joyce moves from the images, the rhyme and the rhythm of the lyric into a fresh use of words: he was creating the epiphany. We can see him developing his theories about art in 'The poet at work' (p. 68), 'The classical temper' (p. 69) and 'The role of the poet' (p. 71) and exemplifying some of them in 'The nature of an epiphany' (p. 108). 'The Sisters', the first story in *Dubliners* (also begun in 1904), from which we have selected 'The Word' (p. 50), presents in miniature Joyce's lifelong preoccupation, a detached contemplation of what he saw as the paralysis of the universe, a fascination which could make him both fearful and fertile. He was to develop, however, from this concept of words denoting paralysis to their capacity in *Finnegans Wake* (see 'In my end is my beginning', p. 254) to convey flowingness, not only the movement of the stream of consciousness but the eternity of fluent narrative.

Stephen Hero, then, gives us more than the temporary scaffolding of direct autobiography; it tests Joyce's expanding artistic theories against the ordinariness of life, creating an objectivity, often by way of dramatic dialogue shot through with a reductive ironic wit still characteristic of much Dublin conversation. 'Improving on Shelley' (p. 80), 'Students' views of love and freedom' (p. 106) and 'The extravagant gesture' (p. 106) add ingredients likely to shock the bourgeoisie, while 'A sultry summer' (p. 93), sardonic and deadpan though it may be, is defensive in its treatment of the situations in which the author finds himself. 'Non credo' (p. 82) gives a jesting treatment to the artist's spiritual wrestling, its nature made clearer in 'The individual conscience' (p. 87). Joyce is struggling to free himself from the fetters of his church, to find himself as an individual. Sometimes, however, there is the counter-pointing, the simple enjoyment of a relevant jest, as in 'The parable of the monkeys and the missionaries; or, the results of chastity' (p. 112).

The epiphanies in *Dubliners* are experimental: they are attempts to capture the nature of an experience; thus the emotional enjoyment of excitement felt by the boys who are miching is largely encapsulated in 'Crossing the Liffey' (p. 51), as the agonies of self-awareness are realised in 'Smiles' (p. 50), 'Happiness' (p. 51), 'Love and Enchantment' (p. 52), 'Leaving home' (p. 54), 'Retreat from escape' (p. 54), or 'Loneliness' (p. 00).

Just as Joyce's writing seemed to transcend the lyric form but did not abandon it – for lyricism runs through his subsequent work (and through several of his letters to Nora, who seemed to him, in his letters of 1909, to be the beauty and the doom of his race, like a dark-blue, rain-drenched wildflower in some wild tangled hedge) – so he moved beyond the limits of the short story; not, however, before showing that genre could be made to include a wide range of emotional experience and culminate in a disturbing denouement in the final episode of 'The Dead', which we have called 'Beyond the Shannon: the romance of the west' (p. 61). Joyce, like Maria Edgeworth, Lady Morgan and Maturin before him, like Yeats and Synge too, realised the great difference between the Irish-speaking west and the English-speaking east of Ireland. Beyond the Shannon lived a passionate people bred upon different customs and values, upon myth, upon the spoken histories of heroes, patterns of thought, legends and sagas invented by poets and passed on through folk tradition. Gabriel in 'The Dead' learns of the young man in Galway who had loved his wife and had, she thought, died for her. Gabriel thinks of how his wife had 'locked in her heart for so many years that image of her lover's eyes when he had told her that he did not wish to live.' Gabriel had 'never felt like that towards any woman but he knew such a feeling must be love.' The prose dissolves the solid world of the story into the snow softly falling into the dark mutinous Shannon waves. Joyce had found his way of blending poetry and prose together in a new freedom of expression that he was to develop still further in *A Portrait of the Artist as a Young Man*.

In this honed, polished and concentrated version of *Stephen Hero*, Joyce finished his preparatory work. He can now convey intensity of perception, can compel language into creative courses within which it can capture ecstasy, despair, desire, ambition. The wordsmith is at work. Indeed he shows how he works, 'Instant inspiration' (p. 123) conveying the way he composes a villanelle. In 'A vision of Hell' (p. 116) alliteration is applied, assurance too, to give deliberate emphasis to the devilish description, whereas in 'An unearthly vision' (p. 118) the 'dappled seaborne clouds' drift across Dublin Bay and pose a question, weighing the pleasure of perception of the sensible word through the prism of a language 'many coloured and richly storied' against the inner vision, the inner world of individual emotion 'mirrored perfectly in a lucid supple periodic prose.' Joyce can ask such questions freely. What did it mean? In 'Ecstasy' (p. 120) he suddenly achieves the result. The reader reads – or, better, the listener hears the description of the girl on the strand, of the faint noise of gently moving water as she stirs it with her foot hither and thither. It broke the silence, 'low and faint and whispering, faint as the bells of sleep; hither and thither, hither and thither: and a faint flame trembled on her cheek.' And Joyce breaks the silence too: 'Heavenly God! cried Stephen's soul, in an outburst of profane joy.'

Joyce's skills are fully at his disposal now: time for going away – 'Away! Away to the reality of experience!' (p. 130). In that experience joy was to be a vital ingredient. The horizons expanded beyond Dublin Bay, beyond the Adriatic, beyond Rome and Zurich and Paris, for Joyce became a cosmic writer, and, beyond that, the great poet of comic epic.

Epic was to give him scope as exile did. He could use the structure of Homer's *Odyssey* and people Homer's heroic world with a new set of characters: twentieth-century people, Leopold Bloom, Molly his wife and Stephen Dedalus, all very different, unheroic characters, different indeed from Homer's larger-than-life Ulysses, Penelope and Telemachus. Joyce's awareness of tradition went back to Homer the storyteller, the creator of epic; it also included Homer's successors, Virgil, Dante and Milton. And in an episode of *Ulysses* he provided a virtual history of English literature in parody of styles, as well as seizing upon the style of Irish epic in 'The rich resources of Gaelic Ireland' (p. 159). The Bible is there, of course, and the Hellenic–Hebraic traditions blend beautifully in 'Citizen Cyclops and Elijah Bloom' (p. 161) – the Dublin dialogue caught so cleverly by Joyce the listener in the repetition of 'Eh, mister! Your fly is open, mister!' – the episode culminating in its crisply comic alliterative anticlimax: 'And they beheld Him, even Him, ben Bloom Elijah, amid clouds of angels ascend to the glory of the brightness at an angle of fortyfive degrees over Donohoe's in Little Green Street like a shot off a shovel.'

Homer could relax tension with comic episodes. In the *Iliad* there is the quarrel of the goddesses, in the *Odyssey* the lay of the love of Ares and Aphrodite, or, in the terms of *Ulysses*, the cuckolding of Hephaestus. But Homer also had moments of intense beauty or poignancy: there is, for instance, the episode in the *Iliad* of Hector playing with his son Astyanax before going out to his death at the hands of Achilles (Bloom's love for his dead son Rudy comes to mind when we remember Priam going to the fierce Achilles to beg back Hector's body); there is all the delicacy of the Nausicaa episode in the *Odyssey* (with its echoes, too, in *Ulysses*). Joyce learned his lessons from the master, from the reciter's need to hold an audience: he realised the need for changes in subject, in the speed and tone of the narrative, the story: and he supplied this need, this demand, through variety not only of style but of substance. The clear lyricism of the early poems and the more personal note of *Pomes Penyeach* shines through the texture of *Ulysses*. He telescoped the events of his epic into a day; he compressed them into the city of Dublin, a city of walkers amid the trams, and horsedrawn drays, and cabs, and outside cars. 'Dublin Bay' (p. 173) encapsulates a summer evening there, while the reverie of 'Nightscape' (p. 175) also embraces Howth settled for slumber, but ends with a reminder of the comicality of life: 'And far on Kish bank the anchored lightship twinkled, winked at Mr Bloom.'

Ulysses, however, is not completely comic in character: it would not, perhaps, gain its surprise effects if it were. It gains by contrast. In 'The cracked lookingglass and its frame' (p. 134) Stephen mourns his mother, dwelling on her dying, her pain, only to have Buck Mulligan ask him what *is* death, his mother's, his own or Buck Mulligan's. Medical student Mulligan reproaches Stephen, justifying his own early remark that Dedalus's mother was 'beastly dead', and telling him he has the cursed Jesuit strain in him 'only it's injected the wrong way.' And in 'Echoes of Dryden to Swift' (p. 144) Joyce remembers Dryden's remark, 'Cousin Swift, you will never be a poet' (justifiable when he made it, for at that time Swift had not found his own poetic voice, had written with great difficulty only a few elaborate artificial poems in the fashionable mode of Cowley), and writes, 'Cousin Stephen, you will never be a saint' with considerable self-mockery. Like Swift – like so many other Irish writers, notably Oliver Goldsmith – Joyce could laugh at himself. It is a dangerous thing for a poet to do. Some dull humourless critics may take such remarks, such self-mockery, such attempts to amuse, seriously. *Ulysses* changed the course of the novel because of its multiplicity and the plasticity it gave to language. It was not just Joyce's use of the stream of consciousness, for that had carried many writers for varying distances: Sterne along most of its length, Maria Edgeworth, Jane Austen and Dickens briefly, Coleridge and Browning for some of its way. Dorothy Richardson and Virginia Woolf made good use of its current, while George Moore and Edouard Dujardin, with their melodic line and intense monologue, also contributed to the development of new styles of communication. Joyce was aware of their work: but he absorbed and used innovation from elsewhere, notably the portman-teau words, the telegram style of Lewis Carroll. He found new ways of focusing his readers' or listeners' attention on aspects of life not made so arresting before – the sensations of sex, perhaps, most obviously, as 'Lovers' encounter' (p. 151), 'At it again' (p. 174) and 'Molly's memories' (p. 190) demonstrate. But in 'The cat' (p. 149) we can hear Mr Bloom's cat cry 'Mrkgnao' as she waits for him to fill her saucer; we enjoy the subtle humour of juxtaposition in 'Affinities' (p. 189); and we appreciate the multiplication of facts in 'Aquacity' (p. 184). We follow the ambulation of argument in 'An instructive discussion' (p. 152); we taste the texture and flavour of food and drink in 'Parturition' (p. 177); we savour a ruthlessness akin to that of the Brothers Grimm in 'A strange legend on an allied theme' (p. 187); or we praise the parody of the press in 'Bloom's benison' (p. 179). Joyce's creative energy sweeps us along, his variety stimulating, his ability to place in juxtaposition echoes of the aristocratic epic model and his presentation of twentieth-century urban people a brilliant *tour de force*.

Ulysses is comic in the way that Fielding's *Tom Jones* is: both authors were very conscious of the need to impose form upon their inventive storytelling, which was not to be contained within any small static frame. Neither, however, could write classical epic, for its day had passed with Homer, however effective Milton's transcending Homer's primary or Virgil's secondary epic had been in the seventeenth century while he pursued 'Things unattempted yet in prose or rhyme.' By the age of reason, the Augustan Age, Swift and Pope had to seek sanction for their exalted writings by parodying previous forms. In his shorter poems Swift mocked the pastoral, in his masterpiece, *Gulliver's Travels*, the genre of the tales of travellers; while Pope could make his money by translating Homer into the neoclassical expression of eighteenth-century English, he had to write mock-epic himself. Joyce managed to write his twentieth-century epic by cleverly using an anti-hero, by drawing upon romanticism as well as classicism, for Blake as well as Homer is in his mind. Blake could sanction the idealism of Bloom, and Joyce treated Bloom sympathetically as well as realistically.

There were, of course, so many sources. Joyce, original as he was, had enough of the classical tradition built into him to know that originality was not necessarily the ultimate criterion, however much he thought in his youth that he was to forge in the smithy of his soul the uncreated conscience of his race. As Fielding put it in the first chapter of *Tom Jones*: 'we do not disdain to borrow wit or wisdom from any man who is capable of lending us either', so Joyce used his vast stock of reading as well as his memories of conversations, concepts and plays in order to enrich his narrative. This creative imagination was ebullient, and matched his serious purposes as an author.

Ulysses finished, he could still progress. Profoundly serious as he was, he had no need to be solemn about it. No one has. He set about creating a dream world in *Finnegans Wake* and did it with brio: here is no wake for dead language, here is a living language laughing at life, using the literature of the past in an entirely new way, here is Joyce the dramatist and poet at his inventive best, in wild exuberance, allusive, punning, singing along like the waters of the Liffey whose story he tells – as well as other stories too, which belong to the area that in some sense he never left. In the triangular romance of Tristram, Mark and Iseult at Chapelizod, is the legend of Finn, the giant hero who is buried somewhere between Howth and Dublin, in the story of Anna Livia Plurabelle, that 'In my end is my beginning' (p. 254) illustrates as the run of the river, Joyce is a poet, who varies the nature of his expression to suit his subjects; in the dialogues of Jute and Mutt he becomes a dramatist; in 'Hosty's rann' (p. 212) he is a ballad singer, in 'Shaun's song of the Ondt and the Gracehoper' (p. 249) he is a modern Aesop, whereas in 'The Mookse he had reason' (p. 217) he lets his fantasy rip.

Here in *Finnegans Wake* is a fine infinity of new words – the thunder, for instance, that could terrify Joyce crackles and crashes out in Aristophanic artistry as 'Ullhodturdenweirmudgaardsringnirurdrmolnirfenrirlukkilokkibaugimandodrrerinsurtkrinmgernrackinarockar! Thor's for you!' And here is a violent exchange of another kind when (with Edward Lear inspiring them?)

> they viterbated each other *canis et coluber* with the wildest ever
> wielded since Tarriestinus lashed Pissasphaltum
> – Unuchon!
> – Ungulant!
> – Uvuloid!
> – Uskybeak!
> and bull folly answered volleyball.

There are echoes, suggestions and twistings of phrases; there are the punnings that go back to Swift's quick ingenuity (punnings that are always more acceptable in Ireland where the word needs to be quicksilvered); there are jestings and jibings and a sophisticated yet simple sense of the absurdity of life with the jealousies of Shem and Shaun – 'heart mysteries there', as Yeats might have said, Yeats whose involved elaborate stories of the 1890s, 'The Adoration of the Magi' and 'The Tables of the Law' so appealed to Joyce, and some of whose phrases and lines attain fresh intense meaning in the Joycean contexts.

There are many ways to read *Finnegans Wake*. It can be a crossword puzzle with clues to follow up, it can be a scholar's livelihood, it can be a delight to a Dubliner with all its local references (the Liffey itself has just been given a magnificent pictorial life in *The Book of the Liffey* by Elizabeth Healy, Christopher Moriarty and Gerard O'Flaherty), but Joyce's comic epic of a novel has the universality of true comedy: Dublin is every city, the Liffey all the rivers of the world, and H. C. Earwicker, the publican of Chapelizod, dreams *Finnegans Wake*. He is the city of Dublin, the Viking who laid down 'before the trotters to my eblanite my stony battered wanggonways, my nordsond circulums, my eastmoreland and westmoreland, running boullowards and syddenly parading.' These are references to Eblana (Dublin), Stoneybatter, the North and South Circular roads, Eastmoreland and Westmoreland Streets, the Bull, a spit of land on the north shore of Dublin Bay, and

Sydney Parade, at Sandymount on the south shore. But the words carry their own meaning, indeed they make it with the rush of the book carrying us on, its rumbustious humour overlapping the often only apparently cryptic meanings. Read it aloud and enjoy its plurality, its punchlines and pellucid poetry.

A. Norman Jeffares and Brendan Kennelly
Fife Ness and Dublin, 1992

CHAMBER MUSIC

I

Strings in the earth and air
    Make music sweet;
Strings by the river where
    The willows meet.

There's music along the river
    For Love wanders there,
Pale flowers on his mantle,
    Dark leaves on his hair.

All softly playing,
    With head to the music bent,
And fingers straying
    Upon an instrument.

II

The twilight turns from amethyst
    To deep and deeper blue,
The lamp fills with a pale green glow
    The trees of the avenue.

The old piano plays an air,
    Sedate and slow and gay;
She bends upon the yellow keys,
    Her head inclines this way.

Shy thoughts and grave wide eyes and hands
    That wander as they list –
The twilight turns to darker blue
    With lights of amethyst.

III

At that hour when all things have repose,
   O lonely watcher of the skies,
   Do you hear the night wind and the sighs
Of harps playing unto Love to unclose
   The pale gates of sunrise?

When all things repose do you alone
   Awake to hear the sweet harps play
   To Love before him on his way,
And the night wind answering in antiphon
   Till night is overgone?

Play on, invisible harps, unto Love
   Whose way in heaven is aglow
   At that hour when soft lights come and go,
Soft sweet music in the air above
   And in the earth below.

IV

When the shy star goes forth in heaven
   All maidenly, disconsolate,
Hear you amid the drowsy even
   One who is singing by your gate.
His song is softer than the dew
   And he is come to visit you.

O bend no more in revery
   When he at eventide is calling
Nor muse: Who may this singer be
   Whose song about my heart is falling?
Know you by this, the lover's chant,
   'Tis I that am your visitant.

V

Lean out of the window,
    Goldenhair,
I heard you singing
    A merry air.

My book is closed,
    I read no more,
Watching the fire dance
    On the floor.

I have left my book:
    I have left my room:
For I heard you singing
    Through the gloom,

Singing and singing
    A merry air.
Lean out of the window,
    Goldenhair.

VI

I would in that sweet bosom be
    (O sweet it is and fair it is!)
Where no rude wind might visit me.
    Because of sad austerities
I would in that sweet bosom be.

I would be ever in that heart
    (O soft I knock and soft entreat her!)
Where only peace might be my part.
    Austerities were all the sweeter
So I were ever in that heart.

VII

My love is in a light attire
  Among the appletrees
Where the gay winds do most desire
  To run in companies.

There, where the gay winds stay to woo
  The young leaves as they pass,
My love goes slowly, bending to
  Her shadow on the grass;

And where the sky's a pale blue cup
  Over the laughing land,
My love goes lightly, holding up
  Her dress with dainty hand.

VIII

Who goes amid the green wood
  With springtide all adorning her?
Who goes amid the merry green wood
  To make it merrier?

Who passes in the sunlight
  By ways that know the light footfall?
Who passes in the sweet sunlight
  With mien so virginal?

The ways of all the woodland
  Gleam with a soft and golden fire –
For whom does all the sunny woodland
  Carry so brave attire?

O, it is for my true love
  The woods their rich apparel wear –
O, it is for my own true love,
  That is so young and fair.

IX

Winds of May, that dance on the sea,
  Dancing a ringaround in glee
From furrow to furrow, while overhead
The foam flies up to be garlanded
In silvery arches spanning the air,
Saw you my true love anywhere?
        Welladay! Welladay!
        For the winds of May!
    Love is unhappy when love is away!

X

Bright cap and streamers,
  He sings in the hollow:
Come follow, come follow
    All you that love.
Leave dreams to the dreamers
  That will not after,
  That song and laughter
    Do nothing move.

With ribbons streaming
  He sings the bolder;
  In troop at his shoulder
  The wild bees hum.
And the time of dreaming
  Dreams is over –
  As lover to lover,
    Sweetheart, I come.

XI

Bid adieu, adieu, adieu,
  Bid adieu to girlish days.
Happy Love is come to woo
  Thee and woo thy girlish ways –
The zone that doth become thee fair,
The snood upon thy yellow hair,

When thou hast heard his name upon
  The bugles of the cherubim
Begin thou softly to unzone
Thy girlish bosom unto him
And softly to undo the snood
That is the sign of maidenhood.

XII

What counsel has the hooded moon
  Put in thy heart, my shyly sweet,
Of Love in ancient plenilune,
  Glory and stars beneath his feet –
A sage that is but kith and kin
With the comedian capuchin?

Believe me rather that am wise
  In disregard of the divine.
A glory kindles in those eyes,
  Trembles to starlight. Mine, O mine!
No more be tears in moon or mist
For thee, sweet sentimentalist.

XIII

Go seek her out all courteously
  And say I come,
Wind of spices whose song is ever
  Epithalamium.
O, hurry over the dark lands
  And run upon the sea
For seas and lands shall not divide us,
  My love and me.

Now, wind, of your good courtesy
  I pray you go
And come into her little garden
  And sing at her window;
Singing: The bridal wind is blowing
  For Love is at his noon;
And soon will your true love be with you,
  Soon, O soon.

XIV

My dove, my beautiful one,
  Arise, arise!
  The nightdew lies
Upon my lips and eyes.

The odorous winds are weaving
  A music of sighs:
  Arise, arise,
My dove, my beautiful one!

I wait by the cedar tree,
  My sister, my love.
  White breast of the dove,
My breast shall be your bed.

The pale dew lies
  Like a veil on my head.
  My fair one, my fair dove,
Arise, arise!

XV

From dewy dreams, my soul, arise,
  From love's deep slumber and from death,
For lo! the trees are full of sighs
  Whose leaves the morn admonisheth.

Eastward the gradual dawn prevails
  Where softly burning fires appear,
Making to tremble all those veils
  Of grey and golden gossamer.

While sweetly, gently, secretly,
  The flowery bells of morn are stirred
And the wise choirs of faery
  Begin (innumerous!) to be heard.

XVI

O cool is the valley now
    And there, love, will we go
For many a choir is singing now
    Where Love did sometime go.
And hear you not the thrushes calling,
    Calling us away?
O cool and pleasant is the valley
    And there, love, will we stay.

XVII

Because your voice was at my side
    I gave him pain,
Because within my hand I held
    Your hand again.

There is no word nor any sign
    Can make amend –
He is a stranger to me now
    Who was my friend.

XVIII

O sweetheart, hear you
    Your lover's tale;
A man shall have sorrow
    When friends him fail.

For he shall know then
   Friends be untrue
And a little ashes
   Their words come to.

But one unto him
   Will softly move
And softly woo him
   In ways of love.

His hand is under
   Her smooth round breast;
So he who has sorrow
   Shall have rest.

XIX

Be not sad because all men
   Prefer a lying clamour before you:
Sweetheart, be at peace again –
   Can they dishonour you?

They are sadder than all tears;
   Their lives ascend as a continual sigh.
Proudly answer to their tears:
   As they deny, deny.

XX

In the dark pinewood
   I would we lay,
In deep cool shadow
   At noon of day.

How sweet to lie there,
 Sweet to kiss,
Where the great pine forest
 Enaisled is!

Thy kiss descending
 Sweeter were
With a soft tumult
 Of thy hair.

O, unto the pinewood
 At noon of day
Come with me now,
 Sweet love, away.

XXI

He who hath glory lost nor hath
 Found any soul to fellow his,
Among his foes in scorn and wrath
 Holding to ancient nobleness,
That high unconsortable one –
His love is his companion.

XXII

Of that so sweet imprisonment
 My soul, dearest, is fain –
Soft arms that woo me to relent
 And woo me to detain.
Ah, could they ever hold me there,
Gladly were I a prisoner!

Dearest, through interwoven arms
  By love made tremulous,
That night allures me where alarms
  Nowise may trouble us
But sleep to dreamier sleep be wed
Where soul with soul lies prisoned.

XXIII

This heart that flutters near my heart
  My hope and all my riches is,
Unhappy when we draw apart
  And happy between kiss and kiss;
My hope and all my riches – yes! –
And all my happiness.

For there, as in some mossy nest
  The wrens will divers treasures keep,
I laid those treasures I possessed
  Ere that mine eyes had learned to weep.
Shall we not be as wise as they
Though love live but a day?

XXIV

Silently she's combing,
  Combing her long hair,
Silently and graciously,
  With many a pretty air.

The sun is in the willow leaves
  And on the dappled grass
And still she's combing her long hair
  Before the lookingglass.

I pray you, cease to comb out,
  Comb out your long hair,
For I have heard of witchery
  Under a pretty air,

That makes as one thing to the lover
  Staying and going hence,
All fair, with many a pretty air
  And many a negligence.

XXV

Lightly come or lightly go
  Though thy heart presage thee woe,
Vales and many a wasted sun,
  Oread let thy laughter run
Till the irreverent mountain air
Ripple all thy flying hair.

Lightly, lightly – ever so:
  Clouds that wrap the vales below
At the hour of evenstar
  Lowliest attendants are:
Love and laughter songconfessed
When the heart is heaviest.

XXVI

Thou leanest to the shell of night,
   Dear lady, a divining ear.
In that soft choiring of delight
   What sound hath made thy heart to fear?
Seemed it of rivers rushing forth
From the grey deserts of the north?

That mood of thine, O timorous,
   Is his, if thou but scan it well,
Who a mad tale bequeaths to us
   At ghosting hour conjurable –
And all for some strange name he read
In Purchas or in Holinshed.

XXVII

Though I thy Mithridates were
   Framed to defy the poisondart,
Yet must thou fold me unaware
   To know the rapture of thy heart
And I but render and confess
The malice of thy tenderness.

For elegant and antique phrase,
   Dearest, my lips wax all too wise;
Nor have I known a love whose praise
   Our piping poets solemnise,
Neither a love where may not be
Ever so little falsity.

XXVIII

Gentle lady, do not sing
　　Sad songs about the end of love;
Lay aside sadness and sing
　　How love that passes is enough.

Sing about the long deep sleep
　　Of lovers that are dead and how
In the grave all love shall sleep.
　　Love is aweary now.

XXIX

Dear heart, why will you use me so?
　　Dear eyes that gently me upbraid
Still are you beautiful – but O,
　　How is your beauty raimented!

Through the clear mirror of your eyes,
　　Through the soft sigh of kiss to kiss,
Desolate winds assail with cries
　　The shadowy garden where love is.

And soon shall love dissolved be
　　When over us the wild winds blow –
But you, dear love, too dear to me,
　　Alas! why will you use me so?

XXX

Love came to us in time gone by
　　When one at twilight shyly played
And one in fear was standing nigh –
　　For Love at first is all afraid.

We were grave lovers. Love is past
　　That had his sweet hours many a one.
Welcome to us now at the last
　　The ways that we shall go upon.

XXXI

O, it was out by Donnycarney
　　When the bat flew from tree to tree
My love and I did walk together
　　And sweet were the words she said to me.

Along with us the summer wind
　　Went murmuring – O, happily! –
But softer than the breath of summer
　　Was the kiss she gave to me.

XXXII

Rain has fallen all the day
　　O come among the laden trees.
The leaves lie thick upon the way
　　Of memories.

Staying a little by the way
  Of memories shall we depart.
Come, my beloved, where I may
  Speak to your heart.

XXXIII

Now, O now, in this brown land
  Where Love did so sweet music make
We two shall wander, hand in hand,
  Forbearing for old friendship' sake
Nor grieve because our love was gay
Which now is ended in this way.

A rogue in red and yellow dress
  Is knocking, knocking at the tree
And all around our loneliness
  The wind is whistling merrily.
The leaves – they do not sigh at all
When the year takes them in the fall.

Now, O now, we hear no more
  The vilanelle and roundelay!
Yet will we kiss, sweetheart, before
  We take sad leave at close of day.
Grieve not, sweetheart, for anything –
The year, the year is gathering.

XXXIV

Sleep now, O sleep now,
   O you unquiet heart!
A voice crying 'Sleep now'
   Is heard in my heart.

The voice of the winter
   Is heard at the door.
O sleep for the winter
   Is crying 'Sleep no more!'

My kiss will give peace now
   And quiet to your heart –
Sleep on in peace now,
   O you unquiet heart!

XXXV

All day I hear the noise of waters
   Making moan
Sad as the seabird is when going
   Forth alone
He hears the winds cry to the waters'
   Monotone.

The grey winds, the cold winds are blowing
   Where I go.
I hear the noise of many waters
   Far below.
All day, all night, I hear them flowing
   To and fro.

XXXVI

I hear an army charging upon the land
   And the thunder of horses plunging,
      foam about their knees.
Arrogant, in black armour, behind them
      stand,
   Disdaining the reins, with fluttering
      whips, the charioteers.

They cry unto the night their battlename:
   I moan in sleep when I hear afar their
      whirling laughter.
They cleave the gloom of dreams, a blinding
      flame,
   Clanging, clanging upon the heart as upon
      an anvil.

They come shaking in triumph their long green hair:
   They come out of the sea and run shouting
      by the shore.
My heart, have you no wisdom thus to
      despair?
   My love, my love, my love, why have you
      left me alone?

POMES
PENYEACH

Tilly

He travels after a winter sun,
Urging the cattle along a cold red road,
Calling to them, a voice they know,
He drives his beasts above Cabra.

The voice tells them home is warm.
They moo and make brute music with their
    hoofs.
He drives them with a flowering branch before
    him,
Smoke pluming their foreheads.

Boor, bond of the herd,
Tonight stretch full by the fire!
I bleed by the black stream
For my torn bough!

Watching the Needleboats
at San Sabba

I heard their young hearts crying
Loveward above the glancing oar
And heard the prairie grasses sighing:
No more, return no more!

O hearts, O sighing grasses,
Vainly your loveblown bannerets mourn!
No more will the wild wind that passes
Return, no more return.

A Flower Given to my Daughter

Frail the white rose and frail are
Her hands that gave
Whose soul is sere and paler
Than time's wan wave.

Rosefrail and fair – yet frailest
A wonder wild
In gentle eyes thou veilest,
My blueveined child.

She Weeps over Rahoon

Rain on Rahoon falls softly, softly falling,
Where my dark lover lies.
Sad is his voice that calls me, sadly calling,
At grey moonrise.

Love, hear thou
How soft, how sad his voice is ever calling,
Ever unanswered, and the dark rain falling,
Then as now.

Dark too our hearts, O love, shall lie and cold
As his sad heart has lain
Under the moongrey nettles, the black mould
And muttering rain.

Tutto è Sciolto

A birdless heaven, seadusk, one lone star
Piercing the west,
As thou, fond heart, love's time, so faint, so far,
Rememberest.

The clear young eyes' soft look, the candid brow,
The fragrant hair,
Falling as through the silence falleth now
Dusk of the air.

Why then, remembering those shy
Sweet lures, repine
When the dear love she yielded with a sigh
Was all but thine?

On the Beach at Fontana

Wind whines and whines the shingle,
The crazy pierstakes groan;
A senile sea numbers each single
Slimesilvered stone.

From whining wind and colder
Grey sea I wrap him warm
And touch his trembling fineboned shoulder
And boyish arm.

Around us fear, descending
Darkness of fear above
And in my heart how deep unending
Ache of love!

Simples

O bella bionda,
Sei come l'onda!

Of cool sweet dew and radiance mild
The moon a web of silence weaves
In the still garden where a child
Gathers the simple salad leaves.

A moondew stars her hanging hair
And moonlight kisses her young brow
And, gathering, she sings an air:
Fair as the wave is, fair, art thou!

Be mine, I pray, a waxen ear
To shield me from her childish croon
And mine a shielded heart for her
Who gathers simples of the moon.

Flood

Goldbrown upon the sated flood
The rockvine clusters lift and sway;
Vast wings above the lambent waters brood
Of sullen day.

A waste of waters ruthlessly
Sways and uplifts its weedy mane
Where brooding day stares down upon the sea
In dull disdain.

Uplift and sway, O golden vine,
Your clustered fruits to love's full flood,
Lambent and vast and ruthless as is thine
Incertitude!

Nightpiece

Gaunt in gloom,
The pale stars their torches,
Enshrouded, wave.
Ghostfires from heaven's far verges faint illume,
Arches on soaring arches,
Night's sindark nave.

Seraphim,
The lost hosts awaken
To service till
In moonless gloom each lapses muted, dim,
Raised when she has and shaken
Her thurible.

And long and loud,
To night's nave upsoaring,
A starknell tolls
As the bleak incense surges, cloud on cloud,
Voidward from the adoring
Waste of souls.

Alone

The moon's greygolden meshes make
All night a veil,
The shorelamps in the sleeping lake
Laburnum tendrils trail.

The sly reeds whisper to the night
A name – her name –
And all my soul is a delight,
A swoon of shame.

A Memory of the Players in a Mirror at Midnight

They mouth love's language. Gnash
The thirteen teeth
Your lean jaws grin with. Lash
Your itch and quailing, nude greed of the flesh.
Love's breath in you is stale, worded or sung,
As sour as cat's breath,
Harsh of tongue.

This grey that stares
Lies not, stark skin and bone.
Leave greasy lips their kissing. None
Will choose her what you see to mouth upon.
Dire hunger holds his hour.
Pluck forth your heart, saltblood, a fruit of tears.
Pluck and devour!

Bahnhofstrasse

The eyes that mock me sign the way
Whereto I pass at eve of day,

Grey way whose violet signals are
The trysting and the twining star.

Ah star of evil! star of pain!
Highhearted youth comes not again

Nor old heart's wisdom yet to know
The signs that mock me as I go.

A Prayer

Again!
Come, give, yield all your strength to me!
From far a low word breathes on the breaking brain
Its cruel calm, submission's misery,
Gentling her awe as to a soul predestined.
Cease, silent love! My doom!

Blind me with your dark nearness, O have
    mercy, beloved enemy of my will!
I dare not withstand the cold touch that I dread.
Draw from me still
My slow life! Bend deeper on me, threatening head,
Proud by my downfall, remembering, pitying
Him who is, him who was!

Again!
Together, folded by the night, they lay on
    earth. I hear
From far her low word breathe on my breaking brain.
Come! I yield. Bend deeper upon me! I am here.
Subduer, do not leave me! Only joy, only anguish,
Take me, save me, soothe me, O spare me!

OTHER
POEMS

The Holy Office

Myself unto myself will give
This name, Katharsis-Purgative.
I, who dishevelled ways forsook
To hold the poets' grammar-book,
Bringing to tavern and to brothel
The mind of witty Aristotle,
Lest bards in the attempt should err
Must here be my interpreter:
Wherefore receive now from my lip
Peripatetic scholarship.
To enter heaven, travel hell,
Be piteous or terrible
One positively needs the ease
Of plenary indulgences.
For every true-born mysticist
A Dante is, unprejudiced,
Who safe at ingle-nook, by proxy,
Hazards extremes of heterodoxy,
Like him who finds a joy at table
Pondering the uncomfortable.
Ruling one's life by common sense
How can one fail to be intense?
But I must not accounted be
One of that mumming company –
With him who hies him to appease
His giddy dames' frivolities
While they console him when he whinges
With gold-embroidered Celtic fringes –
Or him who sober all the day
Mixes a naggin in his play –
Or him whose conduct 'seems to own'
His preference for a man of 'tone' –
Or him who plays the ragged patch
To millionaires in Hazelpatch

But weeping after holy fast
Confesses all his pagan past –
Or him who will his hat unfix
Neither to malt nor crucifix
But show to all that poor-dressed be
His high Castilian courtesy –
Or him who loves his Master dear –
Or him who drinks his pint in fear –
Or him who once when snug abed
Saw Jesus Christ without his head
And tried so hard to win for us
The long-lost works of Æschylus.
But all these men of whom I speak
Make me the sewer of their clique.
That they may dream their dreamy dreams
I carry off their filthy streams
For I can do those things for them
Through which I lost my diadem,
Those things for which Grandmother Church
Left me severely in the lurch.
Thus I relieve their timid arses,
Perform my office of Katharsis.
My scarlet leaves them white as wool:
Through me they purge a bellyful.
To sister mummers one and all
I act as vicar-general
And for each maiden, shy and nervous,
I do a similar kind service.
For I detect without surprise
That shadowy beauty in her eyes,
The 'dare not' of sweet maidenhood
That answers my corruptive 'would.'
Whenever publicly we meet
She never seems to think of it;
At night when close in bed she lies
And feels my hand between her thighs
My little love in light attire

Knows the soft flame that is desire.
But Mammon places under ban
The uses of Leviathan
And that high spirit ever wars
On Mammon's countless servitors
Nor can they ever be exempt
From his taxation of contempt.
So distantly I turn to view
The shamblings of that motley crew,
Those souls that hate the strength that mine has
Steeled in the school of old Aquinas.
Where they have crouched and crawled and prayed
I stand, the self-doomed, unafraid,
Unfellowed, friendless and alone,
Indifferent as the herring-bone,
Firm as the mountain-ridges where
I flash my antlers on the air.
Let them continue as is meet
To adequate the balance-sheet.
Though they may labour to the grave
My spirit shall they never have
Nor make my soul with theirs as one
Till the Mahamanvantara be done:
And though they spurn me from their door
My soul shall spurn them evermore.

Gas from a Burner

Ladies and gents, you are here assembled
To hear why earth and heaven trembled
Because of the black and sinister arts
Of an Irish writer in foreign parts.
He sent me a book ten years ago:
I read it a hundred times or so,
Backwards and forwards, down and up,

Through both the ends of a telescope.
I printed it all to the very last word
But by the mercy of the Lord
The darkness of my mind was rent
And I saw the writer's foul intent.
But I owe a duty to Ireland:
I hold her honour in my hand,
This lovely land that always sent
Her writers and artists to banishment
And in a spirit of Irish fun
Betrayed her own leaders, one by one.
'Twas Irish humour, wet and dry,
Flung quicklime into Parnell's eye;
'Tis Irish brains that save from doom
The leaky barge of the Bishop of Rome
For everyone knows the Pope can't belch
Without the consent of Billy Walsh.
O Ireland my first and only love
Where Christ and Caesar are hand and glove!
O lovely land where the shamrock grows!
(Allow me, ladies, to blow my nose)
To show you for strictures I don't care a button
I printed the poems of Mountainy Mutton
And a play he wrote (you've read it, I'm sure)
Where they talk of 'bastard,' 'bugger' and 'whore,'
And a play on the Word and Holy Paul
And some woman's legs that I can't recall,
Written by Moore, a genuine gent
That lives on his property's ten per cent:
I printed mystical books in dozens:
I printed the table-book of Cousins
Though (asking your pardon) as for the verse
'Twould give you a heartburn on your arse:
I printed folklore from North and South
By Gregory of the Golden Mouth:
I printed poets, sad, silly and solemn:
I printed Patrick What-do-you-Colm:

I printed the great John Milicent Synge
Who soars above on an angel's wing
In the playboy shift that he pinched as swag
From Maunsel's manager's travelling-bag.
But I draw the line at that bloody fellow
That was over here dressed in Austrian yellow,
Spouting Italian by the hour
To O'Leary Curtis and John Wyse Power
And writing of Dublin, dirty and dear,
In a manner no blackamoor printer could bear.
Shite and onions! Do you think I'll print
The name of the Wellington Monument,
Sydney Parade and Sandymount tram,
Downes's cakeshop and Williams's jam?
I'm damned if I do – I'm damned to blazes!
Talk about *Irish Names of Places!*
It's a wonder to me, upon my soul,
He forgot to mention Curly's Hole.
No, ladies, my press shall have no share in
So gross a libel on Stepmother Erin.
I pity the poor – that's why I took
A red-headed Scotchman to keep my book.
Poor sister Scotland! Her doom is fell;
She cannot find any more Stuarts to sell.
My conscience is fine as Chinese silk:
My heart is as soft as buttermilk.
Colm can tell you I made a rebate
Of one hundred pounds on the estimate
I gave him for his *Irish Review*.
I love my country – by herrings I do!
I wish you could see what tears I weep
When I think of the emigrant train and ship.
That's why I publish far and wide
My quite illegible railway guide.
In the porch of my printing institute
The poor and deserving prostitute
Plays every night at catch-as-catch-can

With her tight-breeched British artilleryman
And the foreigner learns the gift of the gab
From the drunken draggletail Dublin drab.
Who was it said: Resist not evil?
I'll burn that book, so help me devil.
I'll sing a psalm as I watch it burn
And the ashes I'll keep in a one-handled urn.
I'll penance do with farts and groans
Kneeling upon my marrowbones.
This very next lent I will unbare
My penitent buttocks to the air
And sobbing beside my printing press
My awful sin I will confess.
My Irish foreman from Bannockburn
Shall dip his right hand in the urn
And sign crisscross with reverent thumb
Memento homo upon my bum.

Ecce Puer

Of the dark past
A child is born;
With joy and grief
My heart is torn.

Calm in his cradle
The living lies.
May love and mercy
Unclose his eyes!

Young life is breathed
On the glass;
The world that was not
Comes to pass.

A child is sleeping:
An old man gone.
O, father forsaken,
Forgive your son!

FROM
DUBLINERS

The Word

FROM 'THE SISTERS'

There was no hope for him this time: it was the third stroke. Night after night I had passed the home (it was vacation time) and studied the lighted square of window: and night after night I had found it lighted in the same way, faintly and evenly. If he was dead, I thought, I would see the reflexion of candles on the darkened blind, for I knew that two candles must be set at the head of a corpse. He had often said to me: 'I am not long for this world,' and I had thought his words idle. Now I knew they were true. Every night as I gazed up at the window I said softly to myself the word paralysis. It had always sounded strangely in my ears, like the word gnomon in the Euclid and the word simony in the Catechism. But now it sounded to me like the name of some maleficent and sinful being. It filled me with fear, and yet I longed to be nearer to it and to look upon its deadly work.

Smiles

FROM 'THE SISTERS'

It was late when I fell asleep. Though I was angry with old Cotter for alluding to me as a child, I puzzled my head to extract meaning from his unfinished sentences. In the dark of my room I imagined that I saw again the heavy grey face of the paralytic. I drew the blankets over my head and tried to think of Christmas. But the grey face still followed me. It murmured; and I understood that it desired to confess something. I felt my soul receding into some pleasant and vicious region; and there again I found it waiting for me. It began to confess to me in a murmuring voice and I wondered why it smiled continually and why the lips were so moist with spittle. But then I remembered that it had died of paralysis and I felt that I too was smiling feebly, as if to absolve the simoniac of his sin.

Happiness

FROM 'AN ENCOUNTER'

That night I slept badly. In the morning I was firstcomer to the bridge, as I lived nearest. I hid my books in the long grass near the ashpit at the end of the garden where nobody ever came, and hurried along the canal bank. It was a mild sunny morning in the first week of June. I sat up on the coping of the bridge, admiring my frail canvas shoes which I had diligently pipeclayed overnight and watching the docile horses pulling a tramload of business people up the hill. All the branches of the tall trees which lined the mall were gay with little light green leaves, and the sunlight slanted through them on to the water. The granite stone of the bridge was beginning to be warm, and I began to pat it with my hands in time to an air in my head. I was very happy.

Crossing the Liffey

FROM 'AN ENCOUNTER'

We crossed the Liffey in the ferryboat, paying our toll to be transported in the company of two labourers and a little Jew with a bag. We were serious to the point of solemnity, but once during the short voyage our eyes met and we laughed. When we landed we watched the discharging of the graceful three-master which we had observed from the other quay. Some bystanders said that she was a Norwegian vessel. I went to the stern and tried to decipher the legend upon it but, failing to do so, I came back and examined the foreign sailors to see had any of them green eyes, for I had some confused notion... The sailors' eyes were blue, and grey, and even black. The only sailor whose eyes could have been called green was a tall man who amused the crowd on the quay by calling out cheerfully every time the planks fell:

'All right! All right!'

Love and enchantment

FROM 'ARABY'

Her image accompanied me even in places the most hostile to romance. On Saturday evenings when my aunt went marketing I had to go to carry some of the parcels. We walked through the flaring streets, jostled by drunken men and bargaining women, amid the curses of labourers, the shrill litanies of shop-boys who stood on guard by the barrels of pigs' cheeks, the nasal chanting of street-singers, who sang a *come-all-you* about O'Donovan Rossa, or a ballad about the troubles in our native land. These noises converged in a single sensation of life for me: I imagined that I bore my chalice safely through a throng of foes. Her name sprang to my lips at moments in strange prayers and praises which I myself did not understand. My eyes were often full of tears (I could not tell why) and at times a flood from my heart seemed to pour itself out into my bosom. I thought little of the future. I did not know whether I would ever speak to her or not or, if I spoke to her, how I could tell her of my confused adoration. But my body was like a harp and her words and gestures were like fingers running upon the wires.

One evening I went into the back drawing-room in which the priest had died. It was a dark rainy evening and there was no sound in the house. Through one of the broken panes I heard the rain impinge upon the earth, the fine incessant needles of water playing in the sodden beds. Some distant lamp or lighted window gleamed below me. I was thankful that I could see so little. All my senses seemed to desire to veil themselves and, feeling that I was about to slip from them, I pressed the palms of my hands together until they trembled, murmuring: *O love! O love!* many times.

At last she spoke to me. When she addressed the first words to me I was so confused that I did not know what to answer. She asked me was I going to *Araby.* I forgot whether I answered yes or no. It would be a splendid bazaar, she said; she would love to go.

– And why can't you? I asked.

While she spoke she turned a silver bracelet round and round her wrist. She could not go, she said, because there would be a retreat that week in her convent. Her brother and two other boys were fighting for their caps and I was alone at the railings. She held one of the spikes, bowing her head towards me. The light from the lamp opposite our door caught the white curve of her neck, lit up her hair that rested there and, falling, lit up the hand upon the railing. It fell over one side of her dress and caught the white border of a petticoat, just visible as she stood at ease.

– It's well for you, she said.

– If I go, I said, I will bring you something.

What innumerable follies laid waste my waking and sleeping thoughts after that evening! I wished to annihilate the tedious intervening days. I chafed against the work of school. At night in my bedroom and by day in the classroom her image came between me and the page I strove to read. The syllables of the word *Araby* were called to me through the silence in which my soul luxuriated and cast an Eastern enchantment over me. I asked for leave to go to the bazaar on Saturday night.

Leaving home

FROM 'EVELINE'

Few people passed. The man out of the last house passed on his way home; she heard his footsteps clacking along the concrete pavement and afterwards crunching on the cinder path before the new red houses. One time there used to be a field there in which they used to play every evening with other people's children. Then a man from Belfast bought the field and built houses in it – not like their little brown houses, but bright brick houses with shining roofs. The children of the avenue used to play together in that field – the Devines, the Waters, the Dunns, little Keogh the cripple, she and her brothers and sisters. Ernest, however, never played: he was too grown up. Her father used often to hunt them in out of the field with his blackthorn stick; but usually little Keogh used to keep *nix* and call out when he saw her father coming. Still they seemed to have been rather happy then. Her father was not so bad then; and besides, her mother was alive. That was a long time ago; she and her brothers and sisters were all grown up; her mother was dead. Tizzie Dunn was dead, too, and the Waters had gone back to England. Everything changes. Now she was going to go away like the others, to leave her home.

Home!

Retreat from escape

FROM 'EVELINE'

She stood among the swaying crowd in the station at the North Wall. He held her hand and she knew that he was speaking to her, saying something about the passage over and over again. The station was full of soldiers with brown baggages. Through the wide doors of the sheds she caught a glimpse of the black mass of the boat, lying in beside the quay wall, with illumined portholes. She answered nothing. She felt her cheek pale and cold and, out of a maze of distress, she prayed to God to direct her, to show her what was her duty. The boat blew a long mournful whistle into the mist. If she went, to-morrow she would be on the sea with Frank, steaming towards Buenos Ayres. Their passage had been booked. Could she still draw back after all he had done for her? Her distress awoke a nausea in her body and she kept moving her lips in silent fervent prayer.

A bell clanged upon her heart. She felt him seize her hand:
– Come!

All the seas of the world tumbled about her heart. He was drawing her into them: he would drown her. She gripped with both hands at the iron railing.
– Come!

No! No! No! It was impossible. Her hands clutched the iron in frenzy. Amid the seas she sent a cry of anguish!
– Eveline! Evvy!

He rushed beyond the barrier and called to her to follow. He was shouted at to go on but he still called to her. She set her white face to him, passive, like a helpless animal. Her eyes gave him no sign of love or farewell or recognition.

August evening in the city

FROM 'TWO GALLANTS'

The grey warm evening of August had descended upon the city, and a mild warm air, a memory of summer, circulated in the streets. The streets, shuttered for the repose of Sunday, swarmed with a gaily coloured crowd. Like illumined pearls the lamps shone from the summits of their tall poles upon the living texture below, which, changing shape and hue unceasingly, sent up into the warm grey evening air an unchanging, unceasing murmur.

A marriage

FROM 'THE BOARDING HOUSE'

M rs Mooney was a butcher's daughter. She was a woman who was quite able to keep things to herself: a determined woman. She had married her father's foreman, and opened a butcher's shop near Spring Gardens. But as soon as his father-in-law was dead Mr Mooney began to go to the devil. He drank, plundered the till, ran headlong into debt. It was no use making him take the pledge: he was sure to break out again a few days after. By fighting his wife in the presence of customers and by buying bad meat he ruined his business. One night he went for his wife with the cleaver, and she had to sleep in a neighbour's house.

A moment of hope

FROM 'THE BOARDING HOUSE'

O n nights when he came in very late it was she who warmed up his dinner. He scarcely knew what he was eating feeling her beside him alone, at night, in the sleeping house. And her thoughtfulness! If the night was anyway cold or wet or windy there was sure to be a little tumbler of punch ready for him. Perhaps they could be happy together . . .

They used to go upstairs together on tiptoe, each with a candle, and on the third landing exchange reluctant good nights. They used to kiss. He remembered well her eyes, the touch of her hand and his delirium . . .

But delirium passes.

The walker through Dublin

FROM 'A LITTLE CLOUD'

When his hour had struck he stood up and took leave of his desk and of his fellow-clerks punctiliously. He emerged from under the feudal arch of the King's Inns, a neat modest figure, and walked swiftly down Henrietta Street. The golden sunset was waning and the air had grown sharp. A horde of grimy children populated the street. They stood or ran in the roadway, or crawled up the steps before the gaping doors, or squatted like mice upon the thresholds. Little Chandler gave them no thought. He picked his way deftly through all that minute vermin-like life and under the shadow of the gaunt spectral mansions in which the old nobility of Dublin had roistered. No memory of the past touched him, for his mind was full of a present joy.

A dream of leaving Dublin

FROM 'A LITTLE CLOUD'

Little Chandler quickened his pace. For the first time in his life he felt himself superior to the people he passed. For the first time his soul revolted against the dull inelegance of Capel Street. There was no doubt about it: if you wanted to succeed you had to go away. You could do nothing in Dublin. As he crossed Grattan Bridge he looked down the river towards the lower quays and pitied the poor stunted houses. They seemed to him a band of tramps, huddled together along the river-banks, their old coats covered with dust and soot, stupefied by the panorama of sunset and waiting for the first chill of night to bid them arise, shake themselves and begone. He wondered whether he could write a poem to express his idea. Perhaps Gallaher might be able to get it into some London paper for him. Could he write something original? He was not sure what idea he wished to express but the thought that a poetic moment had touched him took life within him like an infant hope. He stepped onward bravely.

Every step brought him nearer to London, farther from his own sober inartistic life. A light began to tremble on the horizon of his mind. He was not so old – thirty-two. His temperament might be said to be just at the point of maturity. There were so many different moods and impressions that he wished to express in verse. He felt them within him. He tried to weigh his soul to see if it was a poet's soul. Melancholy was the dominant note of his temperament, he thought, but it was a melancholy tempered by recurrences of faith and resignation and simple joy. If he could give expression to it in a book of poems perhaps men would listen. He would never be popular: he saw that. He could not sway the crowd but he might appeal to a little circle of kindred minds. The English critics, perhaps, would recognize him as one of the Celtic school by reason of the melancholy tone of his poems; besides that, he would put in allusions. He began to invent sentences and phrases from the notices which his book would get. *Mr Chandler has the gift of easy and graceful verse. . . . A wistful sadness pervades these poems. . . . The Celtic note.* It was a pity his name was not more Irish-looking. Perhaps it would be better to insert his mother's name before the surname: Thomas Malone Chandler, or better still: T. Malone Chandler. He would speak to Gallaher about it.

Loneliness

FROM 'A PAINFUL CASE'

He realized that she was dead, that she had ceased to exist, that she had become a memory. He began to feel ill at ease. He asked himself what else could he have done. He could not have carried on a comedy of deception with her; he could not have lived with her openly. He had done what seemed to him best. How was he to blame? Now that she was gone he understood how lonely her life must have been, sitting night after night alone in that room. His life would be lonely too until he, too, died, ceased to exist, became a memory – if anyone remembered him.

It was after nine o'clock when he left the shop. The night was cold and gloomy. He entered the park by the first gate and walked along under the gaunt trees. He walked through the bleak alleys where they had walked four years before. She seemed to be near him in the darkness. At moments he seemed to feel her voice touch his ear, her hand touch his. He stood still to listen. Why had he withheld life from her? Why had he sentenced her to death? He felt his moral nature falling to pieces.

When he gained the crest of the Magazine Hill he halted and looked along the river towards Dublin, the lights of which burned redly and hospitably in the cold night. He looked down the slope and, at the base, in the shadow of the wall of the park, he saw some human figures lying. Those venal and furtive loves filled him with despair. He gnawed the rectitude of his life; he felt that he had been outcast from life's feast. One human being had seemed to love him and he had denied her life and happiness: he had sentenced her to ignominy, a death of shame. He knew that the prostrate creatures down by the wall were watching him and wished him gone. No one wanted him; he was outcast from life's feast. He turned his eyes to the grey gleaming river, winding along towards

Dublin. Beyond the river he saw a goods train winding out of Kingsbridge Station, like a worm with a fiery head winding through the darkness, obstinately and laboriously. It passed slowly out of sight; but still he heard in his ears the laborious drone of the engine reiterating the syllables of her name.

He turned back the way he had come, the rhythm of the engine pounding in his ears. He began to doubt the reality of what memory told him. He halted under a tree and allowed the rhythm to die away. He could not feel her near him in the darkness nor her voice touch his ear. He waited for some minutes listening. He could hear nothing: the night was perfectly silent. He listened again: perfectly silent. He felt that he was alone.

Irish hospitality

FROM 'THE DEAD'

A fat brown goose lay at one end of the table and at the other end, on a bed of creased paper strewn with sprigs of parsley, lay a great ham, stripped of its outer skin and peppered over with crust crumbs, a neat paper frill round its shin and beside this was a round of spiced beef. Between these rival ends ran parallel lines of side-dishes: two little minsters of jelly, red and yellow; a shallow dish full of blocks of blancmange and red jam, a large green leaf-shaped dish with a stalk-shaped handle, on which lay bunches of purple raisins and peeled almonds, a companion dish on which lay a solid rectangle of Smyrna figs, a dish of custard topped with grated nutmeg, a small bowl full of chocolates and sweets wrapped in gold and silver papers and a glass vase in which stood some tall celery stalks. In the centre of the table there stood, as sentries to a fruit-stand which upheld a pyramid of oranges and American apples, two squat old-fashioned decanters of cut glass, one containing port and the other dark sherry. On the closed square piano a pudding in a huge yellow dish lay in waiting and behind it were three squads of bottles of stout and ale and minerals drawn up according to the colours of their uniforms, the first two black, with brown and red labels, the third and smallest squad white, with transverse green sashes.

Beyond the Shannon: the romance of the west

FROM 'THE DEAD'

– What about the song? Why does that make you cry?

She raised her head from her arms and dried her eyes with the back of her hand like a child. A kinder note than he had intended went into his voice.

– Why, Gretta? he asked.

– I am thinking about a person long ago who used to sing that song.

– And who was the person long ago? asked Gabriel, smiling.

– It was a person I used to know in Galway when I was living with my grandmother, she said.

The smile passed away from Gabriel's face. A dull anger began to gather again at the back of his mind and the dull fires of his lust began to glow angrily in his veins.

– Someone you were in love with? he asked ironically.

– It was a young boy I used to know, she answered, named Michael Furey. He used to sing that song, *The Lass of Aughrim*. He was very delicate.

Gabriel was silent. He did not wish her to think that he was interested in this delicate boy.

– I can see him so plainly, she said after a moment. Such eyes as he had: big dark eyes! And such an expression in them – an expression!

– O then, you were in love with him? said Gabriel.

– I used to go out walking with him, she said, when I was in Galway.

A thought flew across Gabriel's mind.

– Perhaps that was why you wanted to go to Galway with that Ivors girl? he said coldly.

She looked at him and asked in surprise:

– What for?

Her eyes made Gabriel feel awkward. He shrugged his shoulders and said:

– How do I know? To see him perhaps.

She looked away from him along the shaft of light towards the window in silence.

– He is dead, she said at length. He died when he was only seventeen. Isn't it a terrible thing to die so young as that?

– What was he? asked Gabriel, still ironically.

– He was in the gasworks, she said.

Gabriel felt humiliated by the failure of his irony and by the evocation of this figure from the dead, a boy in the gasworks. While he had been full of memories of their secret life together, full of tenderness and joy and desire, she had been comparing him in her mind with another. A shameful consciousness of his own person assailed him. He saw himself as a ludicrous figure, acting as a pennyboy for his aunts, a nervous well-meaning sentimentalist, orating to vulgarians and idealizing his own clownish lusts, the pitiable fatuous fellow he had caught a glimpse of in the mirror. Instinctively he turned his back more to the light lest she might see the shame that burned upon his forehead.

He tried to keep up his tone of cold interrogation but his voice when he spoke was humble and indifferent.

– I suppose you were in love with this Michael Furey, Gretta, he said.

– I was great with him at that time, she said.

Her voice was veiled and sad. Gabriel, feeling now how vain it would be to try to lead her whither he had purposed, caressed one of her hands and said, also sadly:

– And what did he die of so young, Gretta? Consumption, was it?

– I think he died for me, she answered.

A vague terror seized Gabriel at this answer as if, at that hour when he had hoped to triumph, some impalpable and vindictive being was coming against him, gathering forces against him in its vague world. But he shook himself free of it with an effort of reason and continued to caress her hand. He did not question her again for he felt that she would tell him of herself. Her hand was warm and moist: it did not respond to his touch but he continued to caress it just as he had caressed her first letter to him that spring morning.

– It was in the winter, she said, about the beginning of the winter when I was going to leave my grandmother's and come up here to the convent. And he was ill at the time in his lodgings in Galway and wouldn't be let out and his people in Oughterard were written to. He was in decline, they said, or something like that. I never knew rightly.

She paused for a moment and sighed.

– Poor fellow, she said. He was very fond of me and he was such a gentle boy. We used to go out together, walking, you know, Gabriel, like the way they do in the country. He was going to study singing only for his health. He had a very good voice, poor Michael Furey.

– Well; and then? asked Gabriel.

– And then when it came to the time for me to leave Galway and come up to the convent he was much worse and I wouldn't be let see him so I wrote a letter saying I was going up to Dublin and would be back in the summer and hoping he would be better then.

She paused for a moment to get her voice under control and then went on:

– Then the night before I left I was in my grandmother's house in Nuns' Island, packing up, and I heard gravel thrown up against the window. The window was so wet I couldn't see so I ran downstairs as I was and slipped out the back into the garden and there was the poor fellow at the end of the garden, shivering.

– And did you not tell him to go back? asked Gabriel.

– I implored of him to go home at once and told him he would get his death in the rain. But he said he did not want to live. I can see his eyes as well as well! He was standing at the end of the wall where there was a tree.

– And did he go home? asked Gabriel.

– Yes, he went home. And when I was only a week in the convent he died and he was buried in Oughterard where his people came from. O, the day I heard that, that he was dead!

She stopped, choking with sobs, and, overcome by emotion, flung herself face downward on the bed, sobbing in the quilt. Gabriel held her hand for a moment longer, irresolutely, and then, shy of intruding on her grief, let it fall gently and walked quietly to the window.

She was fast asleep.

Gabriel, leaning on his elbow, looked for a few moments unresentfully on her tangled hair and half-open mouth, listening to her deep-drawn breath. So she had had that romance in her life: a man had died for her sake. It hardly pained him now to think how poor a part he, her husband, had played in her life. He watched her while she slept as though he and she had never lived together as man and wife. His curious eyes rested long upon her face and on her hair: and, as he thought of what she must have been then, in that time of her first girlish beauty, a strange friendly pity for her entered his soul. He did not like to say even to himself that her face was no longer beautiful but he knew that it was no longer the face for which Michael Furey had braved death.

Perhaps she had not told him all the story. His eyes moved to the chair over which she had thrown some of her clothes. A petticoat string dangled to the floor. One boot stood upright, its limp upper fallen down: the fellow of it lay upon its side. He wondered at his riot of emotions of an hour before. From what had it proceeded? From his aunt's supper, from his own foolish speech, from the wine and dancing, the merry-making when saying good-night in the hall, the pleasure of the walk along the river in the snow. Poor Aunt Julia! She, too, would soon be a shade with the shade of Patrick Morkan and his horse. He had caught that haggard look upon her face for a moment when she was singing *Arrayed for the Bridal*. Soon, perhaps, he would be sitting in that same drawing-room, dressed in black, his silk hat on his knees. The blinds would be drawn down and Aunt Kate would be sitting beside him, crying and blowing her nose and telling him how Julia had died. He would cast about in his mind for some words that might console her, and would find only lame and useless ones. Yes, yes: that would happen very soon.

The air of the room chilled his shoulders. He stretched himself cautiously along under the sheets and lay down beside his wife. One by one they were all becoming shades. Better pass boldly into that other world, in the full glory of some passion, than fade and wither dismally with age. He thought of how she who lay beside him had locked in her heart for so many years that image of her lover's eyes when he had told her that he did not wish to live.

Generous tears filled Gabriel's eyes. He had never felt like that himself towards any woman but he knew that such a feeling must be love. The tears gathered more thickly in his eyes and in the partial darkness he imagined he saw the form of a young man standing under a dripping tree. Other forms were near. His soul had approached that region where dwell the vast hosts of the dead. He was conscious of, but could not apprehend, their wayward and flickering existence. His own identity was fading out into a grey impalpable world: the solid world itself which these dead had one time reared and lived in was dissolving and dwindling.

A few light taps upon the pane made him turn to the window. It had begun to snow again. He watched sleepily the flakes, silver and dark, falling obliquely against the lamplight. The time had come for him to set out on his journey westward. Yes, the newspapers were right: snow was general all over Ireland. It was falling on every part of the dark central plain, on the treeless hills, falling softly upon the Bog of Allen and, farther westward, softly falling into the dark mutinous Shannon waves. It was falling, too, upon every part of the lonely churchyard on the hill where Michael Furey lay buried. It lay thickly drifted on the crooked crosses and headstones, on the spears of the little gate, on the barren thorns. His soul swooned slowly as he heard the snow falling faintly through the universe and faintly falling, like the descent of their last end, upon all the living and the dead.

FROM
STEPHEN HERO

The poet at work

As he walked thus through the ways of the city he had his ears and eyes ever prompt to receive impressions. It was not only in Skeat that he found words for his treasure-house, he found them also at haphazard in the shops, on advertisements, in the mouths of the plodding public. He kept repeating them to himself till they lost all instantaneous meaning for him and became wonderful vocables. He was determined to fight with every energy of soul and body against any possible consignment to what he now regarded as the hell of hells – the region, otherwise expressed, wherein everything is found to be obvious – and the saint who formerly was chary of speech in obedience to a commandment of silence could just be recognised in the artist who schooled himself to silence lest words should return him his discourtesy. Phrases came to him asking to have themselves explained. He said to himself: I must wait for the Eucharist to come to me: and then he set about translating the phrase into common sense. He spent days and nights hammering noisily as he built a house of silence for himself wherein he might await his Eucharist, days and nights gathering the first fruits and every peace-offering and heaping them upon his altar whereon he prayed clamorously the burning token of satisfaction might descend. In class, in the hushed library, in the company of other students he would suddenly hear a command to begone, to be alone, a voice agitating the very tympanum of his ear, a flame leaping into divine cerebral life. He would obey the command and wander up and down the streets alone, the fervour of his hope sustained by ejaculations until he felt sure that it was useless to wander any more: and then he would return home with a deliberate, unflagging step piecing together meaningless words and phrases with deliberate unflagging seriousness.

Their Eminences of the Holy College are hardly more scrupulous solitaries during the ballot for Christ's vicar than was Stephen at this time. He wrote a great deal of verse and, in default of any better contrivance, his verse allowed him to combine the offices of penitent and confessor. He sought in his verses to fix the most elusive of his moods and he put his lines together not word by word but letter by letter. He read Blake and Rimbaud on the values of letters and even permuted and combined the five vowels to construct cries for primitive emotions. To none of his former fervours had he given himself with such a whole heart as to this fervour; the monk now seemed to him no more than half the artist. He persuaded himself that it is necessary for an artist to labour incessantly at his art if he wishes to express completely even the simplest conception and he believed that every moment of inspiration must be paid for in advance. He was not convinced of the truth of the saying 'The poet is born, not made' but he was quite sure of the truth of this at least: 'The poem is made not born.' The burgher notion of the poet Byron in undress pouring out verses just as a city fountain pours out water seemed to him characteristic of most popular judgments on esthetic matters and he combated the notion at its root by saying solemnly to Maurice – Isolation is the first principle of artistic economy.

The classical temper

Having ... established the literary form of art as the most excellent he proceeded to examine it in favour of his theory, or, as he rendered it, to establish the relations which must subsist between the literary image, the work of art itself, and that energy which had imagined and fashioned it, that centre of conscious re-acting, particular life, the artist.

The artist, he imagined, standing in the position of mediator between the world of his experience and the world of his dreams – a mediator, consequently gifted with twin faculties, a selective faculty and a reproductive faculty. To equate these faculties was the secret of artistic success: the artist who could disentangle the subtle soul of the image from its mesh of defining circumstances most exactly and re-embody it in artistic circumstances chosen as the most exact for it in its new office, he was the supreme artist. This perfect coincidence of the two artistic faculties Stephen called poetry and he imagined the domain of an art to be cone-shaped. The term 'literature' now seemed to him a term of contempt and he used it to designate the vast middle region which lies between apex and base, between poetry and the chaos of unremembered writing. Its merit lay in its portrayal of externals; the realm of its princes was the realm of the manners and customs of societies – a spacious realm. But society is itself, he conceived, the complex body in which certain laws are involved and overwrapped and he therefore proclaimed as the realm of the poet the realm of these unalterable laws. Such a theory might easily have led its deviser to the acceptance of spiritual anarchy in literature had he not at the same time insisted on the classical style. A classical style, he said, is the syllogism of art, the only legitimate process from one world to another. Classicism is not the manner of any fixed age or of any fixed country: it is a constant state of the artistic mind. It is a temper of security and satisfaction and patience. The romantic temper, so often and so grievously misinterpreted and not more by others than by its own, is an insecure, unsatisfied, impatient temper which sees no fit abode here for its ideals and chooses therefore to behold them under insensible figures. As a result of this choice it comes to disregard certain limitations. Its figures are blown to wild adventures, lacking the gravity of solid bodies, and the mind that has conceived them ends by disowning them. The classical temper on the other hand, ever mindful of limita-tions, chooses rather to bend upon these present things and so to work upon them and fashion them that the quick intelligence may go beyond them to their meaning which is still unuttered. In this method the sane and joyful spirit issues forth and achieves imperishable perfection, nature assisting with her goodwill and thanks. For so long as this place in nature is given us it is right that art should do no violence to the gift.

The role of the poet

The critic is he who is able, by means of the signs which the artist affords, to approach the temper which has made the work and to see what is well done therein and what it signifies. For him a song by Shakespeare which seems so free and living, as remote from any conscious purpose as rain that falls in a garden or as the lights of evening, discovers itself as the rhythmic speech of an emotion otherwise incommunicable, or at least not so fitly. But to approach the temper which has made art is an act of reverence before the performance of which many conventions must be first put off for certainly that inmost region will never yield its secret to one who is enmeshed with profanities.

Chief among these profanities Stephen set the antique principle that the end of art is to instruct, to elevate, and to amuse. 'I am unable to find even a trace of this Puritanic conception of the esthetic purpose in the definition which Aquinas has given of beauty,' he wrote, 'or in anything which he has written concerning the beautiful. The qualifications he expects for beauty are in fact of so abstract and common a character that it is quite impossible for even the most violent partizan to use the Aquinatian theory with the object of attacking any work of art that we possess from the hand of any artist whatsoever.' This recognition of the beautiful in virtue of the most abstract relations afforded by an object to which the term could be applied so far from giving any support to a commandment of *Noli Tangere* was itself no more than a just sequence from the taking-off of all interdictions from the artist. The limits of decency suggest themselves somewhat too readily to the modern speculator and their effect is to encourage the profane mind to very futile jurisdiction. For it cannot be urged too strongly on the public mind that the tradition of art is with the artists and that even if they do not make it their invariable practice to outrage these limits of decency the public mind has no right to conclude therefrom that they do not arrogate for themselves an entire liberty to do so if they choose. It is as absurd, wrote the fiery-hearted revolutionary, for a criticism itself established upon homilies to prohibit the elective courses of the artist in his *revelation* of the beautiful as it would be for a police-magistrate to prohibit the sum of any two sides of a triangle from being together greater than the third side.

In fine the truth is not that the artist requires a document of licence from householders entitling him to proceed in this or that fashion but that every age must look for its sanction to its poets and philosophers. The poet is the intense centre of the life of his age to which he stands in a relation than which none can be more vital. He alone is capable of absorbing in himself the life that surrounds him and of flinging it abroad again amid planetary music. When the poetic phenomenon is signalled in the heavens, exclaimed this heaven-ascending essayist, it is time for the critics to verify their calculations in accordance with it. It is time for them to acknowledge that here the imagination has contemplated intensely the truth of the being of the visible world and that beauty, the splendour of truth, has been born. The age, though it bury itself fathoms deep in formulas and machinery, has need of these realities which alone give and sustain life and it must await from those chosen centres of vivification the force to live, the security for life which can come to it only from them. Thus the spirit of man makes a continual affirmation.

Poet's foil

It would seem at first somewhat strange and improbable that these two young men should have anything in common beyond an incurable desire for leisure. Stephen had begun to regard himself seriously as a literary artist: he professed scorn for the rabblement and contempt for authority. Cranly's chosen companions represented the rabblement in a stage of partial fermentation when it is midway between vat and flagon and Cranly seemed to please himself in the spectacle of this caricature of his own unreadiness. Anyhow towards rabblement and authority alike he behaved with submissive deference and Stephen would have been disposed to regard this too mature demeanour as a real sign of interior corruption had he not daily evidence that Cranly was willing to endanger his own fair name as a member of the Sodality and as a general lay-servant of the Church by association with one who was known to be contaminated. Cranly, however, might have wished the fathers to suppose that he went with the rebellious young artist with the secret purpose of leading him back again to good ways and, as if from a secret appreciation of his own fitness for such a task, he always enlarged and interpreted the doctrines of the Church side by side with Stephen's theories. Thus confronted, it was a trick of the pleader for orthodoxy to suggest a possible reconciliation between neighbours and to suggest further that the Church would not be over hasty in condemning vagaries of architecture or even the use of pagan emblems and flourishes so long as her ground rent was paid quarterly in advance. These accommodating business terms, which would have seemed of suspicious piety to more simple souls, were not likely to startle two young men who were fond of tracing even moral phenomena back to the region of their primal cells. The moral doctrine of Catholicism so cunningly lined and interwoven with a studious alloy of conscience was capable under the management of a nimble spirit of performing feats of extension and contraction. After a thousand such changes of form this elastic body was suddenly detected in a change of position and a point hitherto external was now seen to be well enclosed within it: and all this imperceptibly, while the eye was lulled by the mere exhibition of so many variations executed with a certain amoeboid instinct.

As for artistic sympathies Cranly could hardly be said to offer these. He had all the rustic's affection for the prosaic things of the six days of the week and, in addition to this, he lacked the hypocritical taste which the rustic affects for the fine arts on the seventh day. In the Library he read nothing but the weekly illustrated papers. Sometimes he took a big book from the counter and carried it solemnly to his place where he opened it and studied the title-page and preface for an hour or so. Of fine literature he had, almost literally speaking, no knowledge. His acquaintance with English prose seemed to be limited to a hazy acquaintance with the beginnings of *Nicholas Nickleby* and of English verse he had certainly read Wordsworth's poem which is called '*Advice to a Father*'. Both of these accomplishments he divulged to Stephen one day when he had been discovered reading with great attention the title-page of a book which was called *Diseases of the Ox*. He offered no comment on what he had read and simply stated the achievement not without wonder at his having achieved it. He had a straggling regiment of words at his command and he was thus enabled to express himself: but he spoke flatly and frequently made childish errors. He had a defiant manner of using technical and foreign terms as if he wished to suggest that for him they were mere conventions of language. His receptiveness was not troubled by any nausea; he received everything that came in his way and it was purely instinctive of Stephen to perceive any special affinity in so indiscriminate a vessel. He was fond of leading a philosophical argument back to the machinery of the intellectual faculty itself and in mundane matters he did likewise, testing everything by its food value.

It was in favour of this young man that Stephen decided to

break his commandment of reticence. Cranly, on his side, must have been above all the accidents of life if he had not suffered a slight commotion from such delicately insistent flattery. Stephen spoke to his impoverished ear out of the plenitude of an amassed vocabulary, and confronted the daring commonplaces of his companion's moods with a complex radiance of thought. Cranly seldom or never obtruded his presence upon these monologues. He listened to all, seemed to understand all, and seemed to think it was the duty of his suppositious character to listen and understand. He never refused his ear. Stephen claimed it in and out of season as he felt the need for intelligent sympathy. They promenaded miles of the streets together, arm-in-arm. They halted in wet weather under spacious porches, desisting at the sight of some inviting triviality. They sat sometimes in the pit of a music-hall and one unfolded to the other the tapestry of his poetical aims while the band bawled to the comedian and the comedian bawled to the band. Cranly grew used to having sensations and impressions recorded and analysed before him at the very instant of their apparition. Such concentration upon oneself was unknown to him and he wondered at first with the joy of solitary possession at Stephen's ingenuous arrogance. This phenomenon, which called all his previous judgments to account, and opened out a new system of life at the last limit of his [Cranly's] world, rankled somewhat in his [Cranly's] mind. It irritated him also because he knew too well the large percentage of Christian sentiment which concealed itself under his veneer of Stoicism to suspect himself of any talent for a similar extravagance. And yet, hearing the whole-hearted young egoist pour out his pride and anger at his feet like some costly ointment, and benefiting by a liberality which seemed to keep nothing in reserve, much as he would have liked to hold himself aloof from such ties he felt himself gradually answering the appeal by a silent, perverse affection. He affected more brutality than was in his nature and, as if infected by his companion's arrogance, seemed to expect that the practice of aggressive criticism would be suspended in his case.

A licence which he allowed himself rather freely was that of impolite abstraction, so deep as to suggest great mental activity but issuing at last in some blunt actuality. If a monologue which had set out from a triviality seemed to him likely to run on unduly he would receive it with a silence through which aversion was just discernible and at a lull bring his hammer down brutally on the poor original object. At times Stephen found this ultra-classical habit very unpalatable. One evening the monologue was interrupted time after time. Stephen had mentioned his sister's illness and had spread out a few leagues of theory on the subject of the tyranny of home. Cranly never actually broke in upon the oration but he continued inserting question after question whenever he had an opening. He asked Isabel's age, her symptoms, her doctor's name, her treatment, her diet, her appearance, how her mother nursed her, whether they had sent for a priest or not, whether she had ever been sick before or not. Stephen answered all these questions and still Cranly was not satisfied. He continued his questions until the monologue had in all decency to be abandoned: and Stephen, thinking over his manner, was unable to decide whether such conduct was to be considered the sign of a deep interest in a human illness or the sign of irritated dissatisfaction with an inhuman theorist.

Rhetoric

Not very far from him in the shelter of one of the pillars Stephen saw his father and two friends. His father had directed his eyeglass upon the distant choir and his face wore an expression of impressed piety. The choir was executing some florid tracery which was intended as an expression of mourning. The walk, the heat, the crush, the darkness of the chapel overcame Stephen and, leaning against the lintel of the door, he half closed his eyes and allowed his thoughts to drift. Rhymes began to make themselves in his head.

He perceived dimly that a white figure had ascended the pulpit and he heard a voice saying *Consummatum est*. He recognised the voice and he knew that Father Dillon was preaching on the Seventh Word. He took no trouble to hear the sermon but every few minutes he heard a new translation of the Word rolling over the congregation. 'It is ended' 'It is accomplished'. This sensation awoke him from his day-dream and as the translations followed [each] one another more and more rapidly he found his gambling instinct on the alert. He wagered with himself as to what word the preacher would select. 'It is . . . accomplished' 'It is . . . consummated' 'It is . . . achieved'. In the few seconds which intervened between the first part and the second part of the phrase Stephen's mind performed feats of divining agility 'It is . . . finished' 'It is . . . completed' 'It is . . . concluded'. At last with a final burst of rhetoric Father Dillon cried out that it was over and the congregation began to pour itself out into the streets. Stephen was borne along in the crowd and everywhere about him he heard the same murmurs of admiration and saw the same expressions of satisfaction, discreet murmurs, subdued expressions. The special charges of the Jesuits were congratulating themselves and one another on a well-spent Good Friday.

To avoid his father Stephen slipped round towards the body of the chapel and waited in the central porch while the common people came shuffling and stumbling past him. Here also there was admiration, satisfaction. A young workman passed out with his wife and Stephen heard the words 'He knows his thayology, I tell ye.' Two women stopped beside the holy water font and after scraping their hands vainly over the bottom crossed themselves in a slovenly fashion with their dry hands. One of them sighed and drew her brown shawl about her:

– An' his language, said the other woman.

–Aw yis.

Here the other woman sighed in her turn and drew her shawl about her:

– On'y, said she, God bless the gintleman, he uses the words that you nor me can't intarprit.

The dying sister

His sister had become almost a stranger to him on account of the way in which she had been brought up. He had hardly spoken a hundred words to her since the time when they had been children together. He could not speak to her now except as to a stranger. She had acquiesced in the religion of her mother; she had accepted everything that had been proposed to her. If she lived she had exactly the temper for a Catholic wife of limited intelligence and of pious docility and if she died she was supposed to have earned for herself a place in the eternal heaven of Christians from which her two brothers were likely to be shut out. Calamities in this world are reported to sit lightly on the shoulders of the true Christian who can bide his time until the Creator institutes the kingdom of the good. Isabel's case moved Stephen's anger and commiseration but he saw at once how hopeless it was and how vain it would be for him to interfere. Her life had been and would always be a trembling walk before God. The slightest interchange of ideas between them must be either a condescension on his part or an attempt to corrupt. No consciousness of their nearness in blood troubled him with natural, unreasoning affection. She was called his sister as his mother was called his mother but there had never been any proof of that relation offered him in their emotional attitude towards him, or any recognition of it permitted in his emotional attitude towards them. The Catholic husband and wife, the Catholic father and mother, are allowed to be natural at discretion but the same grace is not vouchsafed to Catholic children. They must preserve an unquestioning orderliness even at the risk of being upbraided as unnatural by the very preachers who assert that nature is the possession of Satan. Stephen had felt impulses of pity for his mother, for his father, for Isabel, for Wells also but he believed that he had done right in resisting them: he had first of all to save himself and he had no business trying to save others unless his experiment with himself justified him. Cranly had all but formulated serious charges against him, calling up by implication the picture of Isabel with her gradually wasting flame, her long dark hair and great wondering eyes, but Stephen stood up to the charges and answered in his heart that it was injustice to point a finger of reproach at him and that a vague inactive pity from those who upheld a system of mutual servile association towards those who accepted it was only a play upon emotions as characteristic of the egoist as of the man of sentiment. Isabel, moreover, did not seem to Stephen to be in any great danger. He told Cranly she was probably growing too fast; many girls were delicate at that age. He confessed that the subject tired him a little. Cranly stood still and looked at him fixedly:

– My dear man, said he, d'ye know what it is . . . You're an extraordinary . . . man.

Apropos

A week before the examination Cranly explained to Stephen his plan for reading the course in five days. It was a carefully made plan, founded upon an intimate knowledge of examiners and examination papers. Cranly's plan was to study from ten in the morning until half past two in the afternoon, then from four to six, and then from half past seven to ten. Stephen declined to follow this plan as he imagined he had a fair chance of passing on what he called 'roundabout' knowledge but Cranly said that the plan was perfectly safe.

– I don't quite see that, said Stephen, how can you manage to pass – in Latin composition, say – after such a cursory run over it? If you like I'll show you some things – not that I can write so marvellously . . .

Cranly meditated without seeming to observe the offer. Then he averred flatly that his plan would work:

– I'll take my dyin' bible, he said, I'll write them as good a thing, d'ye know, ay – as good a thing as they want. What do they know about Latin prose?

– Not much, I suppose, said Stephen, but they may not be quite ignorant of Latin grammar.

Cranly thought his over and then found his remedy:

– D'ye know what, he said, whenever I can't think of the grammar I'll bring in a piece out of Tacitus.

– Apropos of what?

– What the flamin' hell does it matter what it's apropos of?

– Quite right, said Stephen.

Improving on Shelley

The nights before the examination were spent sitting outside under the porch of the Library. The two young men gazed up into the tranquil sky and discussed how it was possible to live with the least amount of labour. Cranly suggested bees: he seemed to know the entire economy of bee-life and he did not seem as intolerant towards bees as towards men. Stephen said it would be a good arrangement if Cranly were to live on the labour of the bees and allow him (Stephen) to live on the united labours of the bees and of their keeper.

– 'I will watch from dawn to gloom
  The lake-reflected sun illume
  The yellow bees in the ivy bloom.'

– 'Illume'? said Cranly.

– You know the meaning of 'illume'?

– Who wrote that?

– Shelley.

– Illume – it's just the word, d'ye know, for autumn, deep gold colour.

– A spiritual interpretation of landscape is very rare. Some people think they write spiritually if they make their scenery dim and cloudy.

– That bit you said now doesn't seem to me spiritual.

– Nor to me: but sometimes Shelley does not address the eye. He says 'many a lake-surrounded flute.' Does that strike your eye or your sense of colour?

– Shelley has a face that reminds me of a bird. What is it? 'The lake-surrounded sun illume'? . . .

– 'The lake-reflected sun illume
   The yellow bees in the ivy bloom.'

– What are you quoting? asked Glynn who had just come out of the Library after several hours of study.

Cranly surveyed him before answering:

– Shelley.

– O, Shelley? What was the quotation again?

Cranly nodded towards Stephen.

– What was the quotation? asked Glynn. Shelley is an old flame of mine.

Stephen repeated the lines and Glynn nodded his head nervously several times in approval.

– Beautiful poetry Shelley wrote, didn't he? So mystical.

– D'ye know what they call them yellow bees in Wickla? asked Cranly suddenly, turning to Glynn.

– No? what?

– Red-arsed bees.

Cranly laughed loudly at his own remark and struck his heels on the granite steps. Glynn, conscious of a false position, began to fumble with his umbrella and to search for one of his stock witticisms.

– But that is only, he said, if you will pardon the expression, that is only so to speak . . .

> – 'The lake-surrounded sun illume
>   The red-arsed bees in the ivy bloom.'

– It's every bit as good bloody poetry as Shelley's, said Cranly to Glynn. What do you think?

– It seems to me undeniable, said Glynn driving his unsteady umbrella before him as an emphasis, that the bees are in the bloom. Of that we may say that it is distinctly so.

Non credo

The examination ended on Tuesday. On Wednesday morning Stephen's mother seemed to be rather anxious. Stephen had not given his parents much satisfaction as to his conduct at the examination but he could not think that this was the cause of his mother's trouble: he waited, however, for the trouble to declare itself. His mother waited till the room was clear and then she said casually:

– You have not made your Easter duty yet, have you, Stephen?

Stephen answered that he had not.

– It would be better for you to go to confession in the daytime. Tomorrow is Ascension Thursday and the chapels are sure to be crowded tonight by people who have left off making their Easter duty till the last moment. It's a wonder people wouldn't have more shame in them. Goodness knows they have time enough from Ash Wednesday, without waiting till the stroke of twelve to go to the priest . . . I'm not speaking of you, Stephen. I know you have been studying for your examination. But people who have nothing to do . . .

Stephen made no answer to this but went on scraping diligently in his eggshell.

– I have made my Easter duty already – on Holy Thursday – but I'm going to the altar in the morning. I am making a novena and I want you to offer up your communion for a special intention of mine.

– What special intention?

– Well, dear, I'm very much concerned about Isabel ... I don't know what to think ...

Stephen stuck his spoon angrily through the bottom of the shell and asked was there any more tea.

– There's no more in the pot but I can boil some water in a minute.

– O, never mind.

– It won't be a jiffy.

Stephen allowed the water to be put on as it would give him time to put an end to the conversation. He was much annoyed that his mother should try to wheedle him into conformity by using his sister's health as an argument. He felt that such an attempt dishonoured him and freed him from the last dissuasions of considerate piety. His mother put on the water and appeared to be less anxious as if she had expected a blunt refusal. She even ventured on the small talk of religious matrons.

– I must try and get in to town tomorrow in time for High Mass in Marlborough St. Tomorrow is a great feast-day in the Church.

– Why? asked Stephen smiling.

– The Ascension of Our Lord, answered his mother gravely.

– And why is that a great feast-day?

– Because it was on that day he showed Himself Divine: he ascended into Heaven.

Stephen began to plaster butter over a crusty heel of the loaf while his features settled into definite hostility:

– Where did he go off?

– From Mount Olivet, answered his mother reddening under her eyes.

– Head first?

– What do you mean, Stephen?

– I mean he must have been rather giddy by the time he arrived. Why didn't he go by balloon?

– Stephen, are you trying to scoff at Our Lord? I really

thought you had more intelligence than to use that kind of language: it's only what people who believe only in what they can see under their noses say. I'm surprised.

– Tell me, mother, said Stephen between mouthfuls, do you mean to tell me you believe that our friend went up off the mountain as they say he did?

– I do.

– I don't.

– What are you saying, Stephen?

– It's absurd: it's Barnum. He comes into the world God knows how, walks on the water, gets out of his grave and goes up off the Hill of Howth. What drivel is this?

– Stephen!

– I don't believe it: and it would be no credit if I did. It's no credit to me that I don't. It's drivel.

– The most learned doctors of the Church believe it and that's good enough for me.

– He can fast for forty days . . .

– God can do all things.

– There's a fellow in Capel St at present in a show who says he can eat glass and hard nails. He calls himself *The Human Ostrich*.

– Stephen, said his mother, I'm afraid you have lost your faith.

– I'm afraid so too, said Stephen.

Mrs Daedalus looked very discomposed and sat down helplessly on the nearest chair. Stephen fixed his attention on the water and when it was ready made himself another cup of tea.

– I little thought, said his mother, that it would come to this – that a child of mine would lose the faith.

– But you knew some time ago.

– How could I know?

– You knew.

– I suspected something was wrong but I never thought . . .

– And yet you wanted me to receive Holy Communion!

– Of course you cannot receive it now. But I thought you

would make your Easter duty as you have done every year up till now. I do not know what led you astray unless it was those books you read. John, too, your uncle – he was led astray by books when he was young but – only for a time.

– Poor fellow! said Stephen.

– You were religiously brought up by the Jesuits, in a Catholic home . . .

– A very Catholic home!

– None of your people, neither your father's nor mine, have a drop of anything but Catholic blood in their veins.

– Well, I'll make a beginning in the family.

– This is the result of being left too much liberty. You do as you like and believe what you like.

– I don't believe, for example, that Jesus was the only man that ever had pure auburn hair.

– Well?

– Nor that he was the only man that was exactly six feet high, neither more nor less.

– Well?

– Well, you believe that. I heard you tell that years ago to our nurse in Bray – do you remember nurse Sarah?

Mrs Daedalus defended the tradition in a half-hearted way.

– That is what they say.

– O, they say! They say a great deal.

– But you need not believe that if you don't want to.

– Thanks very much.

– All you are asked to believe in is the word of God. Think of the beautiful teachings of Our Lord. Think of your own life when you believed in those teachings. Weren't you better and happier then?

– It was good for me at the time, perhaps, but it is quite useless for me now.

– I know what is wrong with you – you suffer from the pride of the intellect. You forget that we are only worms of the earth. You think you can defy God because you have misused the talents he has given you.

– I think Jehovah gets too high a salary for judging motives. I want to retire him on the plea of old age.

Mrs Daedalus stood up.

– Stephen, you may use that kind of language with your companions whoever they are but I will not allow you to use it with me. Even your father, bad as he is supposed to be, does not speak such blasphemy as you do. I am afraid that you are a changed boy since you went to that University. I suppose you fell in with some of those students . . .

– Good Lord, mother, said Stephen, don't believe that. The students are awfully nice fellows. They love their religion: they wouldn't say boo to a goose.

– Wherever you've learnt it I will not allow you to use such language to me when you speak of holy things. Keep that for the street-corners at night.

– Very well, mother, said Stephen. But you began the conversation.

– I never thought I would see the day when a child of mine would lose the faith. God knows I didn't. I did my best for you to keep you in the right way.

Mrs Daedalus began to cry. Stephen, having eaten and drunk all within his province, rose and went towards the door:

– It's all the fault of those books and the company you keep. Out at all hours of the night instead of in your home, the proper place for you. I'll burn every one of them. I won't have them in the house to corrupt anyone else.

Stephen halted at the door and turned towards his mother who had now broken out into tears:

– If you were a genuine Roman Catholic, mother, you would burn me as well as the books.

– I knew no good would come of your going to that place. You are ruining yourself body and soul. Now your faith is gone!

– Mother, said Stephen from the threshold, I don't see what you're crying for. I'm young, healthy, happy. What is the crying for? . . . It's too silly . . .

The individual conscience

He went up to Cranly who was leaning against a pillar and gazing straight before him and touched him lightly on the shoulder:

– I want to speak to you, he said.

Cranly turned slowly round and looked at him. Then he asked:

– Now?

– Yes.

They walked together up along Kildare St without speaking. When they came to the Green Cranly said:

– I'm going home on Saturday. Will you come as far as Harcourt St Station? I want to see the hour the train goes at.

– All right.

In the station Cranly spent a great deal of time reading the time-tables and making abstruse calculations. Then he went up to the platform and watched for a long time the shunting of the engine of a goods train on to a passenger train. The engine was steaming and blowing a deafening whistle and rolling billows of thick smoke towards the roof of the station. Cranly said that the engine-driver came from his part of the country and that he was the son of a cobbler in Tinahely. The engine executed a series of indecisive movements and finally settled itself on to the train. The engine-driver stuck his head out through the side and gazed languidly along the train:

– I suppose you would call him sooty Jaysus, said Cranly.

– Cranly, said Stephen, I have left the Church.

Cranly took his arm at the word and they turned away from the platform and went down the staircase. As soon as they had emerged into the street he said encouragingly:

– You have left the Church?

Stephen went over the interview phrase by phrase.

– Then you do not believe any longer?

– I cannot believe.

– But you could at one time.

– I cannot now.

– You could now if you wanted to.

– Well, I don't want to.

– Are you sure you do not believe?

– Quite sure.

– Why do you not go to the altar?

– Because I do not believe.

– Would you make a sacrilegious communion?

– Why should I?

– For your mother's sake.

– I don't see why I should.

– Your mother will suffer very much. You say you do not believe. The Host for you is a piece of ordinary bread. Would you not eat a piece of ordinary bread to avoid causing your mother pain?

– I would in many cases.

– And why not in this case? Have you any reluctance to commit a sacrilege? If you do not believe you should not have any.

– Wait a minute, said Stephen. At present I have a reluctance to commit a sacrilege. I am a product of Catholicism; I was sold to Rome before my birth. Now I have broken my slavery but I cannot in a moment destroy every feeling in my nature. That takes time. However if it were a case of needs must – for my life, for instance – I would commit any enormity with the host.

– Many Catholics would do the same, said Cranly, if their lives were at stake.

– Believers?

– Ay, believers. So by your own showing you are a believer.

– It is not from fear that I refrain from committing a sacrilege.

– Why then?

– I see no reason for committing sacrilege.

– But you have always made your Easter Duty. Why do you change? The thing for you is mockery, mummery.

– If I mum it is an act of submission, a public act of submission to the Church. I will not submit to the Church.

– Even so far as to mum?

– It is mumming with an intention. The outward show is nothing but it means a good deal.

– Again you are speaking like a Catholic. The host is nothing in outward show – a piece of bread.

– I admit: but all the same I insist on disobeying the Church. I will not submit any longer.

– But could you not be more diplomatic? Could you not rebel in your heart and yet conform out of contempt? You could be a rebel in spirit.

– That cannot be done for long by anyone who is sensitive. The Church knows the value of her services: her priest must hypnotise himself every morning before the tabernacle. If I get up every morning, go to the looking-glass and say to myself 'You are the Son of God' at the end of twelve months I will want disciples.

– If you could make your religion pay like Christianity I would advise you to get up every morning and go to the looking-glass.

– That would be good for my vicars on earth but I would find crucifixion a personal inconvenience.

– But here in Ireland by following your new religion of unbelief you may be crucifying yourself like Jesus – only socially not physically.

– There is a difference. Jesus was good-humoured over it. I will die hard.

– How can you propose such a future to yourself and yet be afraid to trust yourself to perform even the simplest mumming in a church? said Cranly.

– That is my business, said Stephen, tapping at his forehead.

When they had come to the Green they crossed the streets and began to walk round the enclosure inside the chains. A few mechanics and their sweethearts were sitting on the swinging-chains turning the shadows to account. The footpath was deserted except for the metallic image of a distant policeman who had been posted well in the gaslight as an admonition. When the two young men passed the college they both looked up at the same moment towards the dark windows.

– May I ask you why you left the Church? asked Cranly.

– I could not observe the precepts.

– Not even with grace?

– No.

– Jesus gives very simple precepts. The Church is severe.

– Jesus or the Church – it's all the same to me. I can't follow him. I must have liberty to do as I please.

– No man can do as he pleases.

– Morally.

– No, not morally either.

– You want me, said Stephen, to toe the line with those sycophants and hypocrites in the college. I will never do so.

– No. I mentioned Jesus.

– Don't mention him. I have made it a common noun. They don't believe in him; they don't observe his precepts. In any case let us leave Jesus aside. My sight will only carry me as far as his lieutenant in Rome. It is quite useless: I will not be frightened into paying tribute in money or in thought.

– You told me – do you remember the evening we were standing at the top of the staircase talking about . . .

– Yes, yes, I remember, said Stephen who hated Cranly's method of remembering the past, what did I tell you?

– You told me the idea you had of Jesus on Good Friday, an ugly misshapen Jesus. Did it ever strike you that Jesus may have been a conscious impostor?

– I have never believed in his chastity – that is since I began to think about him. I am sure he was no eunuch priest. His interest in loose women is too persistently humane. All the women associated with him are of dubious character.

– You don't think he was God?

– What a question! Explain it: explain the hypostatic union: tell me if the figure which that policeman worships as the Holy Ghost is intended for a spermatozoon with wings added. What a question! He makes general remarks on life, that's all I know: and I disagree with them.

– For example?

– For example . . . Look here, I cannot talk on this subject. I am not a scholar and I receive no pay as a minister of God. I want to live, do you understand. McCann wants air and food: I want them and a hell of a lot of other things too. I don't care whether I am right or wrong. There is always that risk in human affairs, I suppose. But even if I am wrong at least I shall not have to endure Father Butt's company for eternity.

Cranly laughed.

– Remember he would be glorified.

– Heaven for climate, isn't that it, and hell for society . . . the whole affair is too damn idiotic. Give it up. I am very young. When I have a beard to my middle I will study Hebrew and then write to you about it.

– Why are you so impatient with the Jesuits? asked Cranly.

Stephen did not answer and, when they arrived in the next region of light Cranly exclaimed:

– Your face is red!

– I feel it, said Stephen.

– Most people think you are self-restrained, said Cranly after a pause.

– So I am, said Stephen.

– Not on this subject. Why do you get so excited: I can't understand that. It is a thing for you to think out.

– I can think out things when I like. I have thought this affair out very carefully though you may not believe me when I tell you. But my escape excites me: I must talk as I do. I feel a flame in my face. I feel a wind rush through me.

– 'Like a mighty wind rushing,' said Cranly.

– You urge me to postpone life – till when? Life is now – this is life: if I postpone it I may never live. To walk nobly on the surface of the earth, to express oneself without pretence, to acknowledge one's own humanity! You mustn't think I rhapsodise: I am quite serious. I speak from my soul.

– Soul?

– Yes: from my soul, my spiritual nature. Life is not a yawn. Philosophy, love, art will not disappear from my world because I no longer believe that by entertaining an emotion of desire for the tenth part of a second I prepare for myself an eternity of torture. I am happy.

– Can you say that?

– Jesus is sad. Why is he so sad? He is solitary . . . I say, you must feel the truth of what I say. You are holding up the Church against me . . .

– Allow me . . .

– But what is the Church? It is not Jesus, the magnificent solitary with his inimitable abstinences. The Church is made by me and my like – her services, legends, practices, paintings, music, traditions. These her artists gave her. They made her what she is. They accepted Aquinas' commentary on Aristotle as the Word of God and made her what she is.

– And why will you not help her to be so still – you as an artist?

– I see you recognise the truth of what I say though you won't admit it.

– The Church allows the individual conscience to have great . . . in fact, if you believe . . . believe, that is, said Cranly stamping each heavy foot on the words, honestly and truly . . .

– Enough! said Stephen gripping his companion's arm. You need not defend me. I will take the odds as they are.

They paced along three sides of the Green in silence while the couples began to leave the chains and return meekly to their modest resting-places and after a while Cranly began to explain to Stephen how he too had felt a desire for life – a life of freedom and happiness – when he had been younger and how at that time he too had been about to leave the Church in search of happiness but that many considerations had restrained him.

A sultry summer

The summer was dull and warm. Nearly every day Stephen wandered through the slums watching the sordid lives of the inhabitants. He read all the street-ballads which were stuck in the dusty windows of the Liberties. He read the racing names and prices scrawled in blue pencil outside the dingy tobacco-shops, the windows of which were adorned with scarlet police journals. He examined all the book-stalls which offered old directories and volumes of sermons and unheard-of treatises at the rate of a penny each or three for two-pence. He often posted himself opposite one of the factories in old Dublin at two o'clock to watch the hands coming out to dinner – principally young boys and girls with colourless, expressionless faces, who seized the opportunity to be gallant in their way. He drifted in and out of interminable chapels in which an old man dozed on a bench or a clerk dusted the woodwork or an old woman prayed before the candle she had lighted. As he walked slowly through the maze of poor streets he stared proudly in return for the glances of stupid wonder that he received and watched from under his eyes the great cow-like trunks of police constables swing slowly round after him as he passed them. These wanderings filled him with deep-seated anger and whenever he encountered a burly black-vested priest taking a stroll of pleasant inspection through these warrens full of swarming and cringing believers he cursed the farce of Irish Catholicism: an island the inhabitants of which entrust their wills and minds to others that they may ensure for themselves a life of spiritual paralysis, an island in which all the power and riches are in the keeping of those whose kingdom is not of this world, an island in which Caesar confesses Christ and Christ confesses Caesar that together they may wax fat upon a starveling rabblement which is bidden ironically to take to itself this consolation in hardship 'The Kingdom of God is within you.'

This mood of indignation which was not guiltless of a certain superficiality was undoubtedly due to the excitement of release and it was hardly countenanced by him before he realized the dangers of being a demagogue. The attitude which was constitutional with him was a silent self-occupied, contemptuous manner and his intelligence, moreover, persuaded him that the tomahawk, as an effective instrument of warfare, had become obsolete. He acknowledged to himself in honest egoism that he could not take to heart the distress of a nation, the soul of which was antipathetic to his own, so bitterly as the indignity of a bad line of verse: but at the same time he was nothing in the world so little as an amateur artist. He wished to express his nature freely and fully for the benefit of a society which he would enrich and also for his own benefit, seeing that it was part of his life to do so. It was not part of his life to undertake an extensive alteration of society but he felt the need to express himself such an urgent need, such a real need, that he was determined no conventions of a society, however plausibly mingling pity with its tyranny, should be allowed to stand in his way, and although a taste for elegance and detail unfitted him for the part of demagogue, from his general attitude he might have been supposed not unjustly an ally of the collectivist politicians, who are often very seriously upbraided by opponents who believe in Jehovahs, and decalogues and judgments for sacrificing the reality to an abstraction.

That kind of Christianity which is called Catholicism seemed to him to stand in his way and forthwith he removed it. He had been brought up in the belief of the Roman supremacy and to cease to be a Catholic for him meant to cease to be a Christian. The idea that the power of an empire is weakest at its borders requires some modification for everyone knows that the Pope cannot govern Italy as he governs Ireland nor is the Tsar as terrible an engine to the tradesmen of S. Petersburg as he is to the little Russian of the Steppes. In fact in many cases the government of an empire is strongest at its borders and it is invariably strongest there in the case when its power at the centre is on the wane. The waves of the rise and fall of empires do not travel with the rapidity of waves of light and it will be perhaps a considerable time before Ireland will be able to understand that the Papacy is no longer going through a period of anabolism. The bands of pilgrims who are shepherded safely across the continent by their Irish pastors must shame the jaded reactionaries of the eternal city by their stupefied intensity of worship in much the same way as the staring provincial newly arrived from Spain or Africa may have piqued the loyalty of some smiling Roman for whom the future of his race was becoming uncertain as its past had already become obvious. Though it is evident on the one hand that this persistence of Catholic power in Ireland must intensify very greatly the loneliness of the Irish Catholic who voluntarily outlaws himself yet on the other hand the force which he must generate to propel himself out of so strong and intricate a tyranny may often be sufficient to place him beyond the region of re-attraction. It was, in fact, the very fervour of Stephen's former religious life which sharpened for him now the pains of his solitary position and at the same time hardened into a less pliable, a less appeasable enmity molten rages and glowing transports on which the emotions of helplessness and loneliness and despair had first acted as chilling influences.

Mr Daedalus had not an acute sense of the rights of private property: he paid rent very rarely. To demand money for eatables seemed to him just but to expect people to pay for shelter the exorbitant sums which are demanded annually by houseowners in Dublin seemed to him unjust. He had now been a year in his house in Clontarf and for that year he had paid a quarter's rent. The writ which had been first served on him had contained a legal flaw and this fact enabled him to prolong his term of occupancy. Just now matters were drawing to a head and he was scouring the city for another house. A private message from a friend in the Sheriff's office gave him exactly five days of grace and every morning he brushed his silk hat very diligently and polished his eyeglass and went forth humming derisively to offer himself as a bait to landlords. The halldoor was often banged loudly on these occasions as the only possible close of an altercation. The results of the examination had awarded Stephen a mere pass and his father told him very confidentially that he had better look out for some kind of a doss because in a week's time they would all be out on the street. The funds in the house were very low for the new furniture had fetched very little after its transport piecemeal to a pawn-office. Tradesmen who had seen it depart had begun a game of knocking and ringing which was very often followed by the curious eyes of street-urchins. Isabel was lying upstairs in the backroom, day by day growing more wasted and querulous. The doctor came twice a week now and ordered her delicacies. Mrs Daedalus had to set her wits to work to provide even one substantial meal every day and she certainly had no time to spare between accomplishing this feat, appeasing the clamour at the halldoor, parrying her husband's ill-humour and attending on her dying daughter. As for her sons, one was a freethinker, the other surly.

Stephen had lent his essay to Lynch as he had promised to do and this loan had led to a certain intimacy. Lynch had almost taken the final vows in the order of the discontented but Stephen's unapologetic egoism, his remorseless lack of sentiment for himself no less than for others, gave him pause. His taste for fine arts, which had always seemed to him a taste which should be carefully hidden away, now began to encourage itself timidly. He was also very much relieved to find Stephen's estheticism united with a sane and conscience-less acceptance of the animal needs of young men for, being a shrewd animal himself, he had begun to suspect from Stephen's zeal and loftiness of discourse at least an assertion of that incorrigible virginity which the Irish race demands alike from any John who would baptise it or from any Joan who would set it free as the first heavenly proof of fitness for such high offices. Daniel's household had become so wearisome to Stephen that he had discontinued his Sunday visits there and had substituted rambles with Lynch through the city. They made their way with difficulty along the crowded streets where underpaid young men and flaunting girls were promenading in bands. After a few of these rambles Lynch had absorbed the new terms which expressed the new point of view and he began to feel that he was justifying the contempt to which the spectacle of Dublin manner had always moved him. Many times they stopped to confer in scrupulous slang with the foolish virgins of the city, whose souls were almost terrified out of their naughty intentions by the profundity of the tones of the elder of the young men, and Lynch, sunning himself in a companionship which was so alert and liberal, so free from a taint of secret competition or patronage, began to wonder how he could ever have thought Stephen an affected young man. Everyone, he thought now, who has a character to preserve must have a manner to preserve it with.

There could be no doubt now that the girl was in a bad way. Her eyes were piteously enlarged and her voice had become hollow. She sat half propped-up by pillows in the bed all day, her damp-looking hair hanging in wisps about her face, turning over the pages of an illustrated book. She began to whimper when she was told to eat or when anyone left her bedside. She showed very little animation except when the piano was playing in the room below and then she made them leave the bedroom door open and closed her eyes. Money was still scarce and still the doctor ordered her delicacies. The lingering nature of the illness had spread a hopeless apathy about the household and, though she herself was little more than a child, she must have been aware of this. Stephen alone with persistent kindness preserved his usual manner of selfish cheerfulness and strove to stir a fire out of her embers of life. He even exaggerated and his mother reproved him for

being so noisy. He could not go in to his sister and say to her
'Live! live!' but he tried to touch her soul in the shrillness of a
whistle or the vibration of a note. Whenever he went into the
room he asked questions with an indifferent air as if her
illness was of no importance and once or twice he could have
assured himself that the eyes that looked at him from the bed
had guessed his meaning.

One evening as Stephen was coming down the Library
staircase after idling away a half-hour at a medical treatise on
singing, he heard a dress brushing the steps behind him. The
dress belonged to Emma Clery who, of course, was very much
surprised at seeing Stephen. She had just been working at
some old Irish and now she was going home: her father didn't
like her to stay in the Library until ten o'clock as she had no
escort. The night was so fine that she thought she would not
take the tram. Stephen asked her might he not see her home.
They stood under the porch for a few minutes, talking.
Stephen took out a cigarette and lit it but at once knocked off
the lighted end very meditatively and put the cigarette back
into his case: her eyes were very bright.

   They went up Kildare St and when they came to the corner
of the Green she crossed the road and they continued to walk,
but not quite so quickly, along the gravel path beside the
chains. The chains bore their nightly burden of amorousness.
He offered her his arm which she took, leaning appreciably
upon it. They talked gossip. She discussed the likelihood of
McCann's marrying the eldest of Mr Daniel's daughters. She
seemed to think it very amusing that McCann should have a
desire for matrimony but she added quite seriously that Annie
Daniel was certainly a nice girl. A feminine voice called out
from the dusky region of the couples 'Don't!'

   – 'Don't,' said Emma. Isn't that Mr Punch's advice to young
men who are about to marry . . . I hear you are quite a woman-
hater now, Stephen.

   – Wouldn't that be a change?

– And I heard you read a dreadful paper in the college – all kinds of ideas in it. Isn't that so?

– Please don't mention that paper.

– But I'm sure you're a woman-hater. You've got so standoffish, you know, so reserved. Perhaps you don't like ladies' company?

Stephen pressed her arm a little by way of a disclaimer.

– Are you a believer in the emancipation of women too? she asked.

– To be sure! said Stephen.

– Well, I'm glad to hear you say that, at any rate. I didn't think you were in favour of women.

– O, I am very liberal – like Father Dillon – he is very liberal-minded.

– Yes? Isn't he? she said in a puzzled manner . . . Why do you never go to Daniel's now?

– I . . . don't know.

– What do you do with yourself on Sunday evenings?

– I . . . stay at home, said Stephen.

– You must be morose when you're at home.

– Not I. I'm as happy as if the divil had me.

– I want to hear you sing again.

– O, thanks . . . Some time, perhaps . . .

– Why don't you study music? Have your voice trained?

– Strange to say I was reading a book on singing tonight. It is called . . .

– I am sure you would make a success with your voice, she said quickly, evidently afraid to allow him control of the conversation . . . Have you ever heard Father Moran sing?

– No. Has he a good voice?

– O, very nice: he sings with such taste. He's an awfully nice man, don't you think?

– Very nice indeed. Do you go to confession to him?

She leaned a little more appreciably on his arm and said:

– Now, don't be bold, Stephen.

– I wish you would go to confession to me, Emma, said Stephen from his heart.

– That's a dreadful thing to say ... Why would you like that?

– To hear your sins.

– Stephen!

– To hear you murmur them into my ear and say you were sorry and would never commit them again and ask me to forgive you. And I would forgive you and make you promise to commit them every time you liked and say, 'God bless you, my dear child.'

– O, for shame, Stephen! Such a way to talk of the sacraments!

Stephen had expected that she would blush but her cheek maintained its innocence and her eyes grew brighter and brighter.

– You'd get tired of that too.

– Do you think so? said Stephen making an effort not to be surprised at such an intelligent remark.

– You'd be a dreadful flirt, I'm sure. You get tired of everything so quickly – just the way you did in the Gaelic League.

– People should not think of the end in the beginning of flirtations, should they?

– Perhaps not.

When they came to the corner of her terrace she stopped and said:

– Thanks ever so much.

– Thank *you*.

– Well, you must reform, won't you, and come next Sunday to Daniel's.

– If you expressly ...

– Yes, I insist.

– Very good, Emma. In that case, I'll go.

– Mind. I expect you to obey me.

– Very good.

– Thanks again for your kindness coming across with me. *Au revoir!*

– Good night.

He waited till he had seen her enter the fourth garden of the terrace. She did not turn her head to see if he was watching but he was not cast down because he knew she had a trick of seeing things without using her eyes frankly.

Of course when Lynch heard of this incident he rubbed his hands together and prophesied. By his advice Stephen went to Daniel's on the following Sunday. The old horsehair sofa was there, the picture of the Sacred Heart was there, she was there. The prodigal was welcomed. She spoke to him very little during the evening and seemed to be in deep conversation with Hughes, who had lately been honoured by an invitation. She was dressed in cream colour and the great mass of her hair lay heavily upon her cream-coloured neck. She asked him to sing and when he had sung a song of Dowland's she asked him would he not sing them an Irish song. Stephen glanced from her eyes to Hughes's face and sat down again at the piano. He sang her one of the few Irish melodies which he knew 'My love she was born in the North Countree.' When his song was over she applauded loudly and so did Hughes.

– I love the Irish music, she said a few minutes afterwards, inclining herself towards him with an air of oblivion, it is so soul-stirring.

Stephen said nothing. He remembered almost every word she had said from the first time he had met her and he strove to recall any word which revealed the presence of a spiritual principle in her worthy of so significant a name as soul. He submitted himself to the perfumes of her body and strove to locate a spiritual principle in it: but he could not. She seemed to conform to the Catholic belief, to obey the commandments and the precepts. By all outward signs he was compelled to esteem her holy. But he would not so stultify himself as to misread the gleam in her eyes as holy or to interpret the rise and fall of her bosom as a movement of a sacred intention. He thought of his own spendthrift religiousness and airs of the cloister, he remembered having astonished a labourer in a wood near Malahide by an ecstasy of oriental posture and no more than half-conscious under the influence of her charm he wondered whether the God of the Roman Catholics would put him into hell because he had failed to understand that most marketable goodness which makes it possible to give comfortable assent to propositions without in the least ordering one's life in accordance with them and had failed to appreciate the digestive value of the sacraments.

The young women were all sitting at one end of the table and the young men at the other end with the result that one end of the table was very lively and the other end very serious. Stephen after having failed to engage in conversation a maiden aunt of the family who had fulfilled her office by bringing in two tumblers of punch, one for Father Healy and the other for Mr Daniel, retired silently to the piano where he began to strum old airs and hum them to himself until someone at the table said 'Do sing us something' and then he left the piano and returned to the horsehair sofa.

Her eyes were very bright. Stephen's way through self-examinations had worn him out so much that he could not but long to repose himself in the neighbourhood of her beauty. He remembered the first mood of monstrous dissatisfaction which had overcome him on his entrance into Dublin life and how it was her beauty that had appeased him. Now she seemed to offer him rest. He wondered did she understand him or sympathize with him and was the vulgarity of her manners only a condescension of one who was consciously playing the game. He knew that it was not for such an image that he had constructed a theory of art and life and a garland of verse and yet if he could have been sure of her he would have held his art and verses lightly enough. The longing for a mad night of love came upon him, a desperate willingness to cast his soul away, his life and his art, and to bury them all with her under fathoms of lust-laden slumber. The ugly artificiality of the lives over which Father Healy was comfortably presiding struck this outrageous instant out of him and he went on repeating to himself a line from Dante for no other reason except that it contained the angry disyllable 'frode'. Surely, he thought, I have as much right to use the word as ever Dante had. The spirits of Moynihan and O'Neill and Glynn seemed to him worthy of some blowing about round the verges of a hell which would be a caricature of Dante's. The spirits of the patriotic and religious enthusiasts seemed to him fit to inhabit the fraudulent circles where hidden in hives of immaculate ice they might work their bodies to the due pitch of frenzy. The spirits of the tame sodalists, unsullied and undeserving, he would petrify amid a ring of Jesuits in the circle of foolish and grotesque virginities and ascend above them and their baffled icons to where his Emma, with no detail of her earthly form or vesture abated, invoked him from a Mohammadan paradise.

At the door he had to resign her to others and see her depart with insignificant courtesies and as he came home alone he led his mood through mazes of doubts and misgivings.

His father's days of grace were exciting days. It seemed likely that the family would not have where to lay its heads when at the eleventh hour Mr Daedalus found a roof with a friend from the North of Ireland who was traveller for an ironmonger. Mr Wilkinson was in possession of an old-fashioned house containing perhaps fifteen rooms of which he was nominally a tenant but, the landlord, an old miser without kith or kin in the world, having died very opportunely, Mr Wilkinson's tenancy was untroubled by considerations of time or money. Mr Daedalus was allowed a set of apartments in this dilapidated mansion for a small weekly payment and on the night before the day fixed for his legal eviction he moved his camp by night. The little furniture which remained to them was carried on a float and Stephen and his brother and his mother and his father carried the ancestral portraits themselves as the draymen had drunk a good deal more than was good for them. It was a clear night of late summer freshened with cold as they walked in a body beside the sea-wall. Isabel had been removed earlier in the day and put in Mrs Wilkinson's charge. Mr Daedalus was a long way in front with Maurice and in high spirits with his successful manoeuvre. Stephen followed with his mother and even she was light-hearted. The tide was lapping softly by the wall, being at the full, and through the clear air Stephen heard his father's voice like a muffled flute singing a love-song. He made his mother stop to listen and they both leaned on the heavy picture-frames and listened:

> Shall carry my heart to thee
> Shall carry my heart to thee
> And the breath of the balmy night
> Shall carry my heart to thee

Stephen was very lonely. As at the beginning of the summer so now: he wandered vaguely through the streets. Emma had gone away to the Isles of Aran with a Gaelic party. He was hardly unhappy and yet not happy. His moods were still waited upon and courted and set down in phrases of prose and verse: and when the soles of his feet were too tired his mood too dim a memory or too timid a hope, he would wander into the long lofty dusty drawing-room and sit at the piano while the sunless dusk enwrapped him. He could feel about him and above him the hopeless house and the decay of leaves and in his soul the one bright insistent star of joy trembling at her wane. The chords that floated towards the cobwebs and rubbish and floated vainly to the dust-strewn windows were the meaningless voices of his perturbation and all they could do was flow in meaningless succession through all the chambers of sentience. He breathed an air of tombs.

Even the value of his own life came into doubt with him. He laid a finger upon every falsehood it contained: an egoism which proceeded bravely before men to be frighted by the least challenge of the conscience, freedom which would dress the world anew in the vestments and usages begotten of enslavement, mastery of an art understood by few which owed its very delicacy to a physical decrepitude, itself the brand and sign of vulgar ardours. Cemeteries revealed their ineffectual records to him, records of the lives of all those who with good grace or bad grace had accepted an obvious divinity. The vision of all those failures, and the vision, far more pitiful, of congenital lives, shuffling onwards amid yawn and howl, beset him with evil: and evil, in the similitude of a distorted ritual, called to his soul to commit fornication with her.

One evening he sat at his piano while the dusk enfolded him. The dismal sunset lingered still upon the window-panes in a smoulder of rusty fires. Above him and about him hung the shadow of decay, the decay of leaves and flowers, the decay of hope. He desisted from his chords and waited, bending upon the keyboard in silence: and his soul commingled itself with the assailing, inarticulate dusk. A form which he knew for his mother's appeared far down in the room, standing in the doorway. In the gloom her excited face was crimson. A voice which he remembered as his mother's, a voice of a terrified human being, called his name. The form at the piano answered:

– Yes?

– Do you know anything about the body? . . .

He heard his mother's voice addressing him excitedly like the voice of a messenger in a play:

– What ought I do? There's some matter coming away from the hole in Isabel's . . . stomach . . . Did you ever hear of that happening?

– I don't know, he answered trying to make sense of her words, trying to say them again to himself.

– Ought I send for the doctor . . . Did you ever hear of that? . . . What ought I do?

– I don't know . . . What hole?

– The hole . . . the hole we all have . . . here.

The extravagant gesture

A certain extravagance began to tinge his life. He was aware that though he was nominally in amity with the order of society into which he had been born, he would not be able to continue so. The life of an errant seemed to him far less ignoble than the life of one who had accepted the tyranny of the mediocre because the cost of being exceptional was too high. The young generation which he saw growing up about him regarded his manifestations of spiritual activity as something more than unseemly and he knew that, under their air of fearful amiableness, the representatives of authority cherished the hope that his unguided nature would bring him into such a lamentable conflict with actuality that they would one day have the pleasure of receiving him officially into some hospital or asylum. This would have been no unusual end for the high emprise of youth often brings one to premature senility and a poet's boldness is certainly proved an ill keeper of promises when it induces him to lead a lobster by a bright blue ribbon along the footpath reserved for the citizens. He felt acutely the insidious dangers which conceal themselves under the guise of extravagance but he was convinced also that a dull discharge of duties, neither understood nor congenial, was far more dangerous and far less satisfactory.

Students' views of love and freedom

– For a man of your ordinary intelligence there may be: not for me. Have you ever read the Form of Solemnization of Marriage in the Book of Common Prayer?

– Never.

– You should then. Your everyday life is Protestant: you show yourself a Catholic only when you discuss. Well, to me that ceremony is not acceptable: it is not so sane as you imagine. A man who swears before the world to love a woman till death part him and her is sane neither in the opinion of the philosopher who understands what mutability is nor in the opinion of the man of the world who understands that it is safer to be a witness than an actor in such affairs. A man who swears to do something which it is not in his power to do is not accounted a sane man. For my part I do not believe that there was ever a moment of passion so fierce and energetic that it warranted a man in saying 'I could love you for ever' to the adored object. Please understand the importance of Goethe . . .

– Still marriage is a custom. To follow a custom is a mark of sanity.

– It is a mark of ordinariness. I admit that many ordinary people are sane just as I know that many ordinary people have delusions. But a capacity for being deceived by others or by oneself cannot be said to constitute the essential part of sanity. It is rather a question whether a man does encourage an insane condition in himself by deceiving himself voluntarily or allowing himself to be deceived by others voluntarily.

– Anyhow your move was not diplomatic.

– We all know that, said Stephen standing up, but all genuine diplomacy is with a view to some particularly excellent plum. What plum do you think Cranly is likely to gain by a diplomacy which is highly meritorious in itself? What plum would I be likely to get by proposing a diplomatic marriage except a partner 'to behold my chaste conversation, coupled with fear' – eh?

– The juice of the fruit, answered Lynch standing up in his turn and looking very thirsty and tired.

– The woman herself, you mean?

– Exactly.

Stephen walked along the path without saying anything for about twenty yards: then he said:

– I like a woman to give herself. I like to receive . . . These people count it a sin to sell holy things for money. But surely what they call the temple of the Holy Ghost should not be bargained for! Isn't that simony?

– You want to sell your verses, don't you, said Lynch abruptly, and to a public you say you despise?

– I do not want to sell my poetical mind to the public. I expect reward from the public for my verses because I believe my verses are to be numbered among the spiritual assets of the State. That is not a simoniacal exchange. I do not sell what Glynn calls the divine afflatus: I do not swear to love, honour and obey the public until my dying day – do I? A woman's body is a corporal asset of the State: if she traffic with it she must sell it either as a harlot or as a married woman or as a working celibate or as a mistress. But a woman is (incidentally) a human being and a human being's love and freedom is not a spiritual asset of the State. Can the State buy and sell electricity? It is not possible. Simony is monstrous because it revolts our notion of what is humanly possible. A human being can exert freedom to produce or accept or love to procreate or to satisfy. Love gives and freedom takes. The woman in the black straw hat gave something before she sold her body to the State; Emma will sell herself to the State but give nothing.

– You know even if you had proposed to buy her decently – for State purposes – said Lynch, kicking his toes moodily at the gravel, she would not have sold at the price.

– You think not. Not even if I . . .

– Not likely, said the other definitely. What a damn fool she is!

The nature of an epiphany

He was passing through Eccles' St one evening, one misty evening, with all these thoughts dancing the dance of unrest in his brain when a trivial incident set him composing some ardent verses which he entitled a 'Vilanelle of the

Temptress'. A young lady was standing on the steps of one of those brown brick houses which seem the very incarnation of Irish paralysis. A young gentleman was leaning on the rusty railings of the area. Stephen as he passed on his quest heard the following fragment of colloquy out of which he received an impression keen enough to afflict his sensitiveness very severely.

The Young Lady – (drawling discreetly) . . . O, yes . . . I was . . . at the . . . cha . . . pel. . . .

The Young Gentleman – (inaudibly) . . . I . . . (again inaudibly) . . . I . . .

The Young Lady – (softly) . . . O . . . but you're . . . ve . . . ry . . . wick . . . ed. . . .

This triviality made him think of collecting many such moments together in a book of epiphanies. By an epiphany he meant a sudden spiritual manifestation, whether in the vulgarity of speech or of gesture or in a memorable phase of the mind itself. He believed that it was for the man of letters to record these epiphanies with extreme care, seeing that they themselves are the most delicate and evanescent of moments. He told Cranly that the clock of the Ballast Office was capable of an epiphany. Cranly questioned the inscrutable dial of the Ballast Office with his no less inscrutable countenance.

– Yes, said Stephen. I will pass it time after time, allude to it, refer to it, catch a glimpse of it. It is only an item in the catalogue of Dublin's street furniture. Then all at once I see it and I know at once what it is: epiphany.

– What?

– Imagine my glimpses at that clock as the gropings of a spiritual eye which seeks to adjust its vision to an exact focus. The moment the focus is reached the object is epiphanized. It is just in this epiphany that I find the third, the supreme quality of beauty.

– Yes? said Cranly absently.

– No esthetic theory, pursued Stephen relentlessly, is of any value which investigates with the aid of the lantern of tradition. What we symbolise in black the Chinaman may symbolise in yellow: each has his own tradition. Greek beauty laughs at Coptic beauty and the American Indian derides them both. It is almost impossible to reconcile all tradition whereas it is by no means impossible to find the justification of every form of beauty which has been adored on the earth by an examination into the mechanism of esthetic apprehension whether it be dressed in red, white, yellow or black. We have no reason for thinking that the Chinaman has a different system of digestion from that which we have though our diets are quite dissimilar. The apprehensive faculty must be scrutinized in action.

– Yes . . .

– You know what Aquinas says: The three things requisite for beauty are, integrity, a wholeness, symmetry and radiance. Some day I will expand that sentence into a treatise. Consider the performance of your own mind when confronted with any object, hypothetically beautiful. Your mind to apprehend that object divides the entire universe into two parts, the object, and the void which is not the object. To apprehend it you must lift it away from everything else: and then you perceive that it is one integral thing, that is *a* thing. You recognise its integrity. Isn't that so?

– And then?

– That is the first quality of beauty: it is declared in a simple sudden synthesis of the faculty which apprehends. What then? Analysis then. The mind considers the object in whole and in part, in relation to itself and to other objects, examines the balance of its parts, contemplates the form of the object, traverses every cranny of the structure. So the mind receives the impression of the symmetry of the object. The mind recognises that the object is in the strict sense of the word, a *thing*, a definitely constituted entity. You see?

– Let us turn back, said Cranly.

They had reached the corner of Grafton St and as the footpath was overcrowded they turned back northwards. Cranly had an inclination to watch the antics of a drunkard

who had been ejected from a bar in Suffolk St but Stephen
took his arm summarily and led him away.

– Now for the third quality. For a long time I couldn't make
out what Aquinas meant. He uses a figurative word (a very
unusual thing for him) but I have solved it. *Claritas* is
quidditas. After the analysis which discovers the second
quality the mind makes the only logically possible synthesis
and discovers the third quality. This is the moment which I
call epiphany. First we recognise that the object is *one* integral
thing, then we recognise that it is an organised composite
structure, a *thing* in fact: finally, when the relation of the parts
is exquisite, when the parts are adjusted to the special point,
we recognise that it is *that* thing which it is. Its soul, its
whatness, leaps to us from the vestment of its appearance.
The soul of the commonest object, the structure of which
is so adjusted, seems to us radiant. The object achieves its
epiphany.

Having finished his argument Stephen walked on in
silence. He felt Cranly's hostility and he accused himself of
having cheapened the eternal images of beauty. For the first
time, too, he felt slightly awkward in his friend's company and
to restore a mood of flippant familiarity he glanced up at the
clock of the Ballast Office and smiled:

– It has not epiphanised yet, he said.

Cranly stared stolidly down the river and held his peace for
a few minutes during which the expounder of the new esthetic
repeated his theory to himself all over again. A clock at the far
side of the bridge chimed and simultaneously Cranly's thin
lips parted for speech:

– I wonder, he said . . .

– What?

Cranly continued to stare towards the mouth of the Liffey
like a man in a trance. Stephen waited for the sentence to be
finished and then he said again 'What?' Cranly then faced
about suddenly and said with flat emphasis:

– I wonder did that bloody boat, the *Sea-Queen* ever start?

Stephen had now completed a series of hymns in honour of

extravagant beauty and these he published privately in a manuscript edition of one copy. His last interview with Cranly had been so unsatisfactory that he hesitated to show the manuscript to him. He kept the manuscript by him and its presence tormented him. He wanted to show it to his parents but the examination was approaching and he knew that their sympathy would be incomplete. He wanted to show it to Maurice but he was conscious that his brother resented having been forsaken for plebeian companions. He wanted to show it to Lynch but he dreaded the physical labour of urging that torpid young man into a condition of receptiveness. He even thought for a moment of McCann and Madden.

The parable of the monkeys and the missionaries; or, the results of chastity

– What is the parable, said Stephen.

Temple took off his cap and, bareheaded, he began to recite after the fashion of a country priest, prolonging all the vowels and jerking out the phrases, and dropping his voice at every pause:

– Dearly beloved Brethren: There was once a tribe of monkeys in Barbary. And ... these monkeys were as numerous as the sands of the sea. They lived together in the woods in polygamous ... intercourse ... and reproduced ... their species. ... But, behold there came into Barbary ... the holy missionaries, the holy men of God ... to redeem the people of Barbary. And these holy men preached to the people ... and then ... they went into the woods ... far away into the woods ... to pray to God. And they lived as hermits ... in the woods ... and praying to God. And, behold, the monkeys of Barbary who were in the trees ... saw these holy men living as hermits ... as lonely hermits ... praying to God. And the monkeys who, my dearly beloved brethren, are imitative creatures . . . began to imitate the actions . . . of these holy men . . . and began to do likewise. And so . . . they separated from one another . . . and went away far away, to pray to God . . . and they did as they had seen the holy men do . . . and prayed to God . . . And . . . they did not return . . . any more . . . nor try to reproduce the species . . . And so . . . gradually . . . these po . . . or monkeys . . . grew fewer and fewer . . . and fewer and fewer . . . And today . . . there is no monkey in all Barbary.

FROM
A PORTRAIT OF
THE ARTIST AS
A YOUNG MAN

A vision of Hell

Murmuring faces waited and watched; murmurous voices filled the dark shell of the cave. He feared intensely in spirit and in flesh but, raising his head bravely, he strode into the room firmly. A doorway, a room, the same room, same window. He told himself calmly that those words had absolutely no sense which had seemed to rise murmurously from the dark. He told himself that it was simply his room with the door open.

He closed the door and, walking swiftly to the bed, knelt beside it and covered his face with his hands. His hands were cold and damp and his limbs ached with chill. Bodily unrest and chill and weariness beset him, routing his thoughts. Why was he kneeling there like a child saying his evening prayers? To be alone with his soul, to examine his conscience, to meet his sins face to face, to recall their times and manners and circumstances, to weep over them. He could not weep. He could not summon them to his memory. He felt only an ache of soul and body, his whole being, memory, will, understanding, flesh, benumbed and weary.

That was the work of devils, to scatter his thoughts and overcloud his conscience, assailing him at the gates of the cowardly and sincorrupted flesh: and, praying God timidly to forgive him his weakness, he crawled up on to the bed and, wrapping the blankets closely about him, covered his face again with his hands. He had sinned. He had sinned so deeply against heaven and before God that he was not worthy to be called God's child.

Could it be that he, Stephen Dedalus, had done those things? His conscience sighed in answer. Yes, he had done them, secretly, filthily, time after time, and, hardened in sinful impenitence, he had dared to wear the mask of holiness before the tabernacle itself while his soul within was a living mass of corruption. How came it that God had not struck him dead? The leprous company of his sins closed about him, breathing upon him, bending over him from all sides. He strove to forget them in an act of prayer, huddling his limbs closer together and binding down his eyelids: but the senses of his soul would not be bound and, though his eyes were shut fast, he saw the places where he had sinned and, though his ears were tightly covered, he heard. He desired with all his will not to hear or see. He desired till his frame shook under the strain of his desire and until the senses of his soul closed. They closed for an instant and then opened. He saw.

A field of stiff weeds and thistles and tufted nettlebunches. Thick among the tufts of rank stiff growth lay battered canisters and clots and coils of solid excrement. A faint marshlight struggled upwards from all the ordure through the bristling greygreen weeds. An evil smell, faint and foul as the light, curled upwards sluggishly out of the canisters and from the stale crusted dung.

Creatures were in the field; one, three, six: creatures were moving in the field, hither and thither. Goatish creatures with human faces, hornybrowed, lightly bearded and grey as indiarubber. The malice of evil glittered in their hard eyes, as they moved hither and thither, trailing their long tails behind them. A rictus of cruel malignity lit up greyly their old bony faces. One was clasping about his ribs a torn flannel waistcoat, another complained monotonously as his beard stuck in the tufted weeds. Soft language issued from their spittleless lips as they swished in slow circles round and round the field, winding hither and thither through the weeds, dragging their long tails amid the rattling canisters. They moved in slow circles, circling closer and closer to enclose, to enclose, soft language issuing from their lips, their long swishing tails besmeared with stale shite, thrusting upwards their terrific faces . . .

Help!

He flung the blankets from him madly to free his face and neck. That was his hell. God had allowed him to see the hell reserved for his sins: stinking, bestial, malignant, a hell of lecherous goatish fiends. For him! For him!

An unearthly vision

He drew forth a phrase from his treasure and spoke it softly to himself:
– A day of dappled seaborne clouds.

The phrase and the day and the scene harmonised in a chord. Words. Was it their colours? He allowed them to glow and fade, hue after hue: sunrise gold, the russet and green of apple orchards, azure of waves, the greyfringed fleece of clouds. No, it was not their colours: it was the poise and balance of the period itself. Did he then love the rhythmic rise and fall of words better than their association of legend and colour? Or was it that, being as weak of sight as he was shy of mind, he drew less pleasure from the reflection of the glowing sensible world through the prism of a language manycoloured and richly storied than from the contemplation of an inner world of individual emotions mirrored perfectly in a lucid supple periodic prose?

He passed from the trembling bridge on to firm land again. At that instant, as it seemed to him, the air was chilled and looking askance towards the water he saw a flying squall darkening and crisping suddenly the tide. A faint click at his heart, a faint throb in his throat told him once more of how his flesh dreaded the cold infrahuman odour of the sea: yet he did not strike across the downs on his left but held straight on along the spine of rocks that pointed against the river's mouth.

A veiled sunlight lit up faintly the grey sheet of water where the river was embayed. In the distance along the course of the slowflowing Liffey slender masts flecked the sky and, more distant still, the dim fabric of the city lay prone in haze. Like a scene on some vague arras, old as man's weariness, the image of the seventh city of christendom was visible to him across the timeless air, no older nor more weary nor less patient of subjection than in the days of the thingmote.

Disheartened, he raised his eyes towards the slowdrifting

clouds, dappled and seaborne. They were voyaging across the deserts of the sky, a host of nomads on the march, voyaging high over Ireland, westward bound. The Europe they had come from lay out there beyond the Irish Sea, Europe of strange tongues and valleyed and woodbegirt and citadelled and of entrenched and marshalled races. He heard a confused music within him as of memories and names which he was almost conscious of but could not capture even for an instant; then the music seemed to recede, to recede, to recede: and from each receding trail of nebulous music there fell always one longdrawn calling note, piercing like a star the dusk of silence. Again! Again! Again! A voice from beyond the world was calling.

Stephen Dedalus the artist

Now, as never before, his strange name seemed to him a prophecy. So timeless seemed the grey warm air, so fluid and impersonal his own mood, that all ages were as one to him. A moment before the ghost of the ancient kingdom of the Danes had looked forth through the vesture of the hazewrapped city. Now, at the name of the fabulous artificer, he seemed to hear the noise of dim waves and to see a winged form flying above the waves and slowly climbing the air. What did it mean? Was it a quaint device opening a page of some medieval book of prophecies and symbols, a hawklike man flying sunward above the sea, a prophecy of the end he had been born to serve and had been following through the mists of childhood and boyhood, a symbol of the artist forging anew in his workshop out of the sluggish matter of the earth a new soaring impalpable imperishable being?

His heart trembled; his breath came faster and a wild spirit passed over his limbs as though he were soaring sunward. His heart trembled in an ecstasy of fear and his soul was in flight. His soul was soaring in an air beyond the world and the body he knew was purified in a breath and delivered of incertitude and made radiant and commingled with the element of the spirit. An ecstasy of flight made radiant his eyes and wild his breath and tremulous and wild and radiant his windswept limbs.

Ecstasy

There was a long rivulet in the strand and, as he waded slowly up its course, he wondered at the endless drift of seaweed. Emerald and black and russet and olive, it moved beneath the current, swaying and turning. The water of the rivulet was dark with endless drift and mirrored the highdrifting clouds. The clouds were drifting above him silently and silently the seatangle was drifting below him; and the grey warm air was still: and a new wild life was singing in his veins.

Where was his boyhood now? Where was the soul that had hung back from her destiny, to brood alone upon the shame of her wounds and in her house of squalor and subterfuge to queen it in faded cerements and in wreaths that withered at the touch? Or where was he?

He was alone. He was unheeded, happy and near to the wild heart of life. He was alone and young and wilful and wildhearted, alone amid a waste of wild air and brackish waters and the seaharvest of shells and tangle and veiled grey sunlight and gayclad lightclad figures of children and girls and voices childish and girlish in the air.

A girl stood before him in midstream, alone and still, gazing out to sea. She seemed like one whom magic had changed into the likeness of a strange and beautiful seabird. Her long slender bare legs were delicate as a crane's and pure save where an emerald trail of seaweed had fashioned itself as a sign upon the flesh. Her thighs, fuller and softhued as ivory, were bared almost to the hips where the white fringes of her drawers were like featherings of soft white down. Her slateblue skirts were kilted boldly about her waist and dovetailed behind her. Her bosom was as a bird's soft and slight, slight and soft as the breast of some darkplumaged dove. But her long fair hair was girlish: and girlish, and touched with the wonder of mortal beauty, her face.

She was alone and still, gazing out to sea: and when she felt his presence and the worship of his eyes her eyes turned to him in quiet sufferance of his gaze, without shame or wantonness. Long, long she suffered his gaze and then quietly withdrew her eyes from his and bent them towards the stream, gently stirring the water with her foot hither and thither. The first faint noise of gently moving water broke the silence, low and faint and whispering, faint as the bells of sleep; hither and thither, hither and thither: and a faint flame trembled on her cheek.

– Heavenly God! cried Stephen's soul, in an outburst of profane joy.

He turned away from her suddenly and set off across the strand. His cheeks were aflame; his body was aglow; his limbs were trembling. On and on and on and on he strode, far out over the sands, singing wildly to the sea, crying to greet the advent of the life that had cried to him.

Her image had passed into his soul for ever and no word had broken the holy silence of his ecstasy. Her eyes had called him and his soul had leaped at the call. To live, to err, to fall, to triumph, to recreate life out of life! A wild angel had appeared to him, the angel of mortal youth and beauty, an envoy from the fair courts of life, to throw open before him in an instant of ecstasy the gates of all the ways of error and glory. On and on and on and on!

An acquired speech

– To return to the lamp, he said, the feeding of it is also a nice problem. You must choose the pure oil and you must be careful when you pour it in not to overflow it, not to pour in more than the funnel can hold.

– What funnel? asked Stephen.

– The funnel through which you pour the oil into your lamp.

– That? said Stephen. Is that called a funnel? Is it not a tundish?

– What is a tundish?

– That. The . . . the funnel.

– Is that called a tundish in Ireland? asked the dean. I never heard the word in my life.

– It is called a tundish in Lower Drumcondra, said Stephen laughing, where they speak the best English.

– A tundish, said the dean reflectively. That is a most interesting word. I must look that word up. Upon my word I must. . . .

The dean repeated the word yet again.

– Tundish! Well now, that is interesting!

– The question you asked me a moment ago seems to me more interesting. What is that beauty which the artist struggles to express from lumps of earth, said Stephen coldly.

The little word seemed to have turned a rapier point of his sensitiveness against this courteous and vigilant foe. He felt with a smart of dejection that the man to whom he was speaking was a countryman of Ben Jonson. He thought:

– The language in which we are speaking is his before it is mine. How different are the words *home*, *Christ*, *ale*, *master*, on his lips and on mine! I cannot speak or write these words without unrest of spirit. His language, so familiar and so foreign, will always be for me an acquired speech. I have not made or accepted its words. My voice holds them at bay. My soul frets in the shadow of his language. . . .

13 April: That tundish has been on my mind for a long time. I looked it up and find it English and good old blunt English too. Damn the dean of studies and his funnel! What did he come here for to teach us his own language or to learn it from us? Damn him one way or the other!

Instant inspiration

Towards dawn he awoke. O what sweet music! His soul was all dewy wet. Over his limbs in sleep pale cool waves of light had passed. He lay still, as if his soul lay amid cool waters, conscious of faint sweet music. His mind was waking slowly to a tremulous morning knowledge, a morning inspiration. A spirit filled him, pure as the purest water, sweet as dew, moving as music. But how faintly it was inbreathed, how passionlessly, as if the seraphim themselves were breathing upon him! His soul was waking slowly, fearing to awake wholly. It was that windless hour of dawn when madness wakes and strange plants open to the light and the moth flies forth silently.

An enchantment of the heart! The night had been enchanted. In a dream or vision he had known the ecstasy of seraphic life. Was it an instant of enchantment only or long hours and days and years and ages?

The instant of inspiration seemed now to be reflected from all sides at once from a multitude of cloudy circumstance of what had happened or of what might have happened. The instant flashed forth like a point of light and now from cloud on cloud of vague circumstance confused form was veiling softly its afterglow. O! In the virgin womb of the imagination the word was made flesh. Gabriel the seraph had come to the virgin's chamber. An afterglow deepened within his spirit, whence the white flame had passed, deepening to a rose and ardent light. That rose and ardent light was her strange wilful heart, strange that no man had known or would know, wilful from before the beginning of the world: and lured by that ardent roselike glow the choirs of the seraphim were falling from heaven.

> *Are you now weary of ardent ways,*
> *Lure of the fallen seraphim?*
> *Tell no more of enchanted days.*

The verses passed from his mind to his lips and, murmuring them over, he felt the rhythmic movement of a villanelle pass through them. The roselike glow sent forth its rays of rhyme; ways, days, blaze, praise, raise. Its rays burned up the world, consumed the hearts of men and angels: the rays from the rose that was her wilful heart.

> *Your eyes have set man's heart ablaze*
> *And you have had your will of him.*
> *Are you not weary of ardent ways?*

And then? The rhythm died away, ceased, began again to move and beat. And then? Smoke, incense ascending from the altar of the world.

> *Above the flame the smoke of praise*
> *Goes up from ocean rim to rim.*
> *Tell no more of enchanted days.*

Smoke went up from the whole earth, from the vapoury oceans, smoke of her praise. The earth was like a swinging smoking swaying censer, a ball of incense, an ellipsoidal ball. The rhythm died out at once; the cry of his heart was broken. His lips began to murmur the first verses over and over; then went on stumbling through half verses, stammering and baffled; then stopped. The heart's cry was broken.

The veiled windless hour had passed and behind the panes of the naked window the morning light was gathering. A bell beat faintly very far away. A bird twittered; two birds, three. The bell and the bird ceased: and the dull white light spread itself east and west, covering the world, covering the roselight in his heart.

Fearing to lose all, he raised himself suddenly on his elbow to look for paper and pencil. There was neither on the table; only the soupplate he had eaten the rice from for supper and the candlestick with its tendrils of tallow and its paper socket, singed by the last flame. He stretched his arm wearily towards the foot of the bed, groping with his hand in the pockets of the coat that hung there. His fingers found a pencil and then a cigarette packet. He lay back and, tearing open the packet, placed the last cigarette on the windowledge and began to write out the stanzas of the villanelle in small neat letters on the rough cardboard surface. . . .

The radiant image of the eucharist united again in an instant his bitter and despairing thoughts, their cries arising unbroken in a hymn of thanksgiving.

> *Our broken cries and mournful lays*
> *Rise in one eucharistic hymn.*
> *Are you not weary of ardent ways?*

> *While sacrificing hands upraise*
> *The chalice flowing to the brim,*
> *Tell no more of enchanted days.*

He spoke the verses aloud from the first lines till the music and rhythm suffused his mind, turning it to quiet indulgence; then copied them painfully to feel them the better by seeing them; then lay back on his bolster. . . .

He had written verses for her again after ten years. Ten years before she had worn her shawl cowlwise about her head, sending sprays of her warm breath into the night air, tapping her foot upon the glassy road . . .

Ten years from that wisdom of children to his folly. If he sent her the verses? They would be read out at breakfast amid the tapping of eggshells. Folly indeed! . . .

While his soul had passed from ecstasy to languor where had she been? Might it be, in the mysterious ways of spiritual life, that her soul at those same moments had been conscious of his homage? It might be.

A glow of desire kindled again his soul and fired and fulfilled all his body. Conscious of his desire she was waking from odorous sleep, the temptress of his villanelle. Her eyes, dark and with a look of languor, were opening to his eyes. Her nakedness yielded to him, radiant, warm, odorous and lavish-limbed, enfolded him like a shining cloud, enfolded him like water with a liquid life: and like a cloud of vapour or like waters circumfluent in space the liquid letters of speech, symbols of the element of mystery, flowed forth over his brain.

> *Are you not weary of ardent ways,*
> *Lure of the fallen seraphim?*
> *Tell no more of enchanted days.*
>
> *Your eyes have set man's heart ablaze*
> *And you have had your will of him.*
> *Are you not weary of ardent ways?*
>
> *Above the flame the smoke of praise*
> *Goes up from ocean rim to rim.*
> *Tell no more of enchanted days.*
>
> *Our broken cries and mournful lays*
> *Rise in one eucharistic hymn.*
> *Are you not weary of ardent ways?*
>
> *While sacrificing hands upraise*
> *The chalice flowing to the brim,*
> *Tell no more of enchanted days.*
>
> *And still you hold our longing gaze*
> *With languorous look and lavish limb!*
> *Are you not weary of ardent ways?*
> *Tell no more of enchanted days.*

The birds' augury

W hat birds were they? He stood on the steps of the library to look at them, leaning wearily on his ashplant. They flew round and round the jutting shoulder of a house in Molesworth Street. The air of the late March evening made clear their flight, their dark darting quivering bodies flying clearly against the sky as against a limphung cloth of smoky tenuous blue.

He watched their flight; bird after bird: a dark flash, a swerve, a flash again, a dart aside, a curve, a flutter of wings. He tried to count them before all their darting quivering bodies passed: six, ten, eleven: and wondered were they odd or even in number. Twelve, thirteen: for two came wheeling down from the upper sky. They were flying high and low but ever round and round in straight and curving lines and ever flying from left to right, circling about a temple of air.

He listened to the cries: like the squeak of mice behind the wainscot: a shrill twofold note. But the notes were long and shrill and whirring, unlike the cry of vermin, falling a third or a fourth and trilled as the flying beaks clove the air. Their cry was shrill and clear and fine and falling like threads of silken light unwound from whirring spools.

The inhuman clamour soothed his ears in which his mother's sobs and reproaches murmured insistently and the dark frail quivering bodies wheeling and fluttering and swerving round an airy temple of the tenuous sky soothed his eyes which still saw the image of his mother's face.

Why was he gazing upwards from the steps of the porch, hearing their shrill twofold cry, watching their flight? For an augury of good or evil? A phrase of Cornelius Agrippa flew through his mind and then there flew hither and thither shapeless thoughts from Swedenborg on the correspondence of birds to things of the intellect and of how the creatures of the air have their knowledge and know their times and seasons because they, unlike man, are in the order of their life and have not perverted that order by reason.

And for ages men had gazed upward as he was gazing at birds in flight. The colonnade above him made him think vaguely of an ancient temple and the ashplant on which he leaned wearily of the curved stick of an augur. A sense of fear of the unknown moved in the heart of his weariness, a fear of symbols and portents, of the hawklike man whose name he bore soaring out of his captivity on osierwoven wings, of Thoth, the god of writers, writing with a reed upon a tablet and bearing on his narrow ibis head the cusped moon. . . .

They came back with shrill cries over the jutting shoulder of the house, flying darkly against the fading air. What birds were they? He thought that they must be swallows who had come back from the south. Then he was to go away for they were birds ever going and coming, building ever an unlasting home under the eaves of men's houses and ever leaving the homes they had built to wander.

> *Bend down your faces, Oona and Aleel,*
> *I gaze upon them as the swallow gazes*
> *Upon the nest under the eave before*
> *He wander the loud waters.*

A soft liquid joy like the noise of many waters flowed over his memory and he felt in his heart the soft peace of silent spaces of fading tenuous sky above the waters, of oceanic silence, of swallows flying through the seadusk over the flowing waters.

A soft liquid joy flowed through the words where the soft long vowels hurtled noiselessly and fell away, lapping and flowing back and ever shaking the white bells of their waves in mute chime and mute peal and soft low swooning cry; and he felt that the augury he had sought in the wheeling darting birds and in the pale space of sky above him had come forth from his heart like a bird from a turret quietly and swiftly.

Images of desire

The talk about him ceased for a moment: and a soft hiss fell again from a window above. But no other sound was in the air and the swallows whose flight he had followed with idle eyes were sleeping.

She had passed through the dusk. And therefore the air was silent save for one soft hiss that fell. And therefore the tongues about him had ceased their babble. Darkness was falling.

Darkness falls from the air.

A trembling joy, lambent as a faint light, played like a fairy host around him. But why? Her passage through the darkening air or the verse with its black vowels and its opening sound, rich and lutelike?

He walked away slowly towards the deeper shadows at the end of the colonnade, beating the stone softly with his stick to hide his revery from the students whom he had left: and allowed his mind to summon back to itself the age of Dowland and Byrd and Nash.

Eyes, opening from the darkness of desire, eyes that dimmed the breaking east. What was their languid grace but the softness of chambering? And what was their shimmer but the shimmer of the scum that mantled the cesspool of the court of a slobbering Stuart. And he tasted in the language of memory ambered wines, dying fallings of sweet airs, the proud pavan: and saw with the eyes of memory kind gentlewomen in Covent Garden wooing from their balconies with sucking mouths and the poxfouled wenches of the taverns and young wives that, gaily yielding to their ravishers, clipped and clipped again.

The images he had summoned gave him no pleasure. They were secret and enflaming but her image was not entangled by them. That was not the way to think of her. It was not even the way in which he thought of her. Could his mind then not trust itself?

Away! Away to the reality of experience!

5 April: Wild spring. Scudding clouds. O life! Dark stream of swirling bogwater on which appletrees have cast down their delicate flowers. Eyes of girls among the leaves. Girls demure and romping. All fair or auburn: no dark ones. They blush better. Houp-la!

6 April, later: Michael Robartes remembers forgotten beauty and, when his arms wrap her round, he presses in his arms the loveliness which has long faded from the world. Not this. Not at all. I desire to press in my arms the loveliness which has not yet come into the world.

10 April: Faintly, under the heavy night, through the silence of the city which has turned from dreams to dreamless sleep as a weary lover whom no caress s move, the sound of hoofs upon the road. Not so faintly now as they come near the bridge: and in a moment as they pass the darkened windows the silence is cloven by alarm as by an arrow. They are heard now far away, hoofs that shine amid the heavy night as gems, hurrying beyond the sleeping fields to what journey's end – what heart? – bearing what tidings?

11 April: Read what I wrote last night. Vague words for a vague emotion. Would she like it? I think so. Then I should have to like it also.

16 April: Away! Away!

The spell of arms and voices: the white arms of roads, their promise of close embraces and the black arms of tall ships that stand against the moon, their tale of distant nations. They are held out to say: We are alone. Come. And the voices say with them: We are your kinsmen. And the air is thick with their company as they call to me, their kinsman, making ready to go, shaking the wings of their exultant and terrible youth.

26 April: Mother is putting my new secondhand clothes in order. She prays now, she says, that I may learn in my own life and away from home and friends what the heart is and what it feels. Amen. So be it. Welcome, O life! I go to encounter for the millionth time the reality of experience and to forge in the smithy of my soul the uncreated conscience of my race.

27 April: Old father, old artificer, stand me now and ever in good stead.

FROM
ULYSSES

The cracked lookingglass and its frame

Buck Mulligan frowned at the lather on his razorblade. He hopped down from his perch and began to search his trouser pockets hastily.

– Scutter, he cried thickly.

He came over to the gunrest and, thrusting a hand into Stephen's inner pocket, said:

– Lend us a loan of your noserag to wipe my razor.

Stephen suffered him to pull out and hold up on show by its corner a dirty crumpled handkerchief. Buck Mulligan wiped the razorblade neatly. Then, gazing over the handkerchief, he said:

– The bard's noserag. A new art colour for our Irish poets: snotgreen. You can almost taste it, can't you?

He mounted to the parapet again and gazed out over Dublin bay, his fair oakpale hair stirring slightly.

– God, he said quietly. Isn't the sea what Algy calls it: a grey sweet mother? The snotgreen sea. The scrotumtightening sea. *Epi oinopa ponton.* Ah, Dedalus, the Greeks. I must teach you. You must read them in the original. *Thalatta! Thalatta!* She is our great sweet mother. Come and look.

Stephen stood up and went over to the parapet. Leaning on it he looked down on the water and on the mailboat clearing the harbour mouth of Kingstown.

– Our mighty mother, Buck Mulligan said.

He turned abruptly his great searching eyes from the sea to Stephen's face.

– The aunt thinks you killed your mother, he said. That's why she won't let me have anything to do with you.

– Someone killed her, Stephen said gloomily.

– You could have knelt down, damn it, Kinch, when your dying mother asked you, Buck Mulligan said. I'm hyperborean as much as you. But to think of your mother begging you with her last breath to kneel down and pray for her. And you refused. There is something sinister in you. . .

He broke off and lathered again lightly his farther cheek. A tolerant smile curled his lips.

– But a lovely mummer, he murmured to himself. Kinch, the loveliest mummer of them all.

He shaved evenly and with care, in silence, seriously.

Stephen, an elbow rested on the jagged granite, leaned his palm against his brow and gazed at the fraying edge of his shiny black coat-sleeve. Pain, that was not yet the pain of love, fretted his heart. Silently, in a dream she had come to him after her death, her wasted body within its loose brown graveclothes giving off an odour of wax and rosewood, her breath, that had bent upon him, mute, reproachful, a faint odour of wetted ashes. Across the threadbare cuffedge he saw the sea hailed as a great sweet mother by the wellfed voice beside him. The ring of bay and skyline held a dull green mass of liquid. A bowl of white china had stood beside her deathbed holding the green sluggish bile which she had torn up from her rotting liver by fits of loud groaning vomiting.

Buck Mulligan wiped again his razorblade.

– Ah, poor dogsbody, he said in a kind voice. I must give you a shirt and a few noserags. How are the second-hand breeks?

– They fit well enough, Stephen answered.

Buck Mulligan attacked the hollow beneath his underlip.

– The mockery of it, he said contentedly, secondleg they should be. God knows what poxy bowsy left them off. I have a lovely pair with a hair stripe, grey. You'll look spiffing in them. I'm not joking, Kinch. You look damn well when you're dressed.

– Thanks, Stephen said. I can't wear them if they are grey.

– He can't wear them, Buck Mulligan told his face in the mirror. Etiquette is etiquette. He kills his mother but he can't wear grey trousers.

He folded his razor neatly and with stroking palps of fingers felt the smooth skin.

Stephen turned his gaze from the sea and to the plump face with its smokeblue mobile eyes.

– That fellow I was with in the Ship last night, said Buck Mulligan, says you have g.p.i. He's up in Dottyville with Conolly Norman. General paralysis of the insane.

He swept the mirror a half circle in the air to flash the tidings abroad in sunlight now radiant on the sea. His curling shaven lips laughed and the edges of his white glittering teeth. Laughter seized all his strong wellknit trunk.

– Look at yourself, he said, you dreadful bard.

Stephen bent forward and peered at the mirror held out to him, cleft by a crooked crack, hair on end. As he and others see me. Who chose this face for me? This dogsbody to rid of vermin. It asks me too.

– I pinched it out of the skivvy's room, Buck Mulligan said. It does her all right. The aunt always keeps plain-looking servants for Malachi. Lead him not into temptation. And her name is Ursula.

Laughing again, he brought the mirror away from Stephen's peering eyes.

– The rage of Caliban at not seeing his face in a mirror, he said. If Wilde were only alive to see you.

Drawing back and pointing, Stephen said with bitterness:

– It is a symbol of Irish art. The cracked lookingglass of a servant.

Buck Mulligan suddenly linked his arm in Stephen's and walked with him round the tower, his razor and mirror clacking in the pocket where he had thrust them.

– It's not fair to tease you like that, Kinch, is it? he said kindly. God knows you have more spirit than any of them.

Parried again. He fears the lancet of my art as I fear that of his. The cold steelpen.

– Cracked lookingglass of a servant. Tell that to the oxy chap downstairs and touch him for a guinea. He's stinking with money and thinks you're not a gentleman. His old fellow made his tin by selling jalap to Zulus or some bloody swindle or other. God, Kinch, if you and I could only work together we might do something for the island. Hellenise it.

Cranly's arm. His arm.

– And to think of your having to beg from these swine. I'm the only one that knows what you are. Why don't you trust me more? What have you up your nose against me? Is it Haines? If he makes any noise here I'll bring down Seymour and we'll give him a ragging worse than they gave Clive Kempthorpe.

Young shouts of moneyed voices in Clive Kempthorpe's rooms. Palefaces: they hold their ribs with laughter, one clasping another, O, I shall expire! Break the news to her gently, Aubrey! I shall die! With slit ribbons of his shirt whipping the air he hops and hobbles round the table, with trousers down at heels, chased by Ades of Magdalen with the tailor's shears. A scared calf's face gilded with marmalade. I don't want to be debagged! Don't you play the giddy ox with me!

Shouts from the open window startling evening in the quadrangle. A deaf gardener, aproned, masked with Matthew Arnold's face, pushes his mower on the sombre lawn watching narrowly the dancing motes of grasshalms.

To ourselves . . . new paganism . . . omphalos.

– Let him stay, Stephen said. There's nothing wrong with him except at night.

– Then what is it? Buck Mulligan asked impatiently. Cough it up. I'm quite frank with you. What have you against me now?

They halted, looking towards the blunt cape of Bray Head that lay on the water like the snout of a sleeping whale. Stephen freed his arm quietly.

– Do you wish me to tell you? he asked.

– Yes, what is it? Buck Mulligan answered. I don't remember anything.

He looked in Stephen's face as he spoke. A light wind passed his brow, fanning softly his fair uncombed hair and stirring silver points of anxiety in his eyes.

Stephen, depressed by his own voice, said:

– Do you remember the first day I went to your house after
my mother's death?

Buck Mulligan frowned quickly and said:

– What? Where? I can't remember anything. I remember
only ideas and sensations. Why? What happened in the name
of God?

– You were making tea, Stephen said, and I went across the
landing to get more hot water. Your mother and some visitor
came out of the drawingroom. She asked you who was in your
room.

– Yes? Buck Mulligan said. What did I say? I forget.

– You said, Stephen answered, *O, it's only Dedalus whose
mother is beastly dead.*

A flush which made him seem younger and more engaging
rose to Buck Mulligan's cheek.

– Did I say that? he asked. Well? What harm is that?

He shook his constraint from him nervously.

– And what is death, he asked, your mother's or yours or my
own? You saw only your mother die. I see them pop off every
day in the Mater and Richmond and cut up into tripes in the
dissecting room. It's a beastly thing and nothing else. It simply
doesn't matter. You wouldn't kneel down to pray for your
mother on her deathbed when she asked you. Why? Because
you have the cursed jesuit strain in you, only it's injected the
wrong way. To me it's all a mockery and beastly. Her cerebral
lobes are not functioning. She calls the doctor Sir Peter Teazle
and picks buttercups off the quilt. Humour her till it's over.
You crossed her last wish in death and yet you sulk with me
because I don't whinge like some hired mute from Lalouette's.
Absurd! I suppose I did say it. I didn't mean to offend the
memory of your mother.

He had spoken himself into boldness. Stephen, shielding
the gaping wounds which the words had left in his heart, said
very coldly:

– I am not thinking of the offence to my mother.

– Of what, then? Buck Mulligan asked.

– Of the offence to me, Stephen answered.

Buck Mulligan swung round on his heel.

– O, an impossible person! he exclaimed.

He walked off quickly round the parapet. Stephen stood at his post, gazing over the calm sea towards the headland. Sea and headland now grew dim. Pulses were beating in his eyes, veiling their sight, and he felt the fever of his cheeks.

A voice within the tower called loudly:

– Are you up there, Mulligan?

– I'm coming, Buck Mulligan answered.

He turned towards Stephen and said:

– Look at the sea. What does it care about offences? Chuck Loyola, Kinch, and come on down. The Sassenach wants his morning rashers.

His head halted again for a moment at the top of the staircase, level with the roof.

– Don't mope over it all day, he said. I'm inconsequent. Give up the moody brooding.

His head vanished but the drone of his descending voice boomed out of the stairhead:

> *And no more turn aside and brood*
> *Upon love's bitter mystery*
> *For Fergus rules the brazen cars.*

Woodshadows floated silently by through the morning peace from the stairhead seaward where he gazed. Inshore and farther out the mirror of water whitened, spurned by lightshod hurrying feet. White breast of the dim sea. The twining stresses, two by two. A hand plucking the harpstrings merging their twining chords. Wavewhite wedded words shimmering on the dim tide.

A cloud began to cover the sun slowly, shadowing the bay in deeper green. It lay behind him, a bowl of bitter waters. Fergus' song: I sang it alone in the house, holding down the long dark chords. Her door was open: she wanted to hear my music. Silent with awe and pity I went to her bedside. She was crying in her wretched bed. For those words, Stephen: love's bitter mystery.

Where now?

Her secrets: old feather fans, tasselled dancecards, powdered with musk, a gaud of amber beads in her locked drawer. A birdcage hung in the sunny window of her house when she was a girl. She heard old Royce sing in the pantomime of Turko the terrible and laughed with others when he sang:

> *I am the boy*
> *That can enjoy*
> *Invisibility.*

Phantasmal mirth, folded away: muskperfumed.

And no more turn aside and brood

Folded away in the memory of nature with her toys. Memories beset his brooding brain. Her glass of water from the kitchen tap when she had approached the sacrament. A cored apple, filled with brown sugar, roasting for her at the hob on a dark autumn evening. Her shapely fingernails reddened by the blood of squashed lice from the children's shirts.

In a dream, silently, she had come to him, her wasted body within its loose graveclothes giving off an odour of wax and rosewood, her breath bent over him with mute secret words, a faint odour of wetted ashes.

Her glazing eyes, staring out of death, to shake and bend my soul. On me alone. The ghostcandle to light her agony. Ghostly light on the tortured face. Her hoarse loud breath rattling in horror, while all prayed on their knees. Her eyes on me to strike me down. *Liliata rutilantium te confessorum turma circumdet: iubilantium te virginum chorus excipiat.*

Ghoul! Chewer of corpses!

No mother. Let me be and let me live.

– Kinch ahoy!

Buck Mulligan's voice sang from within the tower. It came nearer up the staircase, calling again. Stephen, still trembling at his soul's cry, heard warm running sunlight and in the air behind him friendly words.

– Dedalus, come down, like a good mosey. Breakfast is ready. Haines is apologizing for waking us last night. It's all right.

– I'm coming, Stephen said, turning.

– Do, for Jesus' sake, Buck Mulligan said. For my sake and for all our sakes.

His head disappeared and reappeared.

– I told him your symbol of Irish art. He says it's very clever. Touch him for a quid, will you? A guinea, I mean.

– I get paid this morning, Stephen said.

– The school kip? Buck Mulligan said. How much? Four quid? Lend us one.

– If you want it, Stephen said.

– Four shining sovereigns, Buck Mulligan cried with delight. We'll have a glorious drunk to astonish the druidy druids. Four omnipotent sovereigns.

He flung up his hands and tramped down the stone stairs, singing out of tune with a Cockney accent:

> *O, won't we have a merry time*
> *Drinking whisky, beer and wine,*
> *On coronation,*
> *Coronation day?*
> *O, won't we have a merry time*
> *On coronation day?*

Warm sunshine merrying over the sea. The nickel shaving-bowl shone, forgotten, on the parapet. Why should I bring it down? Or leave it there all day, forgotten friendship?

He went over to it, held it in his hands awhile, feeling its coolness, smelling the clammy slaver of the lather in which the brush was stuck. So I carried the boat of incense then at

Clongowes. I am another now and yet the same. A servant too. A server of a servant.

In the gloomy domed livingroom of the tower Buck Mulligan's gowned form moved briskly about the hearth to and fro, hiding and revealing its yellow glow. Two shafts of soft daylight fell across the flagged floor from the high barbicans: and at the meeting of their rays a cloud of coalsmoke and fumes of fried grease floated, turning.

Belief

– It's a wonderful tale, Haines said, bringing them to halt again.

Eyes, pale as the sea the wind had freshened, paler, firm and prudent. The seas' ruler, he gazed southward over the bay, empty save for the smokeplume of the mailboat, vague on the bright skyline, and a sail tacking by the Muglins.

– I read a theological interpretation of it somewhere, he said bemused. The Father and the Son idea. The Son striving to be atoned with the Father.

Buck Mulligan at once put on a blithe broadly smiling face. He looked at them, his wellshaped mouth open happily, his eyes, from which he had suddenly withdrawn all shrewd sense, blinking with mad gaiety. He moved a doll's head to and fro, the brims of his Panama hat quivering, and began to chant in a quiet happy foolish voice:

> – *I'm the queerest young fellow that ever you heard.*
> *My mother's a jew, my father's a bird.*
> *With Joseph the joiner I cannot agree,*
> *So here's to disciples and Calvary.*

He held up a forefinger of warning.

  - *If anyone thinks that I amn't divine*
    He'll get no free drinks when I'm making the wine
    But have to drink water and wish it were plain
    That I make when the wine becomes water again.

He tugged swiftly at Stephen's ashplant in farewell and, running forward to a brow of the cliff, fluttered his hands at his sides like fins or wings of one about to rise in the air, and chanted:

  - *Goodbye, now, goodbye. Write down all I said*
    And tell Tom, Dick and Harry I rose from the dead.
    What's bred in the bone cannot fail me to fly
    And Olivet's breezy . . . Goodbye, now, goodbye.

He capered before them down towards the fortyfoot hole, fluttering his winglike hands, leaping nimbly, Mercury's hat quivering in the fresh wind that bore back to them his brief birdlike cries.

Haines, who had been laughing guardedly, walked on beside Stephen and said:

– We oughtn't to laugh, I suppose, He's rather blasphemous. I'm not a believer myself, that is to say. Still his gaiety takes the harm out of it somehow, doesn't it? What did he call it? Joseph the Joiner?

– The ballad of Joking Jesus, Stephen answered.

– O, Haines said, you have heard it before?

– Three times a day, after meals, Stephen said drily.

– You're not a believer, are you? Haines asked. I mean, a believer in the narrow sense of the word. Creation from nothing and miracles and a personal God.

– There's only one sense of the word, it seems to me, Stephen said.

The soul

A swarthy boy opened a book and propped it nimbly under the breastwork of his satchel. He recited jerks of verse with odd glances at the text:

> – *Weep no more, woful shepherd, weep no more*
> *For Lycidas, your sorrow, is not dead,*
> *Sunk though he be beneath the watery floor . . .*

It must be a movement then, an actuality of the possible as possible. Aristotle's phrase formed itself within the gabbled verses and floated out into the studious silence of the library of Saint Genevieve where he had read, sheltered from the sin of Paris, night by night. By his elbow a delicate Siamese conned a handbook of strategy. Fed and feeding brains about me: under glowlamps, impaled, with faintly beating feelers: and in my mind's darkness a sloth of the underworld, reluctant, shy of brightness, shifting her dragon scaly folds. Thought is the thought of thought. Tranquil brightness. The soul is in a manner all that is: the soul is the form of forms. Tranquillity sudden, vast, candescent: form of forms.

Talbot repeated:

> – *Through the dear might of Him that walked the*
>   *waves,*
> *Through the dear might . . .*

Echoes of Dryden to Swift

B ringing his host down and kneeling he heard twine with his second bell the first bell in the transept (he is lifting his) and, rising, heard (now I am lifting) their two bells (he is kneeling) twang in diphthong.

Cousin Stephen, you will never be a saint. Isle of saints. You were awfully holy, weren't you? You prayed to the Blessed

Virgin that you might not have a red nose. You prayed to the devil in Serpentine avenue that the fubsy widow in front might lift her clothes still more from the wet street. *O si, certo!* Sell your soul for that, do, dyed rags pinned round a squaw. More tell me, more still! On top of the Howth tram alone crying to the rain: *naked women!* What about that, eh?

What about what? What else were they invented for?

Reading two pages apiece of seven books every night, eh? I was young. You bowed to yourself in the mirror, stepping forward to applause earnestly, striking face. Hurray for the Goddamned idiot! Hray! No-one saw: tell no-one. Books you were going to write with letters for titles. Have you read his F? O yes, but I prefer Q. Yes, but W is wonderful. O yes, W. Remember your epiphanies on green oval leaves, deeply deep, copies to be sent if you died to all the great libraries of the world, including Alexandria? Someone was to read them there after a few thousand years, a mahamanvantara. Pico della Mirandola like. Ay, very like a whale. When one reads these strange pages of one long gone one feels that one is at one with one who once . . .

The grainy sand had gone from under his feet. His boots trod again a damp crackling mast, razorshells, squeaking pebbles, that on the unnumbered pebbles beats, wood sieved by the shipworm, lost Armada. Unwholesome sandflats waited to suck his treading soles, breathing upward sewage breath. He coasted them, walking warily. A porter-bottle stood up, stogged to its waist, in the cakey sand dough. A sentinel: isle of dreadful thirst. Broken hoops on the shore; at the land a maze of dark cunning nets; farther away chalk-scrawled backdoors and on the higher beach a dryingline with two crucified shirts. Ringsend: wigwams of brown steersmen and master mariners. Human shells.

He halted. I have passed the way to aunt Sara's. Am I not going there? Seems not. No-one about. He turned northeast and crossed the firmer sand towards the Pigeonhouse.

– *Qui vous a mis dans cette fichue position?*

– *C'est le pigeon, Joseph.*

Rogue words for Romanies

Shouldering their bags they trudged, the red Egyptians. His blued feet out of turnedup trousers slapped the clammy sand, a dull brick muffler strangling his unshaven neck. With woman steps she followed: the ruffian and his strolling mort. Spoils slung at her back. Loose sand and shellgrit crusted her bare feet. About her windraw face her hair trailed. Behind her lord his helpmate, bing awast, to Romeville. When night hides her body's flaws calling under her brown shawl from an archway where dogs have mired. Her fancyman is treating two Royal Dublins in O'Loughlin's of Blackpitts. Buss her, wap in rogue's rum lingo, for, O, my dimber wapping dell. A shefiend's whiteness under her rancid rags. Fumbally's lane that night: the tanyard smells.

> *White thy fambles, red thy gan*
> *And thy quarrons dainty is.*
> *Couch a hogshead with me then.*
> *In the darkness clip and kiss.*

Morose delectation Aquinas tunbelly calls this, *frate porcos-pino*. Unfallen Adam rode and not rutted. Call away let him: *thy quarrons dainty is*. Language no whit worse than his. Monkwords, marybeads jabber on their girdles: roguewords, tough nuggets patter in their pockets.

Passing now.

Sea death

Touch me. Soft eyes. Soft soft soft hand. I am lonely here.
O, touch me soon, now. What is that word known to all
men? I am quiet here alone. Sad too. Touch, touch me.

He lay back at full stretch over the sharp rocks, cramming
the scribbled note and pencil into a pocket, his hat tilted down
on his eyes. That is Kevin Egan's movement I made nodding
for his nap, sabbath sleep. *Et vidit Deus. Et erant valde bona.*
Alo! *Bonjour,* welcome as the flowers in May. Under its leaf he
watched through peacocktwittering lashes the southing sun. I
am caught in this burning scene. Pan's hour, the faunal noon.
Among gumheavy serpentplants, milkoozing fruits, where on
the tawny waters leaves lie wide. Pain is far.

And no more turn aside and brood.

His gaze brooded on his broadtoed boots, a buck's castoffs
nebeneinander. He counted the creases of rucked leather
wherein another's foot had nested warm. The foot that beat
the ground in tripudium, foot I dislove. But you were delighted
when Esther Osvalt's shoe went on you: girl I knew in Paris.
Tiens, quel petit pied! Staunch friend, a brother soul: Wilde's
love that dare not speak its name. He now will leave me. And
the blame? As I am. As I am. All or not at all.

In long lassoes from the Cock lake the water flowed full,
covering greengoldenly lagoons of sand, rising, flowing. My
ashplant will float away. I shall wait. No, they will pass on,
passing chafing against the low rocks, swirling, passing.
Better get this job over quick. Listen: a fourworded wave-
speech: seesoo, hrss, rsseeiss, ooos. Vehement breath of
waters amid seasnakes, rearing horses, rocks. In cups of rocks
it slops: flop, slop, slap: bounded in barrels. And, spent, its
speech ceases. It flows purling, widely flowing, floating
foampool, flower unfurling.

Under the upswelling tide he saw the writhing weeds lift
languidly and sway reluctant arms, hising up their petticoats,
in whispering water swaying and upturning coy silver fronds.

Day by day: night by night: lifted, flooded and let fall. Lord, they are weary: and, whispered to, they sigh. Saint Ambrose heard it, sigh of leaves and waves, waiting, awaiting the fullness of their times, *diebus ac noctibus iniurias patiens ingemiscit*. To no end gathered: vainly then released, forth flowing, wending back: loom of the moon. Weary too in sight of lovers, lascivious men, a naked woman shining in her courts, she draws a toil of waters.

Five fathoms out there. Full fathom five thy father lies. At one he said. Found drowned. High water at Dublin bar. Driving before it a loose drift of rubble, fanshoals of fishes, silly shells. A corpse rising saltwhite from the undertow, bobbing landward, a pace a pace a porpoise. There he is. Hook it quick. Sunk though he be beneath the watery floor. We have him. Easy now.

Bag of corpsegas sopping in foul brine. A quiver of minnows, fat of a spongy titbit, flash through the slits of his buttoned trouserfly. God becomes man becomes fish becomes barnacle goose becomes featherbed mountain. Dead breaths I living breathe, tread dead dust, devour a urinous offal from all dead. Hauled stark over the gunwale he breathes upward the stench of his green grave, his leprous nosehole snoring to the sun.

A seachange this, brown eyes saltblue. Seadeath, mildest of all deaths known to man. Old Father Ocean. *Prix de Paris:* beware of imitations. Just you give it a fair trial. We enjoyed ourselves immensely.

Come. I thirst. Clouding over. No black clouds anywhere, are there? Thunderstorm. Allbright he falls, proud lightning of the intellect, *Lucifer, dico, qui nescit occasum*. No. My cockle hat and staff and his my sandal shoon. Where? To evening lands. Evening will find itself.

He took the hilt of his ashplant, lunging with it softly, dallying still. Yes, evening will find itself in me, without me. All days make their end. By the way next when is it? Tuesday will be the longest day. Of all the glad new year, mother, the rum tum tiddledy tum. Lawn Tennyson, gentleman poet.

Già. For the old hag with the yellow teeth. And Monsieur Drumont, gentleman journalist. *Già.* My teeth are very bad. Why, I wonder? Feel. That one is going too. Shells. Ought I go to a dentist, I wonder, with that money? That one. Toothless Kinch, the superman. Why is that, I wonder, or does it mean something perhaps?

My handkerchief. He threw it. I remember. Did I not take it up?

His hand groped vainly in his pockets. No, I didn't. Better buy one.

He laid the dry snot picked from his nostril on a ledge of rock, carefully. For the rest let look who will.

Behind. Perhaps there is someone.

He turned his face over a shoulder, rere regardant. Moving through the air high spars of a threemaster, her sails brailed up on the crosstrees, homing, upstream, silently moving, a silent ship.

The cat

The cat walked stiffly round a leg of the table with tail on high.

– Mkgnao!

– O, there you are, Mr Bloom said, turning from the fire.

The cat mewed in answer and stalked again stiffly round a leg of the table, mewing. Just how she stalks over my writingtable. Prr. Scratch my head. Prr.

Mr Bloom watched curiously, kindly, the lithe black form. Clean to see: the gloss of her sleek hide, the white button under the butt of her tail, the green flashing eyes. He bent down to her, his hands on his knees.

– Milk for the pussens, he said.

– Mrkgnao! the cat cried.

They call them stupid. They understand what we say better than we understand them. She understands all she wants to.

Vindictive too. Wonder what I look like to her. Height of a tower? No, she can jump me.

– Afraid of the chickens she is, he said mockingly. Afraid of the chookchooks. I never saw such a stupid pussens as the pussens.

Cruel. Her nature. Curious mice never squeal. Seem to like it.

– Mrkrgnao! the cat said loudly.

She blinked up out of her avid shameclosing eyes, mewing plaintively and long, showing him her milk-white teeth. He watched the dark eyeslits narrowing with greed till her eyes were green stones. Then he went to the dresser, took the jug Hanlon's milkman had just filled for him, poured warm-bubbled milk on a saucer and set it slowly on the floor.

– Gurrhr! she cried, running to lap.

He watched the bristles shining wirily in the weak light as she tipped three times and licked lightly. Wonder is it true if you clip them they can't mouse after. Why? They shine in the dark, perhaps, the tips. Or kind of feelers in the dark, perhaps.

He listened to her licking lap. Ham and eggs, no. No good eggs with this drouth. Want pure fresh water. Thursday: not a good day either for a mutton kidney at Buckley's. Fried with butter, a shake of pepper. Better a pork kidney at Dlugacz's. While the kettle is boiling. She lapped slower, then licking the saucer clean. Why are their tongues so rough? To lap better, all porous holes. Nothing she can eat? He glanced round him. No.

Last day

Mr Kernan said with solemnity:
– *I am the resurrection and the life.* That touches a man's inmost heart.

– It does, Mr Bloom said.

Your heart perhaps but what price the fellow in the six feet by two with his toes to the daisies? No touching that. Seat of the affections. Broken heart. A pump after all, pumping thousands of gallons of blood every day. One fine day it gets bunged up and there you are. Lots of them lying around here: lungs, hearts, livers. Old rusty pumps: damn the thing else. The resurrection and the life. Once you are dead you are dead. That last day idea. Knocking them all up out of their graves. Come forth, Lazarus! And he came fifth and lost the job. Get up! Last day! Then every fellow mousing around for his liver and his lights and the rest of his traps. Find damn all of himself that morning. Pennyweight of powder in a skull. Twelve grammes one pennyweight. Troy measure.

Lovers' encounter

S tuck on the pane two flies buzzed, stuck.
　　Glowing wine on his palate lingered swallowed. Crushing in the winepress grapes of Burgundy. Sun's heat it is. Seems to a secret touch telling me memory. Touched his sense moistened remembered. Hidden under wild ferns on Howth. Below us bay sleeping sky. No sound. The sky. The bay purple by the Lion's head. Green by Drumleck. Yellowgreen towards Sutton. Fields of undersea, the lines faint brown in grass, buried cities. Pillowed on my coat she had her hair, earwigs in the heather scrub my hand under her nape, you'll toss me all. O wonder! Coolsoft with ointments her hand touched me, caressed: her eyes upon me did not turn away. Ravished over her I lay, full lips full open, kissed her mouth. Yum. Softly she gave me in my mouth the seedcake warm and chewed. Mawkish pulp her mouth had mumbled sweet and sour with spittle. Joy: I ate it: joy. Young life, her lips that gave me pouting. Soft, warm, sticky gumjelly lips. Flowers her eyes were, take me, willing eyes. Pebbles fell. She lay still. A goat. No-one. High on Ben Howth rhododendrons a nannygoat walking surefooted, dropping currants. Screened under ferns

she laughed warmfolded. Wildly I lay on her, kissed her; eyes, her lips, her stretched neck, beating, woman's breasts full in her blouse of nun's veiling, fat nipples upright. Hot I tongued her. She kissed me. I was kissed. All yielding she tossed my hair. Kissed, she kissed me.

Me. And me now.

Stuck, the flies buzzed.

An instructive discussion

He thous and thees her with grave husbandwords. Dost love, Miriam? Dost love thy man?

– That may be too, Stephen said. There is a saying of Goethe's which Mr Magee likes to quote. Beware of what you wish for in youth because you will get it in middle life. Why does he send to one who is a *buonaroba*, a bay where all men ride, a maid of honour with a scandalous girlhood, a lordling to woo for him? He was himself a lord of language and had made himself a coistrel gentleman and had written *Romeo and Juliet*. Why? Belief in himself has been untimely killed. He was overborne in a cornfield first (ryefield, I should say) and he will never be a victor in his own eyes after nor play victoriously the game of laugh and lie down. Assumed dongiovannism will not save him. No later undoing will undo the first undoing. The tusk of the boar has wounded him there where love lies ableeding. If the shrew is worsted yet there remains to her woman's invisible weapon. There is, I feel in the words, some goad of the flesh driving him into a new passion, a darker shadow of the first, darkening even his own understanding of himself. A like fate awaits him and the two rages commingle in a whirlpool.

They list. And in the porches of their ears I pour.

– The soul has been before stricken mortally, a poison poured in the porch of a sleeping ear. But those who are done to death in sleep cannot know the manner of their quell unless their Creator endow their souls with that knowledge in the life to come. The poisoning and the beast with two backs that urged it king Hamlet's ghost could not know of were he not endowed with knowledge by his creator. That is why the speech (his lean unlovely English) is always turned elsewhere, backward. Ravisher and ravished, what he would but would not, go with him from Lucrece's bluecircled ivory globes to Imogen's breast, bare, with its mole cinquespotted. He goes back, weary of the creation he has piled up to hide him from himself, an old dog licking an old sore. But, because loss is his gain, he passes on towards eternity in undiminished personality, untaught by the wisdom he has written or by the laws he has revealed. His beaver is up. He is a ghost, a shadow now, the wind by Elsinore's rocks or what you will, the sea's voice, a voice heard only in the heart of him who is the substance of his shadow, the son consubstantial with the father.

– Amen! responded from the doorway.

Has thou found me, O mine enemy?

Entr'acte.

A ribald face, sullen as a dean's, Buck Mulligan came forwards then blithe in motley, towards the greeting of their smiles. My telegram.

– You were speaking of the gaseous vertebrate, if I mistake not? he asked of Stephen.

Primrosevested he greeted gaily with his doffed Panama as with a bauble.

They make him welcome. *Was Du verlachst wirst Du noch dienen.*

Brood of mockers: Photius, pseudomalachi, Johann Most.

He Who Himself begot, middler the Holy Ghost, and Himself sent himself, Agenbuyer, between Himself and others, Who, put upon by His fiends, stripped and whipped, was nailed like bat to barndoor, starved on crosstree, Who let Him bury, stood up, harrowed hell, fared into heaven and there these nineteen hundred years sitteth on the right hand of His Own Self but yet shall come in the latter day to doom the quick and dead when all the quick shall be dead already.

Glo—o—ri—a in ex—cel—sis De—o

He lifts hands. Veils fall. O, flowers! Bells with bells with bells acquiring.

– Yes, indeed, the quaker librarian said. A most instructive discussion. Mr Mulligan, I'll be bound, has his theory too of the play and of Shakespeare. All sides of life should be represented.

Penelope at Stratford

– We want to hear more, John Eglinton decided with Mr Best's approval. We begin to be interested in Mrs S. Till now we had thought of her, if at all, as a patient Griselda, a Penelope stayathome.

– Antisthenes, pupil of Gorgias, Stephen said, took the palm of beauty from Kyrios Menelaus' brooddam, Argive Helen, the wooden mare of Troy in whom a score of heroes slept, and handed it to poor Penelope. Twenty years he lived in London and, during part of that time, he drew a salary equal to that of the lord chancellor of Ireland. His life was rich. His art, more than the art of feudalism, as Walt Whitman called it, is the art of surfeit. Hot herringpies, green mugs of sack, honeysauces, sugar of roses, marchpane, gooseberried pigeons, ringocandies. Sir Walter Raleigh, when they arrested him, had half a million francs on his back including a pair of fancy stays. The gombeen woman Eliza Tudor had underlinen enough to vie with her of Sheba. Twenty years he dallied there between conjugal love and its chaste delights and scortatory love and its foul pleasures. You know Manningham's story of the burgher's wife who bade Dick Burbage to her bed after she had seen him in *Richard III* and how Shakespeare, overhearing, without more ado about nothing, took the cow by the horns and, when Burbage came knocking at the gate, answered from the capon's blankets: *William the conqueror came before Richard III.* And the gay lakin, mistress Fitton, mount and cry O, and his dainty birdsnies, lady Penelope Rich, a clean quality woman is suited for a player, and the punks of the bankside, a penny a time.

Cours-la-Reine. *Encore vingt sous. Nous ferons de petites cochonneries. Minette? Tu veux?*

– The height of fine society. And sir William Davenant of Oxford's mother with her cup of canary for every cockcanary.

Buck Mulligan, his pious eyes upturned, prayed:

– Blessed Margaret Mary Anycock!

– And Harry of six wives' daughter and other lady friends from neighbour seats, as Lawn Tennyson, gentleman poet, sings. But all those twenty years what do you suppose poor Penelope in Stratford was doing behind the diamond panes?

Do and do. Thing done. In a rosery of Fetter Lane of Gerard, herbalist, he walks, greyedauburn. An azured harebell like her veins. Lids of Juno's eyes, violets. He walks. One life is all. One body. Do. But do. Afar, in a reek of lust and squalor, hands are laid on whiteness.

Buck Mulligan rapped John Eglinton's desk sharply.

– Whom do you suspect? he challenged.

– Say that he is the spurned lover in the sonnets. Once spurned twice spurned. But the court wanton spurned him for a lord, his dearmylove.

Love that dare not speak its name.

– As an Englishman, you mean, John sturdy Eglinton put in, he loved a lord.

Old wall where sudden lizards flash. At Charenton I watched them.

– It seems so, Stephen said, when he wants to do for him, and for all other and singular uneared wombs, the holy office an ostler does for the stallion. Maybe, like Socrates, he had a midwife to mother as he had a shrew to wife. But she, the giglot wanton, did not break a bedvow. Two deeds are rank in that ghost's mind: a broken vow and the dullbrained yokel on whom her favour has declined, deceased husband's brother. Sweet Ann I take it, was hot in the blood. Once a wooer twice a wooer.

Stephen turned boldly in his chair.

– The burden of proof is with you not with me, he said, frowning. If you deny that in the fifth scene of *Hamlet* he has branded her with infamy, tell me why there is no mention of her during the thirtyfour years between the day she married him and the day she buried him. All those women saw their men down and under: Mary, her goodman John, Ann, her poor dear Willun, when he went and died on her, raging that he was the first to go, Joan, her four brothers, Judith, her husband and all her sons, Susan, her husband too, while Susan's daughter, Elizabeth, to use granddaddy's words, wed her second, having killed her first.

O yes, mention there is. In the years when he was living richly in royal London to pay a debt she had to borrow forty shillings from her father's shepherd. Explain you then. Explain the swansong too wherein he has commended her to posterity.

He faced their silence.

To whom thus Eglinton:

> You mean the will.
> That has been explained, I believe, by jurists.
> She was entitled to her widow's dower
> At common law. His legal knowledge was great
> Our judges tell us.

> Him Satan fleers,

Mocker:

> And therefore he left out her name
> From the first draft but he did not leave out
> The presents for his granddaughter, for his daughters,

For his sister, for his old cronies in Stratford
And in London. And therefore when he was urged,
As I believe, to name her
He left her his
Secondbest
Bed.

Punkt

Leftherhis
Secondbest
Bestabed
Secabest
Leftabed.

Woa!

– Pretty countryfolk had few chattels then, John Eglinton observed, as they have still if our peasant plays are true to type.

– He was a rich countrygentleman, Stephen said, with a coat of arms and landed estate at Stratford and a house in Ireland yard, a capitalist shareholder, a bill promoter, a tithefarmer. Why did he not leave her his best bed if he wished her to snore away the rest of her nights in peace?

– It is clear that there were two beds, a best and a secondbest, Mr Secondbest Best said finely.

– *Separatio a mensa et a thalamo*, bettered Buck Mulligan and was smiled on.

– Antiquity mentions famous beds, Second Eglinton puckered, bedsmiling. Let me think.

– Antiquity mentions that Stagyrite schoolurchin and bald heathen sage, Stephen said, who when dying in exile frees and endows his slaves, pays tribute to his elders, wills to be laid in earth near the bones of his dead wife and bids his friends be kind to an old mistress (don't forget Nell Gwynn Herpyllis) and let her live in his villa.

– Do you mean he died so? Mr Best asked with slight concern. I mean . . .

– He died dead drunk, Buck Mulligan capped. A quart of ale is a dish for a king. O, I must tell you what Dowden said!

– What? asked Besteglinton.

William Shakespeare and company, limited. The people's William. For terms apply: E. Dowden, Highfield house . . .

– Lovely! Buck Mulligan suspired amorously. I asked him what he thought of the charge of pederasty brought against the bard. He lifted his hands and said: *All we can say is that life ran very high in those days.* Lovely!

Catamite.

– The sense of beauty leads us astray, said beautifulinsadness Best to ugling Eglinton.

Steadfast John replied severe:

– The doctor can tell us what those words mean. You cannot eat your cake and have it.

Sayest thou so? Will they wrest from us, from me the palm of beauty?

– And the sense of property, Stephen said. He drew Shylock out of his own long pocket. The son of a maltjobber and moneylender he was himself a cornjobber and moneylender with ten tods of corn hoarded in the famine riots. His borrowers are no doubt those divers of worship mentioned by Chettle Falstaff who reported his uprightness of dealing. He sued a fellowplayer for the price of a few bags of malt and exacted his pound of flesh in interest for every money lent. How else could Aubrey's ostler and callboy get rich quick? All events brought grist to his mill. Shylock chimes with the jewbaiting that followed the hanging and quartering of the queen's leech Lopez, his jew's heart being plucked forth while the sheeny was yet alive: *Hamlet* and *Macbeth* with the coming to the throne of a Scotch philosophaster with a turn for witchroasting. The lost armada is his jeer in *Love's Labour Lost*. His pageants, the histories, sail fullbellied on a tide of Mafeking enthusiasm. Warwickshire jesuits are tried and we have a porter's theory of equivocation. The *Sea Venture* comes home from Bermuda and the play Renan admired is written with Patsy Caliban, our American cousin. The sugared sonnets follow Sidney's. As for fay Elizabeth, otherwise carroty Bess, the gross virgin who inspired *The Merry Wives of Windsor*, let some meinherr from Almany grope his life long for deephid meanings in the depth of the buckbasket.

I think you're getting on very nicely. Just mix up a mixture of theolologicophilolological. *Mingo, minxi, mictum, mingere.*

Jest on

Puck Mulligan footed featly, trilling:

> *I hardly hear the purlieu cry*
> *Or a Tommy talk as I pass one by*
> *Before my thoughts begin to run*
> *On F. M'Curdy Atkinson,*
> *The same that had the wooden leg*
> *And that filibustering fillibeg*
> *That never dared to slake his drouth,*
> *Magee that had the chinless mouth.*
> *Being afraid to marry on earth*
> *They masturbated for all they were worth.*

Jest on. Know thyself.

The rich resources of Gaelic Ireland

In Inisfail the fair there lies a land, the land of holy Michan. There rises a watchtower beheld of men afar. There sleep the mighty dead as in life they slept, warriors and princes of high renown. A pleasant land it is in sooth of murmuring waters, fishful streams where sport the gunnard, the plaice, the roach, the halibut, the gibbed haddock, the grilse, the dab, the brill, the flounder, the mixed coarse fish generally and other denizens of the aqueous kingdom too numerous to be enumerated. In the mild breezes of the west and of the east the lofty trees wave in different directions their first class foliage, the wafty sycamore, the Lebanonian cedar, the exalted planetree, the eugenic eucalyptus and other ornaments of the arboreal world with which that region is thoroughly well supplied. Lovely maidens sit in close proximity to the roots of the lovely trees singing the most lovely songs while they play with all kinds of lovely objects as for example golden ingots, silvery fishes, crans of herrings, drafts of eels, codlings, creels of fingerlings, purple seagems and playful insects. And heroes voyage from afar to woo them, from Elbana to Slievemargy, the peerless princes of unfettered Munster and of Connacht the just and of smooth sleek Leinster and of Cruachan's land and of Armagh the splendid and of the noble district of Boyle, princes, the sons of kings.

And there rises a shining palace whose crystal glittering roof is seen by mariners who traverse the extensive sea in barks built expressly for that purpose and thither come all herds and fatlings and first fruits of that land for O'Connell Fitzsimon takes toll of them, a chieftain descended from chieftains. Thither the extremely large wains bring foison of the fields, flaskets of cauliflowers, floats of spinach, pineapple chunks, Rangoon beans, strikes of tomatoes, drums of figs, drills of Swedes, spherical potatoes and tallies of iridescent kale, York and Savoy, and trays of onions, pearls of the earth, and punnets of mushrooms and custard marrows and fat vetches and bere and rape and red green yellow brown russet sweet big bitter ripe pomellated apples and chips of strawberries and sieves of gooseberries, pulpy and pelurious, and strawberries fit for princes and raspberries from their canes.

– I dare him, says he, and I doubledare him. Come out here, Geraghty, you notorious bloody hill and dale robber!

And by that way wend the herds innumerable of bellwethers and flushed ewes and shearling rams and lambs and stubble geese and medium steers and roaring mares and polled calves and longwools and storesheep and Cuffe's prime springers and culls and sowpigs and baconhogs and the various different varieties of highly distinguished swine and Angus heifers and polly bullocks of immaculate pedigree together with prime premiated milchcows and beeves: and there is ever heard a trampling, cackling, roaring, lowing, bleating, bellowing, rumbling, grunting, champing, chewing, of sheep and pigs and heavyhooved kine from pasturelands of Lush and Rush and Carrickmines and from the streamy vales of Thomond, from M'Gillicuddy's reeks the inaccessible and lordly Shannon the unfathomable, and from the gentle declivities of the place of the race of Kiar, their udders distended with superabundance of milk and butts of butter and rennets of cheese and farmer's firkins and targets of lamb and crannocks of corn and oblong eggs, in great hundreds, various in size, the agate with the dun.

Citizen Cyclops and Elijah Bloom

– I know where he's gone, says Lenehan, cracking his fingers.

– Who? says I.

– Bloom, says he, the courthouse is a blind. He had a few bob on *Throwaway* and he's gone to gather in the shekels.

– Is it that whiteyed kaffir? says the citizen, that never backed a horse in anger in his life.

– That's where he's gone, says Lenehan. I met Bantam Lyons going to back that horse only I put him off it and he told me Bloom gave him the tip. Bet you what you like he has a hundred shillings to five on. He's the only man in Dublin has it. A dark horse.

– He's a bloody dark horse himself, says Joe.

– Mind, Joe, says I. Show us the entrance out.

– There you are, says Terry.

Goodbye Ireland I'm going to Gort. So I just went round to the back of the yard to pumpship and begob (hundred

shillings to five) while I was letting off my (*Throwaway*
twenty to) letting off my load gob says I to myself I knew he
was uneasy in his (two pints off of Joe and one in Slattery's
off) in his mind to get off the mark to (hundred shillings is
five quid) and when they were in the (dark horse) Pisser
Burke was telling me card party and letting on the child was
sick (gob, must have done about a gallon) flabbyarse of a wife
speaking down the tube *she's better* or *she's* (ow!) all a plan so
he could vamoose with the pool if he won or (Jesus, full up I
was) trading without a licence (ow!) Ireland my nation says he
(hoik! phthook!) never be up to those bloody (there's the last
of it) Jerusalem (ah!) cuckoos.

So anyhow when I got back they were at it dingdong, John
Wyse saying it was Bloom gave the idea for Sinn Fein to
Griffith to put in his paper all kinds of jerrymandering,
packed juries and swindling the taxes off of the Government
and appointing consuls all over the world to walk about
selling Irish industries. Robbing Peter to pay Paul. Gob, that
puts the bloody kybosh on it if old sloppy eyes is mucking up
the show. Give us a bloody chance. God save Ireland from the
likes of that bloody mouseabout. Mr Bloom with his argol
bargol. And his old fellow before him perpetrating frauds, old
Methusalem Bloom, the robbing bagman, that poisoned
himself with the prussic acid after he swamping the country
with his baubles and his penny diamonds. Loans by post on
easy terms. Any amount of money advanced on note of hand.
Distance no object. No security. Gob he's like Lanty
MacHale's goat that'd go a piece of the road with every one.

– Well, it's a fact, says John Wyse. And there's the man now
that'll tell you about it, Martin Cunningham.

Sure enough the castle car drove up with Martin on it and
Jack Power with him and a fellow named Crofter or Crofton,
pensioner out of the collector general's, an orangeman
Blackburn does have on the registration and he drawing his
pay or Crawford gallivanting around the country at the king's
expense.

Our travellers reached the rustic hostelry and alighted from their palfreys.

– Ho, varlet! cried he, who by his mien seemed the leader of the party. Saucy knave! To us!

So saying he knocked loudly with his swordhilt upon the open lattice.

Mine host came forth at the summons girding him with his tabard.

– Give you good den, my masters, said he with an obsequious bow.

– Bestir thyself, sirrah! cried he who had knocked. Look to our steeds. And for ourselves give us of your best for ifaith we need it.

– Lackaday, good masters, said the host, my poor house has but a bare larder. I know not what to offer your lordships.

– How now, fellow? cried the second of the party, a man of pleasant countenance, so servest thou the king's messengers, Master Taptun?

An instantaneous change overspread the landlord's visage.

– Cry you mercy, gentlemen, he said humbly. An you be the king's messengers (God shield His Majesty!) you shall not want for aught. The king's friends (God bless His Majesty!) shall not go afasting in my house I warrant me.

– Then about! cried the traveller who had not spoken, a lusty trencherman by his aspect. Hast aught to give us?

Mine host bowed again as he made answer:

– What say you, good masters, to a squab pigeon pasty, some collops of venison, a saddle of veal, widgeon with crisp hog's bacon, a boar's head with pistachios, a bason of jolly custard, a medlar tansy and a flagon of old Rhenish?

– Gadzooks! cried the last speaker. That likes me well. Pistachios!

– Aha! cried he of the pleasant countenance. A poor house and a bare larder, quotha! 'Tis a merry rogue.

So in comes Martin asking where was Bloom.

– Where is he? says Lenehan. Defrauding widows and orphans.

– Isn't that a fact, says John Wyse, what I was telling the citizen about Bloom and the Sinn Fein?

– That's so, says Martin. Or so they allege.

– Who made those allegations? says Alf.

– I, says Joe. I'm the alligator.

– And after all, says John Wyse, why can't a jew love his country like the next fellow?

– Why not? says J. J., when he's quite sure which country it is.

– Is he a jew or a gentile or a holy Roman or a swaddler or what the hell is he? says Ned. Or who is he? No offence, Crofton.

– We don't want him, says Crofter the Orangeman or presbyterian.

– Who is Junius? says J. J.

– He's a perverted jew, says Martin, from a place in Hungary and it was he drew up all the plans according to the Hungarian system. We know that in the castle.

– Isn't he a cousin of Bloom the dentist? says Jack Power.

– Not at all, says Martin. Only namesakes. His name was Virag. The father's name that poisoned himself. He changed it by deed poll, the father did.

– That's the new Messiah for Ireland! says the citizen. Island of saints and sages!

– Well, they're still waiting for their redeemer, says Martin. For that matter so are we.

– Yes, says J. J., and every male that's born they think it may be their Messiah. And every jew is in a tall state of excitement, I believe, till he knows if he's a father or a mother.

– Expecting every moment will be his next, says Lenehan.

– O, by God, says Ned, you should have seen Bloom before that son of his that died was born. I met him one day in the south city markets buying a tin of Neave's food six weeks before the wife was delivered.

– *En ventre sa mère*, says J. J.

– Do you call that a man? says the citizen.

– I wonder did he ever put it out of sight, says Joe.

– Well, there were two children born anyhow, says Jack Power.

– And who does he suspect? says the citizen.

Gob, there's many a true word spoken in jest. One of those mixed middlings he is. Lying up in the hotel Pisser was telling me once a month with headache like a totty with her courses. Do you know what I'm telling you? It'd be an act of God to take a hold of a fellow the like of that and throw him in the bloody sea. Justifiable homicide, so it would. Then sloping off with his five quid without putting up a pint of stuff like a man. Give us your blessing. Not as much as would blind your eye.

– Charity to the neighbour, says Martin. But where is he? We can't wait.

– A wolf in sheep's clothing, says the citizen. That's what he is. Virag from Hungary! Ahasuerus I call him. Cursed by God.

– Have you time for a brief libation, Martin? says Ned.

– Only one, says Martin. We must be quick. J. J. and S.

– You Jack? Crofton? Three half ones, Terry.

– Saint Patrick would want to land again at Ballykinlar and convert us, says the citizen, after allowing things like that to contaminate our shores.

– Well, says Martin, rapping for his glass. God bless all here is my prayer.

– Amen, says the citizen.

– And I'm sure he will, says Joe.

And at the sound of the sacring bell, headed by a crucifer with acolytes, thurifers, boatbearers, readers, ostiarii, deacons and subdeacons, the blessed company drew nigh of mitred abbots and priors and guardians and monks and friars: the monks of Benedict of Spoleto, Carthusians and Camaldolesi, Cistercians and Olivetans, Oratorians and Vallombrosans, and the friars of Augustine, Brigittines, Premonstratesians, Servi, Trinitarians, and the children of Peter Nolasco: and therewith from Carmel mount the children of Elijah prophet led by Albert bishop and by Teresa of Avila, calced and other: and friars brown and grey, sons of poor Francis, capuchins, cordeliers, minimes and observants and the daughters of

Clara: and the sons of Dominic, the friars preachers, and the sons of Vincent: and the monks of S. Wolstan: and Ignatius his children: and the confraternity of the christian brothers led by the reverend brother Edmund Ignatius Rice. And after came all saints and martyrs, virgins and confessors: S. Cyr and S. Isidore Arator and S. James the Less and S. Phocas of Sinope and S. Julian Hospitator and S. Felix de Cantalice and S. Simon Stylites and S. Stephen Protomartyr and S. John of God and S. Ferreol and S. Leugarde and S. Theodotus and S. Vulmar and S. Richard and S. Vincent de Paul and S. Martin of Todi and S. Martin of Tours and S. Alfred and S. Joseph and S. Denis and S. Cornelius and S. Leopold and S. Bernard and S. Terence and S. Edward and S. Owen Caniculus and S. Anonymous and S. Eponymous and S. Pseudonymous and S. Homonymous and S. Paronymous and S. Synonymous and S. Laurence O'Toole and S. James of Dingle and Compostella and S. Columcille and S. Columba and S. Celestine and S. Colman and S. Kevin and S. Brendan and S. Frigidian and S. Senan and S. Fachtna and S. Columbanus and S. Gall and S. Fursey and S. Fintan and S. Fiacre and S. John Nepomuc and S. Thomas Aquinas and S. Ives of Brittany and S. Michan and S. Herman-Joseph and the three patrons of holy youth S. Aloysius Gonzaga and S. Stanislaus Kostka and S. John Berchmans and the saints Gervasius, Servasius and Bonifacius and S. Bride and S. Kieran and S. Canice of Kilkenny and S. Jarlath of Tuam and S. Finbarr and S. Pappin of Ballymun and Brother Aloysius Pacificus and Brother Louis Bellicosus and the saints Rose of Lima and of Viterbo and S. Martha of Bethany and S. Mary of Egypt and S. Lucy and S. Brigid and S. Attracta and S. Dympna and S. Ita and S. Marion Calpensis and the Blessed Sister Teresa of the Child Jesus and S. Barbara and S. Scholastica and S. Ursula with eleven thousand virgins. And all came with nimbi and aureoles and gloriae, bearing palms and harps and swords and olive crowns, in robes whereon were woven the blessed symbols of their efficacies, inkhorns, arrows, loaves, cruses, fetters, axes, trees, bridges, babes in a bathtub, shells, wallets, shears, keys, dragons, lilies, buckshot, beards, hogs, lamps, bellows, beehives, soupladles, stars, snakes, anvils, boxes of vaseline, bells, crutches, forceps, stags' horns, watertight boots, hawks, millstones, eyes on a dish, wax candles, aspergills, unicorns. And as they wended their way by Nelson's Pillar, Henry Street, Mary Street, Capel Street, Little Britain Street, chanting the introit in *Epiphania Domini* which beginneth *Surge, illuminare* and thereafter most sweetly the gradual *Omnes* which saith *de Saba venient* they did divers wonders such as casting out devils, raising the dead to life, multiplying fishes, healing the halt and the blind, discovering various articles which had been mislaid, interpreting and fulfilling the scriptures, blessing and prophesying. And last, beneath a canopy of cloth of gold came the reverend Father O'Flynn attended by Malachi and Patrick. And when the good fathers had reached the appointed place, the house of Bernard Kiernan and Co, limited, 8, 9 and 10 little Britain street, wholesale grocers, wine and brandy shippers, licensed for the sale of beer, wine and spirits for consumption on the premises, the celebrant blessed the house and censed the mullioned windows and the groynes and the vaults and the arrises and the capitals and the pediments and the cornices and the engrailed arches and the spires and the cupolas and sprinkled the lintels thereof with blessed water and prayed that God might bless that house as he had blessed the house of Abraham and Isaac and Jacob and make the angels of His light to inhabit therein. And entering he blessed the viands and the beverages and the company of all the blessed answered his prayers.

– *Adiutorium nostrum in nomine Domini.*

– *Que fecit cœlum et terram.*

– *Dominus vobiscum.*

– *Et cum spiritu tuo.*

And he laid his hands upon the blessed and gave thanks and he prayed and they all with him prayed:

– *Deus, cuius verbo sanctificantur omnia, benedictionem tuam effunde super creaturas istas: et præsta ut quisquis eis secundum legem et voluntatem Tuan cum gratiarum actione*

*usus fuerit per invocationem sanctissimi nominis Tui corporis
sanitatem et animæ tutelam Te auctore percipiat per Chris-
tum Dominum nostrum.*

– And so say all of us, says Jack.

– Thousand a year, Lambert, says Crofton or Crawford.

– Right, says Ned, taking up his John Jameson. And butter
for fish.

I was just looking round to see who the happy thought
would strike when be damned but in he comes again letting on
to be in a hell of a hurry.

– I was just round at the courthouse, says he, looking for
you. I hope I'm not . . .

– No, says Martin, we're ready.

Courthouse my eye and your pockets hanging down with
gold and silver. Mean bloody scut. Stand us a drink itself. Devil
a sweet fear! There's a jew for you! All for number one. Cute
as a shithouse rat. Hundred to five.

– Don't tell anyone, says the citizen.

– Beg your pardon, says he.

– Come on boys, says Martin, seeing it was looking blue.
Come along now.

– Don't tell anyone, says the citizen, letting a bawl out of
him. It's a secret.

And the bloody dog woke up and let a growl.

– Bye bye all, says Martin.

And he got them out as quick as he could, Jack Power and
Crofton or whatever you call him and him in the middle of
them letting on to be all at sea up with them on the bloody
jaunting car.

Off with you, says Martin to the jarvey.

The milkwhite dolphin tossed his mane and, rising in the
golden poop, the helmsman spread the bellying sail upon the
wind and stood off forward with all sail set, the spinnaker to
larboard. A many comely nymphs drew nigh to starboard and
to larboard and, clinging to the sides of the noble bark, they
linked their shining forms as doth the cunning wheelwright
when he fashions about the heart of his wheel the equidistant

rays whereof each one is sister to another and he binds them
all with an outer ring and giveth speed to the feet of men
whenas they ride to a hosting or contend for the smile of
ladies fair. Even so did they come and set them, those willing
nymphs, the undying sisters. And they laughed, sporting in a
circle of their foam: and the bark clave the waves.

But begob I was just lowering the heel of the pint when I
saw the citizen getting up to waddle to the door, puffing and
blowing with the dropsy and he cursing the curse of Cromwell
on him, bell, book and candle in Irish, spitting and spatting
out of him and Joe and little Alf round him like a leprechaun
trying to peacify him.

– Let me alone, says he.

And begob he got as far as the door and they holding him
and he bawls out of him:

– Three cheers for Israel!

Arrah, sit down on the parliamentary side of your arse for
Christ sake and don't be making a public exhibition of
yourself. Jesus, there's always some bloody clown or other
kicking up a bloody murder about bloody nothing. Gob, it'd
turn the porter sour in your guts, so it would.

And all the ragamuffins and sluts of the nation round the
door and Martin telling the jarvey to drive ahead and the
citizen bawling and Alf and Joe at him to whisht and he on his
high horse about the jews and the loafers calling for a speech
and Jack Power trying to get him to sit down on the car and
hold his bloody jaw and a loafer with a patch over his eye
starts singing *If the man in the moon was a jew, jew, jew* and
a slut shouts out of her:

– Eh, mister! Your fly is open, mister!

And says he:

– Mendelssohn was a jew and Karl Marx and Mercadante
and Spinoza. And the Saviour was a jew and his father was a
jew. Your God.

– He had no father, says Martin. That'll do now. Drive
ahead.

– Whose God? says the citizen.

– Well, his uncle was a jew, says he. Your God was a jew.
Christ was a jew like me.

Gob, the citizen made a plunge back into the shop.

– By Jesus, says he, I'll brain that bloody jewman for using
the holy name. By Jesus, I'll crucify him so I will. Give us that
biscuitbox here.

– Stop! Stop! says Joe.

A large and appreciative gathering of friends and acquain-
tances from the metropolis and greater Dublin assembled in
their thousands to bid farewell to Nagyaságos uram Lipóti
Virag, late of Messrs Alexander Thom's, printers to His
Majesty, on the occasion of his departure for the distant clime
of Százharminczbrojúgulyás-Dugulás (Meadow of Murmur-
ing Waters). The ceremony which went off with great *éclat*
was characterised by the most affecting cordiality. An illumi-
nated scroll of ancient Irish vellum, the work of Irish artists,
was presented to the distinguished phenomenologist on be-
half of a large section of the community and was accompanied
by the gift of a silver casket, tastefully executed in the style of
ancient Celtic ornament, a work which reflects every credit on
the makers, Messrs Jacob *agus* Jacob. The departing guest was
the recipient of a hearty ovation, many of those who were
present being visibly moved when the select orchestra of Irish
pipes struck up the wellknown strains of *Come back to Erin*,
followed immediately by *Rakoczy's March*. Tar-barrels and
bonfires were lighted along the coastline of the four seas on
the summits of the Hill of Howth, Three Rock Mountain,
Sugarloaf, Bray Head, the mountains of Mourne, the Galtees,
the Ox and Donegal and Sperrin peaks, the Nagles and the
Bograghs, the Connemara hills, the reeks of M'Gillicuddy,
Slieve Aughty, Slieve Bernagh and Slieve Bloom. Amid cheers
that rent the welkin, responded to by answering cheers from
a big muster of henchmen on the distant Cambrian and
Caledonian hills, the mastodontic pleasureship slowly moved
away saluted by a final floral tribute from the representatives
of the fair sex who were present in large numbers while, as it
proceeded down the river, escorted by a flotilla of barges, the

flags of the Ballast office and Custom House were dipped in salute as were also those of the electrical power station at the Pigeonhouse. *Visszontlátásra, kedvés baráton! Visszontlátásra!* Gone but not forgotten.

Gob, the devil wouldn't stop him till he got hold of the bloody tin anyhow and out with him and little Alf hanging on to his elbow and he shouting like a stuck pig, as good as any bloody play in the Queen's royal theatre.

– Where is he till I murder him?

And Ned and J. G. paralysed with the laughing.

– Bloody wars, says I, I'll be in for the last gospel.

But as luck would have it the jarvey got the nag's head round the other way and off with him.

– Hold on, citizen, says Joe. Stop.

Begob he drew his hand and made a swipe and let fly. Mercy of God the sun was in his eyes or he'd have left him for dead. Gob, he near sent it into the county Longford. The bloody nag took fright and the old mongrel after the car like bloody hell and all the populace shouting and laughing and the old tinbox clattering along the street.

The catastrophe was terrific and instantaneous in its effect. The observatory of Dunsink registered in all eleven shocks, all of the fifth grade of Mercalli's scale, and there is no record extant of a similar seismic disturbance in our island since the earthquake of 1534, the year of the rebellion of Silken Thomas. The epicentre appears to have been that part of the metropolis which constitutes the Inn's Quay ward and parish of Saint Michan covering a surface of fortyone acres, two roods and one square pole or perch. All the lordly residences in the vicinity of the palace of justice were demolished and that noble edifice itself, in which at the time of the catastrophe important legal debates were in progress, is literally a mass of ruins beneath which it is to be feared all the occupants have been buried alive. From the reports of eyewitnesses it transpires that the seismic waves were accompanied by a violent atmospheric perturbation of cyclonic character. An article of headgear since ascertained to belong to the much

respected clerk of the crown and peace Mr George Fottrell and
a silk umbrella with gold handle with the engraved initials,
coat of arms and house number of the erudite and worshipful
chairman of quarter sessions sir Frederick Falkiner, recorder
of Dublin, have been discovered by search parties in remote
parts of the island, respectively, the former on the third
basaltic ridge of the giant's causeway, the latter embedded to
the extent of one foot three inches in the sandy beach of
Holeopen bay near the old head of Kinsale. Other eye-
witnesses depose that they observed an incandescent object of
enormous proportions hurtling through the atmosphere at a
terrifying velocity in a trajectory directed south west by west.
Messages of condolence and sympathy are being hourly
received from all parts of the different continents and the
sovereign pontiff has been graciously pleased to decree that a
special *missa pro defunctis* shall be celebrated simultaneously
by the ordinaries of each and every cathedral church of all the
episcopal dioceses subject to the spiritual authority of the
Holy See in suffrage of the souls of those faithful departed
who have been so unexpectedly called away from our midst.
The work of salvage, removal of *débris* human remains etc
has been entrusted to Messrs Michael Meade and Son, 159,
Great Brunswick Street and Messrs T. C. Martin, 77, 78, 79
and 80, North Wall, assisted by the men and officers of the
Duke of Cornwall's light infantry under the general supervi-
sion   of
H. R. H., rear admiral the right honourable sir Hercules
Hannibal Habeas Corpus Anderson K.G., K.P., K.T., P.C.,
K.C.B., M.P., J.P., M.B., D.S.O., S.O.D., M.F.H., M.R.I.A., B.L.,
Mus. Doc., P.L.G., F.T.C.D., F.R.U.I., F.R.C.P.I. and F.R.C.S.I.

   You never saw the like of it in all your born puff. Gob, if he
got that lottery ticket on the side of his poll he'd remember the
gold cup, he would so, but begob the citizen would have been
lagged for assault and battery and Joe for aiding and abetting.
The jarvey saved his life by furious driving as sure as God
made Moses. What? O, Jesus, he did. And he let a volley of
oaths after him.

– Did I kill him, says he, or what?

And he shouting to the bloody dog:

– After him, Garry! After him, boy!

And the last we saw was the bloody car rounding the corner and old sheepface on it gesticulating and the bloody mongrel after it with his lugs back for all he was bloody well worth to tear him limb from limb. Hundred to five! Jesus, he took the value of it out of him, I promise you.

When, lo, there came about them all a great brightness and they beheld the chariot wherein He stood ascend to heaven. And they beheld Him in the chariot, clothed upon in the glory of the brightness, having raiment as of the sun, fair as the moon and terrible that for awe they durst not look upon Him. And there came a voice out of heaven, calling: *Elijah! Elijah!* And he answered with a main cry: *Abba! Adonai!* And they beheld Him even Him, ben Bloom Elijah, amid clouds of angels ascend to the glory of the brightness at an angle of fortyfive degrees over Donohoe's in Little Green Street like a shot off a shovel.

Dublin Bay

The summer evening had begun to fold the world in its mysterious embrace. Far away in the west the sun was setting and the last glow of all too fleeting day lingered lovingly on sea and strand, on the proud promontory of dear old Howth guarding as ever the waters of the bay, on the weedgrown rocks along Sandymount shore and, last but not least, on the quiet church whence there streamed forth at times upon the stillness the voice of prayer to her who is in her pure radiance a beacon ever to the storm-tossed heart of man, Mary, star of the sea.

At it again

And Jacky Caffrey shouted to look, there was another and she leaned back and the garters were blue to match on account of the transparent and they all saw it and shouted to look, look there it was and she leaned back ever so far to see the fireworks and something queer was flying about through the air, a soft thing to and fro, dark. And she saw a long Roman candle going up over the trees, up, up, and, in the tense hush, they were all breathless with excitement as it went higher and higher and she had to lean back more and more to look up after it, high, high, almost out of sight, and her face was suffused with a divine, an entrancing blush from straining back and he could see her other things too, nainsook knickers, the fabric that caresses the skin, better than those other pettiwidth, the green, four and eleven, on account of being white and she let him and she saw that he saw and then it went so high it went out of sight a moment and she was trembling in every limb from being bent so far back he had a full view high up above her knee no-one ever not even on the swing or wading and she wasn't ashamed and he wasn't either to look in that immodest way like that because he couldn't resist the sight of the wondrous revealment half offered like those skirtdancers behaving so immodest before gentlemen looking and he kept on looking, looking. She would fain have cried to him chokingly, held out her snowy slender arms to him to come, to feel his lips laid on her white brow the cry of a young girl's love, a little strangled cry, wrung from her, that cry that has rung through the ages. And then a rocket sprang and bang shot blind and O! then the Roman candle burst and it was like a sigh of O! and everyone cried O! O! in raptures and it gushed out of it a stream of rain gold hair threads and they shed and ah! they were all greeny dewy stars falling with golden, O so lively! O so soft, sweet, soft!

Then all melted away dewily in the grey air: all was silent. Ah! She glanced at him as she bent forward quickly, a pathetic little glance of piteous protest, of shy reproach under which he coloured like a girl. He was leaning back against the rock behind. Leopold Bloom (for it is he) stands silent, with bowed head before those young guileless eyes. What a brute he had been! At it again? A fair unsullied soul had called to him and, wretch that he was, how had he answered? An utter cad he had been. He of all men! But there was an infinite store of mercy in those eyes, for him too a word of pardon even though he had erred and sinned and wandered. Should a girl tell? No, a thousand times no. That was their secret, only theirs, alone in the hiding twilight and there was none to know or tell save the little bat that flew so softly through the evening to and fro and little bats don't tell.

Nightscape

Ba. What is that flying about? Swallow? Bat probably. Thinks I'm a tree, so blind. Have birds no smell? Metempsychosis. They believed you could be changed into a tree from grief. Weeping willow. Ba. There he goes. Funny little beggar. Wonder where he lives. Belfry up there. Very likely. Hanging by his heels in the odour of sanctity. Bell scared him out, I suppose. Mass seems to be over. Could hear them all at it. Pray for us. And pray for us. And pray for us. Good idea the repetition. Same thing with ads. Buy from us. And buy from us. Yes, there's the light in the priest's house. Their frugal meal. Remember about the mistake in the valuation when I was in Thom's. Twentyeight it is. Two houses they have. Gabriel Conroy's brother is curate. Ba. Again. Wonder why they come out at night like mice. They're a mixed breed. Birds are like hopping mice. What frightens them, light or noise? Better sit still. All instinct like the bird in drouth got water out of the end of a jar by throwing in pebbles. Like a little man in a cloak he is with tiny hands. Weeny bones. Almost see them shimmering, kind of a bluey white. Colours depend on the light you see. Stare the sun for example like the eagle then look at a shoe see a blotch blob yellowish. Wants to stamp his trademark on everything. Instance, that cat this morning on the staircase. Colour of brown turf. Say you never see them with three colours. Not true. That half tabbywhite tortoiseshell in the *City Arms* with the letter em on her forehead. Body fifty different colours. Howth a while ago amethyst. Glass flashing. That's how that wise man what's his name with the burning glass. Then the heather goes on fire. It can't be tourists' matches. What? Perhaps the sticks dry rub together in the wind and light. Or broken bottles in the furze act as a burning glass in the sun. Archimedes. I have it! My memory's not so bad.

Ba. Who knows what they're always flying for. Insects? That bee last week got into the room playing with his shadow on the ceiling. Might be the one bit me, come back to see. Birds too never find out what they say. Like our small talk. And says she and says he. Nerve? they have to fly over the ocean and back. Lot must be killed in storms, telegraph wires. Dreadful life sailors have too. Big brutes of ocean-going steamers floundering along in the dark, lowing out like seacows. *Faugh a ballagh.* Out of that, bloody curse to you. Others in vessels, bit of a handkerchief sail, pitched about like snuff at a wake when the stormy winds do blow. Married too. Sometimes away for years at the ends of the earth somewhere. No ends really because it's round. Wife in every port they say. She has a good job if she minds it till Johnny comes marching home again. If ever he does. Smelling the tail end of ports. How can they like the sea? Yet they do. The anchor's weighed. Off he sails with a scapular or a medal on him for luck. Well? And the tephilim no what's this they call it poor papa's father had on his door to touch. That brought us out of the land of Egypt and into the house of bondage. Something in all those superstitions because when you go out never know what dangers. Hanging on to a plank or astride of a beam for grim life, lifebelt round round him, gulping salt water, and that's the last of his nibs till the sharks catch hold of him. Do fish ever get seasick?

Then you have a beautiful calm without a cloud, smooth sea, placid, crew and cargo in smithereens, Davy Jones' locker. Moon looking down. Not my fault, old cockalorum.

A lost long candle wandered up the sky from Mirus bazaar in search of funds for Mercer's hospital and broke, drooping, and shed a cluster of violet but one white stars. They floated, fell: they faded. The shepherd's hour: the hour of holding: hour of tryst. From house to house, giving his everwelcome double knock, went the nine o'clock postman, the glowworm's lamp at his belt gleaming here and there through the laurel hedges. And among the five young trees a hoisted lintstock lit the lamp at Leahy's terrace. By screens of lighted windows, by equal gardens a shrill voice went crying, wailing: *Evening Telegraph, stop press edition! Result of the Gold Cup race!* and from the door of Dignam's house a boy ran out and called. Twittering the bat flew here, flew there. Far out over the sands the coming surf crept, grey. Howth settled for slumber tired of long days, of yumyum rhododendrons (he was old) and felt gladly the night breeze lift, ruffle his fell of ferns. He lay but opened a red eye unsleeping, deep and slowly breathing, slumberous but awake. And far on Kish bank the anchored lightship twinkled, winked at Mr Bloom.

Parturition

The air without is impregnated with raindew moisture, life essence celestial, glistering on Dublin stone there under starshiny *coelum*. God's air, the Allfather's air, scintillant circumambient cessile air. Breathe it deep into thee. By heaven, Theodore Purefoy, thou hast done a doughty deed and no botch! Thou art, I vow, the remarkablest progenitor barring none in this chaffering allincluding most farraginous chronicle. Astounding! In her lay a Godframed Godgiven

preformed possibility which thou hast fructified with thy
modicum of man's work. Cleave to her! Serve! Toil on, labour
like a very bandog and let scholarment and all Malthusiasts go
hang. Thou art all their daddies, Theodore. Art drooping
under thy load, bemoiled with butcher's bills at home and
ingots (not thine!) in the countinghouse? Head up! For every
newbegotten thou shalt gather thy homer of ripe wheat. See,
thy fleece is drenched. Dost envy Darby Dullman there with
his Joan? A canting jay and a rheumeyed curdog is all their
progeny. Pshaw, I tell thee! He is a mule, a dead gasteropod,
without vim or stamina, not worth a cracked kreutzer.
Copulation without population! No, say I! Herod's slaughter
of the innocents were the truer name. Vegetables, forsooth,
and sterile cohabitation! Give her beefsteaks, red, raw,
bleeding! She is a hoary pandemonium of ills, enlarged glands,
mumps, quinsy, bunions, hayfever, bedsores, ringworm,
floating kidney, Derbyshire neck, warts, bilious attacks,
gallstones, cold feet, varicose veins. A truce to threnes and
trentals and jeremies and all such congenital defunctive music.
Twenty years of it, regret them not. With thee it was not as
with many that will and would and wait and never do. Thou
sawest thy America, thy lifetask, and didst charge to cover like
the transpontine bison. How saith Zarathusthra? *Deine Kuh
Trübsal melkest Du. Nun Trinkst Du die süsse Milch des
Euters.* See! It displodes for thee in abundance. Drink, man, an
udderful! Mother's milk, Purefoy, the milk of human kin, milk
too of those burgeoning stars overhead, rutilant in thin
rainvapour, punch milk, such as those rioters will quaff in
their guzzlingden, milk of madness, the honeymilk of
Canaan's land. Thy cow's dug was tough, what? Ay, but her
milk is hot and sweet and fattening. No dollop this but thick
rich bonny-claber. To her, old patriarch! Pap! *Per deam
Partulam et Pertundam nunc est bibendum!*

Bloom's benison

B LOOM: My beloved subjects, a new era is about to dawn. I, Bloom, tell you verily it is even now at hand. Yea, on the word of a Bloom, ye shall ere long enter into the golden city which is to be, the new Bloomusalem in the Nova Hibernia of the future.

(Thirtytwo workmen wearing rosettes, from all the counties of Ireland, under the guidance of Derwan the builder, construct the new Bloomusalem. It is a colossal edifice, with crystal roof, built in the shape of a huge pork kidney, containing forty thousand rooms. In the course of its extension several buildings and monuments are demolished. Government offices are temporarily transferred to railway sheds. Numerous houses are razed to the ground. The inhabitants are lodged in barrels and boxes, all marked in red with the letters: L. B. Several paupers fall from a ladder. A part of the walls of Dublin, crowded with loyal sightseers, collapses.)

THE SIGHTSEERS: *(Dying)* Morituri te salutant. *(They die)*

Bloom's manifesto

B LOOM: I stand for the reform of municipal morals and the plain ten commandments. New worlds for old. Union of all, jew, moslem and gentile. Three acres and a cow for all children of nature. Saloon motor hearses. Compulsory manual labour for all. All parks open to the public day and night. Electric dishscrubbers. Tuberculosis, lunacy, war and mendicancy must now cease. General amnesty, weekly carnival, with masked licence, bonuses for all, esperanto the universal brotherhood. No more patriotism of barspongers and dropsical impostors. Free money, free love and a free lay church in a free lay state.

Bloom in despair

BLOOM: (*In a seamless garment marked I. H. S. stands upright amid phoenix flames*) Weep not for me, O daughters of Erin.

(*He exhibits to Dublin reporters traces of burning. The daughters of Erin, in black garments with large prayerbooks and long lighted candles in their hands, kneel down and pray.*)

THE DAUGHTERS OF ERIN:

> Kidney of Bloom, pray for us.
> Flower of the Bath, pray for us.
> Mentor of Menton, pray for us.
> Canvasser for the Freeman, pray for us.
> Charitable Mason, pray for us.
> Wandering Soap, pray for us.
> Sweets of Sin, pray for us.
> Music without Words, pray for us.
> Reprover of the Citizen, pray for us.
> Friend of all Frillies, pray for us.
> Midwife Most Merciful, pray for us.
> Potato Preservative against Plague and Pestilence,
>   pray for us.

(*A choir of six hundred voices, conducted by Mr Vincent O'Brien, sings the Alleluia chorus, accompanied on the organ by Joseph Glynn. Bloom becomes mute, shrunken, carbonised.*)

ZOE: Talk away till you're black in the face.

BLOOM: (*In caubeen with clay pipe stuck in the band, dusty brogues, an emigrant's red handkerchief bundle in his hand, leading a black bogoak pig by a sugaun, with a smile in his eye*) Let me be going now, woman of the house, for by all the goats in Connemara I'm after having the father and mother of a bating. (*With a tear in his eye*) All insanity. Patriotism, sorrow for the dead, music, future of the race. To be or not to be. Life's dream is o'er. End it peacefully. They can live on. (*He *gazes far away mournfully*) I am ruined. A few pastilles of aconite. The blinds drawn. A letter. Then lie back to rest. (*He breathes softly*) No more. I have lived. Fare. Farewell.

ZOE: (*Stiffly, her finger in her neckfillet*) Honest? Till the next time. (*She sneers*) Suppose you got up the wrong side of the bed or came too quick with your best girl. O, I can read your thoughts.

BLOOM: (*Bitterly*) Man and woman, love, what is it? A cork and bottle.

Spoiled dream

FLORRY: (*To Stephen*) I'm sure you are a spoiled priest. Or a monk.

LYNCH: He is. A Cardinal's son.

STEPHEN: Cardinal sin. Monks of the screw.

(*His Eminence, Simon Stephen Cardinal Dedalus, Primate of all Ireland, appears in the doorway, dressed in red soutane, sandals and socks. Seven dwarf simian acolytes, also in red, cardinal sins, uphold his train, peeping under it. He wears a battered silk hat sideways on his head. His thumbs are stuck in his armpits and his palms outspread. Round his neck hangs a rosary of corks ending on his breast in a corkscrew cross. Releasing his thumbs, he invokes grace from on high with large wave gestures and proclaims with bloated pomp.*)

THE CARDINAL:

> Conservio lies captured.
> He lies in the lowest dungeon
> With manacles and chains around his limbs
> Weighing upwards of three tons.

(*He looks at all for a moment, his right eye closed tight, his left cheek puffed out. Then, unable to repress his merriment, he rocks to and fro, arms akimbo, and sings with broad rollicking humour.*)

O, the poor little fellow
Hi-hi-hi-hi-his legs they were yellow
He was plump, fat and heavy and brisk as a snake
But some bloody savage
To graize his white cabbage
He murdered Nell Flaherty's duckloving drake.

(*A multitude of midges swarms over his robe. He scratches himself with crossed arms at his ribs, grimacing, and exclaims.*)
I'm suffering the agony of the damned. By the hoky fiddle, thanks be to Jesus those funny little chaps are not unanimous. If they were they'd walk me off the face of the bloody globe.
(*His head aslant, he blesses curtly with fore and middle fingers, imparts the Easter kiss and doubleshuffles off comically, swaying his hat from side to side, shrinking quickly to the size of his trainbearers. The dwarf acolytes, giggling, peeping, nudging, ogling, Easterkissing, zigzag behind him. His voice is heard mellow from afar, merciful, male, melodious.*)

Shall carry my heart to thee,
Shall carry my heart to thee,
And the breath of the balmy night
Shall carry my heart to thee.

(*The trick doorhandle turns*)
THE DOORHANDLE: Theeee.
ZOE: The devil is in that door.

Points of view

Did Bloom discover common factors of similarity between their respective like and unlike reactions to experience?
Both were sensitive to artistic impressions musical in

preference to plastic or pictorial. Both preferred a continental to an insular manner of life, a cisatlantic to a transatlantic place of residence. Both indurated by early domestic training and an inherited tenacity of heterodox resistance professed their disbelief in many orthodox religious, national, social and ethical doctrines. Both admitted the alternately stimulating and obtunding influence of heterosexual magnetism.

Were their views on some points divergent?

Stephen dissented openly from Bloom's view on the importance of dietary and civic selfhelp while Bloom dissented tacitly from Stephen's views on the eternal affirmation of the spirit of man in literature. Bloom assented covertly to Stephen's rectification of the anachronism involved in assigning the date of the conversion of the Irish nation to christianity from druidism by Patrick son of Calpornus, son of Potitus, son of Odyssus, sent by pope Celestine I in the year 432 in the reign of Leary to the year 260 or thereabouts in the reign of Cormac MacArt († 266 A.D.) suffocated by imperfect deglutition of aliment at Sletty and interred at Rossnaree. The collapse which Bloom ascribed to gastric inanition and certain chemical compounds of varying degrees of adulteration and alcoholic strength, accelerated by mental exertion and the velocity of rapid circular motion in a relaxing atmosphere, Stephen attributed to the reapparition of a matutinal cloud (perceived by both from two different points of observation, Sandycove and Dublin) at first no bigger than a woman's hand.

Was there one point on which their views were equal and negative?

The influence of gaslight or electric light on the growth of adjoining paraheliotropic trees.

Aquacity

What did Bloom do at the range?
     He removed the saucepan to the left hob, rose and carried the iron kettle to the sink in order to tap the current by turning the faucet to let it flow.

Did it flow?
Yes. From Roundwood reservoir in county Wicklow of a cubic capacity of 2,400 million gallons, percolating through a subterranean aqueduct of filter mains of single and double pipeage constructed at an initial plant cost of £5 per linear yard by way of the Dargle, Rathdown, Glen of the Downs and Callowhill to the 26 acre reservoir at Stillorgan, a distance of 22 statute miles, and thence, through a system of relieving tanks, by a gradient of 250 feet to the city boundary at Eustace bridge, upper Leeson street, though from prolonged summer drouth and daily supply of 12½ million gallons the water had fallen below the sill of the overflow weir for which reason the borough surveyor and waterworks engineer, Mr Spencer Harty, C. E., on the instructions of the waterworks committee, had prohibited the use of municipal water for purposes other than those of consumption (envisaging the possibility of recourse being had to the impotable water of the Grand and Royal canals as in 1893) particularly as the South Dublin Guardians, notwithstanding their ration of 15 gallons per day per pauper supplied through a 6 inch meter, had been convicted of a wastage of 20,000 gallons per night by a reading of their meter on the affirmation of the law agent of the corporation, Mr Ignatius Rice, solicitor, thereby acting to the detriment of another section of the public, selfsupporting taxpayers, solvent, sound.

What in water did Bloom, waterlover, drawer of water, watercarrier returning to the range, admire?
Its universality: its democratic equality and constancy to its nature in seeking its own level: its vastness in the ocean of

Mercator's projection: its unplumbed profundity in the Sundam trench of the Pacific exceeding 8,000 fathoms: the restlessness of its waves and surface particles visiting in turn all points of its seaboard: the independence of its units: the variability of states of sea: its hydrostatic quiescence in calm: its hydrokinetic turgidity in neap and spring tides: its subsidence after devastation: its sterility in the circumpolar icecaps, arctic and antarctic: its climatic and commercial significance: its preponderance of 3 to 1 over the dry land of the globe: its indisputable hegemony extending in square leagues over all the region below the subequatorial tropic of Capricorn: the multisecular stability of its primeval basin: its luteofulvous bed: its capacity to dissolve and hold in solution all soluble substances including millions of tons of the most precious metals: its slow erosions of peninsulas and downwardtending promontories: its alluvial deposits: its weight and volume and density: its imperturbability in lagoons and highland tarns: its gradation of colours in the torrid and temperate and frigid zones: its vehicular ramifications in continental lakecontained streams and confluent oceanflowing rivers with their tributaries and transoceanic currents: gulf-stream, north and south equatorial courses: its violence in seaquakes, waterspouts, artesian wells, eruptions, torrents, eddies, freshets, spates, groundswells, watersheds, waterpartings, geysers, cataracts, whirlpools, maelstroms, inundations, deluges, cloudbursts: its vast circumterrestrial ahorizontal curve: its secrecy in springs, and latent humidity, revealed by rhabdomantic or hygrometric instruments and exemplified by the hole in the wall at Ashtown gate, saturation of air, distillation of dew: the simplicity of its composition, two constituent parts of hydrogen with one constituent part of oxygen: its healing virtues: its buoyancy in the waters of the Dead Sea: its persevering penetrativeness in runnels, gullies, inadequate dams, leaks on shipboard: its properties for cleansing, quenching thirst and fire, nourishing vegetation: its infallibility as paradigm and paragon: its metamorphoses as vapour, mist, cloud, rain, sleet, snow, hail: its strength in rigid hydrants: its variety of forms in loughs and bays and gulfs and bights and guts and lagoons and atolls and archipelagos and sounds and fjords and minches and tidal estuaries and arms of sea: its solidity in glaciers, icebergs, icefloes: its docility in working hydraulic millwheels, turbines, dynamos, electric power stations, bleachworks, tanneries, scutchmills: its utility in canals, rivers, if navigable, floating and graving docks: its potentiality derivable from harnessed tides or watercourses falling from level to level: its submarine fauna and flora (anacoustic, photophobe) numerically, if not literally, the inhabitants of the globe: its ubiquity as constituting 90% of the human body: the noxiousness of its effluvia in lacustrine marshes, pestilential fens, faded flowerwater, stagnant pools in the waning moon.

Having set the halffilled kettle on the now burning coals, why did he return to the stillflowing tap?

To wash his soiled hands with a partially consumed tablet of Barrington's lemonflavoured soap, to which paper still adhered (bought thirteen hours previously for fourpence and still unpaid for), in fresh cold neverchanging everchanging water and dry them, face and hands, in a long redbordered holland cloth passed over a wooden revolving roller.

What reason did Stephen give for declining Bloom's offer?

That he was hydrophobe, hating partial contact by immersion or total by submersion in cold water (his last bath having taken place in the month of October of the preceding year), disliking the aqueous substances of glass and crystal, distrusting aquacities of thought and language.

What impeded Bloom from giving Stephen counsels of hygiene and prophylactic to which should be added suggestions concerning a preliminary wetting of the head and contraction of the muscles with rapid splashing of the face and neck and thoracic and epigastric region in case of sea or river bathing, the parts of the human anatomy most sensitive to cold being the nape, stomach, and thenar or sole of foot?

The incompatibility of aquacity with the erratic originality of genius.

A strange legend on an allied theme

Recite the first (major) part of this chanted legend?

Little Henry Hughes and his schoolfellows all
Went out for to play ball.
And the very first ball little Harry Hughes played
He drove it o'er the jew's garden wall.
And the very second ball little Harry Hughes played
He broke the jew's windows all.

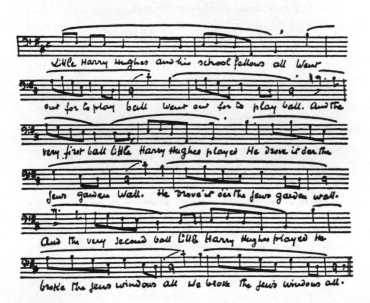

How did the son of Rudolph receive this first part?

With unmixed feeling. Smiling, a jew, he heard with pleasure and saw the unbroken kitchen window.

Recite the second part (minor) of the legend.

> *Then out there came the jew's daughter*
> *And she all dressed in green.*
> *'Come back, come back, you pretty little boy,*
> *And play your ball again.'*
>
> *'I can't come back and I won't come back*
> *Without my schoolfellows all,*
> *For if my master he did hear*
> *He'd make it a sorry ball.'*
>
> *She took him by the lilywhite hand*
> *And led him along the hall*
> *Until she led him to a room*
> *Where none could hear him call.*
>
> *She took a penknife out of her pocket*
> *And cut off his little head,*
> *And now he'll play his ball no more*
> *For he lies among the dead.*

Affinities

What special affinities appeared to him to exist between the moon and woman?

Her antiquity in preceding and surviving successive tellurian generations: her nocturnal predominance: her satellitic dependence: her luminary reflection: her constancy under all her phases, rising, and setting by her appointed times, waxing and waning: the forced invariability of her aspect: her indeterminate response to inaffirmative interrogation: her potency over effluent and refluent waters: her power to enamour, to mortify, to invest with beauty, to render insane, to incite to and aid delinquency: the tranquil inscrutability of her visage: the terribility of her isolated dominant implacable resplendent propinquity: her omens of tempest and of calm: the stimulation of her light, her motion and her presence: the admonition of her craters, her arid seas, her silence: her splendour, when visible: her attraction, when invisible.

Attractive places

What considerations rendered it [departure] desirable?

The attractive character of certain localities in Ireland and abroad, as represented in general geographical maps of polychrome design or in special ordnance survey charts by employment of scale numerals and hachures.

In Ireland?

The cliffs of Moher, the windy wilds of Connemara, lough Neagh with submerged petrified city, the Giant's Causeway, Fort Camden and Fort Carlisle, the Golden Vale of Tipperary, the islands of Aran, the pastures of royal Meath, Brigid's elm in Kildare, the Queen's Island shipyard in Belfast, the Salmon Leap, the lakes of Killarney.

Abroad?

Ceylon (with spicegardens supplying tea to Thomas Kernan, agent for Pulbrook, Robertson and Co, 2 Mincing lane, London, E. C., 5 Dame street, Dublin), Jerusalem, the holy city (with mosque of Omar and gate of Damascus, goal of aspiration), the straits of Gibraltar (the unique birthplace of Marion Tweedy), the Parthenon (containing statues, nude Grecian divinities), the Wall street money market (which controlled international finance), the Plaza de Toros at La Linea, Spain (where O'Hara of the Camerons had slain the bull), Niagara (over which no human being had passed with impunity), the land of the Eskimos (eaters of soap), the forbidden country of Thibet (from which no traveller returns), the bay of Naples (to see which was to die), the Dead Sea.

Under what guidance, following what signs?

At sea, septentrional, by night the polestar, located at the point of intersection of the right line from beta to alpha in Ursa Major produced and divided externally at omega and the hypotenuse of the rightangled triangle formed by the line alpha omega so produced and the line alpha delta of Ursa Major. On land, meridional, a bispherical moon, revealed in imperfect varying phases of lunation through the posterior interstice of the imperfectly occluded skirt of a carnose negligent perambulating female, a pillar of the cloud by day.

Molly's memories

Ill go out Ill have him eyeing up at the ceiling where is she gone now make him want me thats the only way a quarter after what an unearthly hour I suppose theyre just getting up in China now combing out their pigtails for the day well soon have the nuns ringing the angelus theyve nobody coming in to spoil their sleep except an odd priest or two for his night

office the alarmclock next door at cockshout clattering the
brains out of itself let me see if I can doze off 1 2 3 4 5 what
kind of flowers are those they invented like the stars the
wallpaper in Lombard street was much nicer the apron he
gave me was like that something only I only wore it twice
better lower this lamp and try again so as I can get up early Ill
go to Lambes there beside Findlaters and get them to send us
some flowers to put about the place in case he brings him
home tomorrow today I mean no no Fridays an unlucky day
first I want to do the place up someway the dust grows in it I
think while Im asleep then we can have music and cigarettes
I can accompany him first I must clean the keys of the piano
with milk whatll I wear shall I wear a white rose or those fairy
cakes in Liptons I love the smell of a rich big shop at 7 1/2d
a lb or the other ones with the cherries in them and the pinky
sugar 11d a couple of lbs of course a nice plant for the middle
of the table Id get that cheaper in wait wheres this I saw them
not long ago I love flowers Id love to have the whole place
swimming in roses God of heaven theres nothing like nature
the wild mountains then the sea and the waves rushing then
the beautiful country with fields of oats and wheat and all
kinds of things and all the fine cattle going about that would
do your heart good to see rivers and lakes and flowers all sorts
of shapes and smells and colours springing up even out of the
ditches primroses and violets nature it is as for them saying
theres no God I wouldnt give a snap of my two fingers for all
their learning why dont they go and create something I often
asked him atheists or whatever they call themselves go and
wash the cobbles off themselves first then they go howling for
the priest and they dying and why why because theyre afraid
of hell on account of their bad conscience ah yes I know them
well who was the first person in the universe before there was
anybody that made it all who ah that they dont know neither
do I so there you are they might as well try to stop the sun
from rising tomorrow the sun shines for you he said the day
we were lying among the rhododendrons on Howth head in
the grey tweed suit and his straw hat the day I got him to

propose to me yes first I gave him the bit of seedcake out of my mouth and it was leapyear like now yes 16 years ago my God after that long kiss I near lost my breath yes he said I was a flower of the mountain yes so we are flowers all a womans body yes that was one true thing he said in his life and the sun shines for you today yes that was why I liked him because I saw he understood or felt what a woman is and I knew I could always get round him and I gave him all the pleasure I could leading him on till he asked me to say yes and I wouldnt answer first only looked out over the sea and the sky I was thinking of so many things he didnt know of Mulvey and Mr Stanhope and Hester and father and old captain Groves and the sailors playing all birds fly and I say stoop and washing up dishes they called it on the pier and the sentry in front of the governors house with the thing round his white helmet poor devil half roasted and the Spanish girls laughing in their shawls and their tall combs and the auctions in the morning the Greeks and the jews and the Arabs and the devil knows who else from all the ends of Europe and Duke street and the fowl market all clucking outside Larby Sharons and the poor donkeys slipping half asleep and the vague fellows in the cloaks asleep in the shade on the steps and the big wheels of the carts of the bulls and the old castle thousands of years old yes and those handsome Moors all in white and turbans like kings asking you to sit down in their little bit of a shop and Ronda with the old windows of the posadas glancing eyes a lattice hid for her lover to kiss the iron and the wineshops half open at night and the castanets and the night we missed the boat at Algeciras the watchman going about serene with his lamp and O that awful deepdown torrent O and the sea the sea crimson sometimes like fire and the glorious sunsets and the figtrees in the Alameda gardens yes and all the queer little streets and pink and blue and yellow houses and the rosegardens and the jessamine and geraniums and cactuses and Gibraltar as a girl where I was a Flower of the mountain yes when I put the rose in my hair like the Andalusian girls used or shall I wear a red yes and how he kissed me under the

Moorish wall and I thought well as well him as another and then I asked him with my eyes to ask again yes and then he asked me would I yes to say yes my mountain flower and first I put my arms around him yes and drew him down to me so he could feel my breasts all perfume yes and his heart was going like mad and yes I said yes I will Yes.

FROM
LETTERS

To Stanislaus Joyce

(9 Oct. 1906)

Yesterday being the anniversary of the day of my espousal and of the day of the gladness of my heart, we went out into the country and ate and drank the greater portion of several larders. Here is the full and exact list of what we ate yesterday.

10.30 a.m.   Ham, bread and butter, coffee
 1.30 p.m.   Soup, roast lamb and potatoes, bread and wine
 4.– p.m.   Beef-stew, bread and wine
 6.– p.m.   Roast veal, bread, gorgonzola cheese and wine
 8.30 p.m.   Roast veal, bread and grapes and vermouth
 9.30 a.m.   Veal cutlets, bread, salad, grapes and wine

There is literally no end to our appetites. I don't believe I ever was in better health except for the sedentary life I lead. I stand fascinated before the windows of grocers' shops. My salary, I am afraid will not be sufficient to feed me in the winter.

To Ezra Pound

(9 April 1917)

Perhaps it [Exiles] would be more successful than *A Portrait of the Artist*. I send you a limerick thereon:

> *There once was a lounger named Stephen*
> *Whose youth was most odd and uneven.*
> *He throve on the smell*
> *Of a horrible hell*
> *That a Hottentot wouldn't believe in.*

To Harriet Shaw Weaver

(24 May 1924)

Dr Rosenbach sent me a message asking me what would be my price for the corrected proofs of *Ulysses*. When he receives a reply from me all the rosy brooks will have run dry.

> *Rosy Brook he bought a book*
> *Though he didn't know how to spell it.*
> *Such is the lure of literature*
> *To the lad who can buy it and sell it.*

To Harriet Shaw Weaver

(15 Aug. 1925)

Rouen is the rainiest place getting
Inside all impermeables, wetting
Damp marrow in drenched bones.
Midwinter soused us coming over Le Mans
Our inn at Niort was the Grape of Burgundy
But the winepress of the Lord thundered over that grape of
    Burgundy
And we left it in a hurgundy.
    (Hurry up, Joyce, it's time!)
I heard mosquitoes swarm in old Bordeaux
So many!
I had not thought the earth contained so many
    (Hurry up, Joyce, it's time)
Mr Anthologos, the local gardener,
Greycapped, with politeness full of cunning
Has made wine these fifty years
And told me in his southern French
Le petit vin is the surest drink to buy

For if 'tis bad
Vous ne l'avez pas payé
   (Hurry up, hurry up, now, now, now!)
But we shall have great times,
When we return to Clinic, that waste land
O Esculapios!
   (Shan't we? Shan't we? Shan't we?)

To Harriet Shaw Weaver

(20 Jan. 1926)

I will just add an epigram I made. To a person asking if I go
to church: O, yes, I go to mass every morning at Notre
Dame de Siam and to vespers every evening at Saint Louis le
Debonair.

And this limerick:

> *There's a coughmixture scopolamine*
> *And its equal has never been seen*
>   *'Twould make staid Tutankamen*
>   *Laugh and leap like a salmon*
> *And his mummy hop Scotch on the green.*

Advertisement for
Anna Livia Plurabelle

Buy a book in brown paper
From Faber & Faber
To see Annie Liffey trip, tumble and caper.
Sevensinns in her singthings,
Plurabelle on her prose,
Seashell ebb music wayriver she flows.

Advertisement for Haveth Childers Everywhere

Humptydump Dublin squeaks through his norse,
Humptydump Dublin hath a horrible vorse
And with all his kinks english
Plus his irismanx brogues
Humptydump Dublin's grandada of all rogues.

To James Stephens

(7 May 1932)

Dear Stephens: Here is your poem ['Stephen's Green'] in German, Latin, Norwegian, Italian and French. Can you add your Irish version so as, with the English, to make a rainbow and we might present it to ourselves in a brochure for our jubilee year [both were born on 2 Feb. 1882].

The Latin contains violations of quantity (lines 4 and 5 for example) but this really does not matter in the rhymed doggerel which a classic poet would call church verse.

In the German 'liess los' sounds rather free and vulgar. It is really 'let a shout' but I prefer it to the verb 'stossen' which is more elegant.

In the Italian I made the wind a bandit cousin of Fra Diavolo. He puts three fingers in his mouth to balance the three 'kills'. This I also balanced by the collision of 3 vowels in line 5.

As regards the Norwegian that language has changed in spelling almost as much (I mean since I began to study it in Dublin) as English has since 1600. I have followed the orthography Ibsen used which is now nearer Danish than Norwegian. Those two races still preserve pagan terms. They have no word for Christmas (which they call 'Jul') or for the Last Day or General Judgment. This they call 'Ragnarok'. So line 4 means that the trees think the crack of doom is upon them. Also this typewriter cannot reproduce such Norwegian letters as 'ø' or 'å'.

[The five versions (with the original prefixed) are as follows:]

The wind stood up and gave a shout.
He whistled on his fingers and

Kicked the withered leaves about
And thumped the branches with his hand

And said he'd kill and kill.
And so he will and so he will.

　Les Verts de Jacques

Le vent d'un saut lance son cri,
Se siffle sur les doigts et puis

Trépigne les feuilles d'automne,
Craque les branches qu'il assomme.

Je tuerai, crie-t-il, holà!
Et vous verrez s'il le fera!

J.J.

Der Wind stand auf, liess los einen Schrei,
Pfiff mit den Fingern schrill dabei

Wirbelte duerres Laub durch den Wald
Und haemmerte Aeste mit Riesengewalt.

Zum tod, heult, zu Tod and Mord!
Und meint es ernst: ein Wind, ein Wort.

J.J.

Surgit Boreas digitorum
Fistulam faciens et clamorem.

Pes pugno certat par (oremus!)
Foliis quatit omne nemus.

Caedam, ait, caedam, caedam!
Nos ne habeat ille praedam.

J.J.

Vinden staar op med en vild Huru,
Han piber paa fingerne og nu

Sparker bladenes flyvende flok.
Traeerne troer han er Ragnarok.

Skovens liv og blod vil han draebe og drikke.
Hvad der bliver at goere, det ved jeg ikke.

J.J.

Balza in piè Fra Vento e grida.
Tre dita in bocca fischia la sfida.

Tira calci, pesta botte:
Ridda di foglie e frasche rotte.

Ammazzerò, ei urla, O gente!
E diuraddio costui non mente.

J.J.

To Giorgio and Helen Joyce
(28 Nov. 1934)

Goodbye, Zürich, I must leave you
Though it breaks my head to shreds
[indecipherable]
Something tells me I am needed
In Paree to hump the beds.
Bump! I hear the trunks a tumbling
And I'm frantic for the fray.
Farewell, dolce far niente!
Goodbye, Zürichsee!

This is a parody of 'Dolly Gray'

> *Good-bye, Dolly, I must leave you,*
> *Though it breaks my heart to go.*
> *Something tells me I am needed*
> *In the front to face the foe.*
> *Hark! I hear the bugles calling*
> *And I must no longer stay.*
> *Good-bye, Dolly, I must leave you,*
> *Good-bye, Dolly Gray.*

FROM
FINNEGANS WAKE

Here comes everybody

Yet may we not see still the brontoichthyan form outlined aslumbered, even in our own nighttime by the sedge of the troutling stream that Bronto loved and Brunto has a lean on. *Hic cubat edilis. Apud libertinam parvulam.* Whatif she be in flags or flitters, reekierags or sundyechosies, with a mint of mines or beggar a pinnyweight. Arrah, sure, we all love little Anny Ruiny, or, we mean to say, lovelittle Anna Rayiny, when unda her brella, mid piddle med puddle, she ninny-nannygoes nancing by. Yoh! Brontolone slaaps, yoh snoores. Upon Benn Heather, in Seeple Isout too. The cranic head on him, caster of his reasons, peer yuthner in yondmist. Whooth? His clay feet, swarded in verdi-grass, stick up starck where he last fellonem, by the mund of the magazine wall, where our maggy seen all, with her sisterin shawl. While over against this belles' alliance beyind Ill Sixty, ollollowed ill! bagsides of the fort, bom, tarabom, tarabom, lurk the ombushes, the site of the lyffing-in-wait of the upjock and hockums. Hence when the clouds roll by, jamey, a proudseye view is enjoyable of our mound-ing's mass, now Wallinstone national museum, with, in some greenish distance, the charmful waterloose country and the two quitewhite villagettes who hear show of themselves so gigglesomes minxt the follyages, the prettilees! Penetrators are permitted into the museomound free. Welsh and the Paddy Patkinses, one shelenk! Redismembers invalids of old guard find poussepousse pousseypram to sate the sort of their butt. For her passkey supply to the janitrix, the mistress Kathe. Tip.

This the way to the museyroom. Mind your hats goan in! Now yiz are in the Willingdone Museyroom. This is a Prooshious gunn. This is a ffrinch. Tip. This is the flag of the Prooshious, the Cap and Soracer. This is the bullet that byng the flag of the Prooshious. This is the ffrinch that fire on the Bull that bang the flag of the Prooshious. Saloos the Crossgunn! Up with your pike and fork! Tip. (Bullsfoot!

Fine!) This is the triplewon hat of Lipoleum. Tip. Lipoleum-
hat. This is the Willingdone on his same white harse, the
Cokenhape. This is the big Sraughter Willingdone, grand and
magentic in his goldtin spurs and his ironed dux and his
quarterbrass woodyshoes and his magnate's gharters and his
bangkok's best and goliar's goloshes and his pulluponeasyan
wartrews. This is his big wide harse. Tip. This is the three
lipoleum boyne grouching down in the living detch. This is an
inimyskilling inglis, this is a scotcher grey, this is a davy,
stooping. This is the bog lipoleum mordering the lipoleum
beg. A Gallawghurs argaumunt. This is the petty lipoleum boy
that was nayther bag nor bug. Assaye, assaye! Touchole Fitz
Tuomush. Dirty MacDyke. And Hairy O'Hurry. All of them
arminusvarminus. This is Delian alps. This is Mont Tivel, this
is Mont Tipsey, this is the Grand Mons Injun. This is the
crimealine of the alps hooping to sheltershock the three
lipoleums. This is the jinnies with their legahorns feinting to
read in their handmade's book of stralegy while making their
war undisides the Willingdone. The jinnies is a cooin her
hand and the jinnies is a ravin her hair and the Willingdone
git the band up. This is big Willingdone mormorial tallows-
coop Wounderworker obscides on the flanks of the jinnies.
Sexcaliber hrosspower. Tip. This is me Belchum sneaking his
phillippy out of his most Awful Grimmest Sunshat Crom-
welly. Looted. This is the jinnies' hastings dispatch for to
irrigate the Willingdone. Dispatch in thin red lines cross the
shortfront of me Belchum. Yaw, yaw, yaw! Leaper Orthor.
Fear siecken! Fieldgaze thy tiny frow. Hugacting. Nap. That
was the tictacs of the jinnies for to fontannoy the Willing-
done. Shee, shee, shee! The jinnies is jillous agincourting all
the lipoleums. And the lipoleums is gonn boycottoncrezy onto
the one Willingdone. And the Willingdone git the band up.
This is bode Belchum, bonnet to busby, breaking his secred
word with a ball up his ear to the Willingdone. This is the
Willingdone's hurold dispitchback. Dispitch desployed on the
regions rare of me Belchum. Salamangra! Ayi, ayi, ayi! Cherry
jinnies. Figtreeyou! Damn fairy ann, Voutre. Willingdone.

That was the first joke of Willingdone, tic for tac. Hee, hee, hee! This is me Belchum in his twelvemile cowchooks, weet, tweet and stampforth foremost, footing the camp for the jinnies. Drink a sip, drankasup, for he's as sooner buy a guinness than he'd stale store stout. This is Rooshious balls. This is a ttrinch. This is mistletropes. This is Canon Futter with the popynose. After his hundred days' indulgence. This is the blessed. Tarra's widdars! This is jinnies in the bonny bawn blooches. This is lipoleums in the rowdy howses. This is the Willingdone, by the splinters of Cork, order fire. Tonnerre! (Bullsear! Play!) This is camelry, this is floodens, this is the sophereens in action, this is their mobbily, this is panickburns. Almeidagad! Arthiz too loose! This is Willingdone cry. Brum! Brum! Cumbrum! This is jinnies cry. Underwetter! Goat strip Finnlambs! This is jinnies rinning away to their ousterlists dowan a bunkersheels. With a nip nippy nip and a trip trippy trip so airy. For their heart's right there. Tip. This is me Belchum's tinkyou tankyou silvoor plate for citchin the crapes in the cool of his canister. Poor the pay! This is the bissmark of the marathon merry of the jinnies they left behind them. This is the Willingdone branlish his same marmorial tallowscoop Sophy-Key-Po for his royal divorsion on the rinnaway jinnies. Gambariste della porca! Dalaveras fimmieras! This is the pettiest of the lipoleums, Toffeethief, that spy on the Willingdone from his big white harse, the Capeinhope. Stonewall Willingdone is an old maxy montrumeny. Lipoleums is nice hung bushellors. This is hiena hinnessy laughing alout at the Willingdone. This is lipsyg dooley krieging the funk from the hinnessy. This is the hinndoo Shimar Shin between the dooley boy and the hinnessy. Tip. This is the wixy old Willingdone picket up the half of the threefoiled hat of lipoleums fromoud of the bluddle filth. This is the hinndoo waxing ranjymad for a bombshoob. This is the Willingdone hanking the half of the hat of lipoleums up the tail on the buckside of his big white harse. Tip. That was the last joke of Willingdone. Hit, hit, hit! This is the same white harse of the Willingdone, Culpenhelp, waggling his tailoscrupp with the half of a hat of lipoleums to insoult on the hinndoo seeboy. Hney, hney, hney! (Bullsrag! Foul!) This is the seeboy, madrashattaras, upjump and pumpim, cry to the Willingdone: Ap Pukkaru! Pukka Yurap! This is the Willingdone, bornstable ghentleman, tinders his maxbotch to the cursigan Shimar Shin. Basucker youstead! This is the dooforhim seeboy blow the whole of the half of the hat of lipoleums off of the top of the tail on the back of his big wide harse. Tip (Bullseye! Game!) How Copenhagen ended. This way the museyroom. Mind your boots goan out.

A dialogue

In the name of Anem this carl on the kopje in pelted thongs a parth a lone who the joebiggar be he? Forshapen his pigmaid hoagshead, shroonk his plodsfoot. He hath locktoes, this shortshins, and, Obeold that's pectoral, his mamma-muscles most mousterious. It is slaking nuncheon out of some thing's brain pan. Me seemeth a dragon man. He is almonthst on the kiep fief by here, is Comestipple Sacksoun, be it junipery or febrewery, marracks or alebrill or the ramping riots of pouriose and froriose. What a quhare soort of a mahan. It is evident the michindaddy. Lets we overstep his fire defences and these kraals of slitsucked marrogbones. (Cave!) He can prapsposterus the pillory way to Hirculos pillar. Come on, fool porterfull, hosiered women blown monk sewer? Scuse us, chorley guy! You tollerday donsk? N. You tolkatiff scowegian? Nn. You spigotty anglease? Nnn. You phonio saxo? Nnnn. Clear all so! 'Tis a Jute. Let us swop hats and excheck a few strong verbs weak oach eather yapyazzard abast the blooty creeks.

Jute. – Yutah!
Mutt. – Mukk's pleasurad.
Jute. – Are you jeff?
Mutt. – Somehards.

Jute.   – But you are not jeffmute?

Mutt.   – Noho. Only an utterer.

Jute.   – Whoa? Whoat is the mutter with you?

Mutt.   – I became a stun a stummer.

Jute.   – What a hauhauhauhaudibble thing, to be cause! How, Mutt?

Mutt.   – Aput the buttle, surd.

Jute.   – Whose poddle? Wherein?

Mutt.   – The Inns of Dungtarf where Used awe to be he.

Jute.   – You that side your voise are almost inedible to me. Become a bitskin more wiseable, as if I were you.

Mutt.   – Has? Has at? Hasatency? Urp, Boohooru! Booru Usurp! I trumple from rath in mine mines when I rimimirim!

Jute.   – One eyegonblack. Bisons is bisons. Let me fore all your hasitancy cross your qualm with trink gilt. Here have sylvan coyne, a piece of oak. Ghinees hies good for you.

Mutt.   – Louee, louee! How wooden I not know it, the intelligible greytcloak of Cedric Silkyshag! Cead mealy faulty rices for one dabblin bar. Old grilsy growlsy! He was poached on in that eggtentical spot. Here where the liveries, Monomark. There where the missers moony, Minnikin passe.

Jute.   – Simply because as Taciturn pretells, our wrong-storyshortener, he dumptied the wholeborrow of rubbages on to soil here.

Mutt.   – Just how a puddinstone inat the brookcells by a riverpool.

Jute.   – Load Allmarshy! Wid wad for a norse like?

Mutt.   – Somular with a bull on a clompturf. Rooks roarum rex roome! I could snore to him of the spumy horn, with his woolseley side in, by the neck I am sutton on, did Brian d' of Linn.

Jute.   – Boildoyle and rawhoney on me when I can beuraly forsstand a weird from sturk to finnic in

such a patwhat as your rutterdamrotter. Onheard
of and umscene! Gut aftermeal! See you doomed.

Mutt. – Quite agreem. Bussave a sec. Walk a dun blink
roundward this albutisle and you skull see how
olde ye plaine of my Elters, hunfree and ours,
where wone to wail whimbrel to peewee o'er the
saltings, where wilby citie by law of isthmon,
where by a droit of signory, icefloe was from his
Inn the Byggning to whose Finishthere Punct. Let
erehim ruhmuhrmuhr. Mearmerge two races,
swete and brack. Morthering rue. Hither, crach-
ing eastuards, they are in surgence: hence, cool at
ebb, they requiesce. Countlessness of livestories
have netherfallen by this plage, flick as flowflakes,
litters from aloft, like a waast wizzard all of
whirlworlds. Now are all tombedto the mound,
isges to isges, erde from erde. Pride, O pride, thy
prize!

Jute. – 'Stench!

Mutt. – Fiatfuit! Hereinunder lyethey. Llarge by the smal
an' everynight life olso th'estrange, babylone the
greatgrandhotelled with tit tit tittlehouse, alp on
earwig, drukn on ild, likeas equal to anequal in
this sound seemetery which iz leebez luv.

Jute. – 'Zmorde!

Mutt. – Meldundleize! By the fearse wave behoughted.
Despond's sung. And thanacestross mound have
swollup them all. This ourth of years is not save
brickdust and being humus the same roturns. He
who runes may rede it on all fours. O'c'stle,
n'wc'stle, tr'c'stle, crumbling! Sell me sooth the
fare for Humblin! Humblady Fair. But speak it
allsosiftly, moulder! Be in your whisht!

Jute. – Whysht?

Mutt. – The gyant Forficules with Amni the fay.

Jute. – Howe?

Mutt. – Here is viceking's graab.

Jute.   – Hwaad!
Mutt.   – Ore you astoneaged, jute you?
Jute.   – Oye am thonthorstrok, thing mud.

Illiterative porthery

It was of a night, late, lang time agone, in an auldstane eld, when Adam was delvin and his madameen spinning watersilts, when mulk mountynotty man was everybully and the first leal ribberrobber that ever had her ainway everybuddy to his lovesaking eyes and everybilly lived alove with everybiddy else, and Jarl van Hoother had his burnt head high up in his lamphouse, laying cold hands on himself. And his two little jiminies, cousins of ourn, Tristopher and Hilary, were kickaheeling their dummy on the oil cloth flure of his homerigh, castle and earthenhouse. And, be dermot, who come to the keep of his inn only the niece-of-his-in-law, the prankquean. And the prankquean pulled a rosy one and made her wit foreninst the dour. And she lit up and fireland was ablaze. And spoke she to the dour in her petty perusienne: Mark the Wans, why do I am alook alike a poss of porterpease? And that was how the skirtmisshes began. But the dour handworded her grace in dootch nossow: Shut! So her grace o'malice kidsnapped up the jiminy Tristopher and into the shandy westerness she rain, rain, rain. And Jarl van Hoother warlessed after her with soft dovesgall: Stop deef stop come back to my earin stop. But she swaradid to him: Unlikelihud. And there was a brannewail that same sabboath night of falling angles somewhere in Erio. And the prankquean went for her forty years' walk in Tourlemonde and she washed the blessings of the lovespots off the jiminy with soap sulliver suddles and she had her four owlers masters for to tauch him his tickles and she converted him to the onesure allgood and he became a luderman. So then she started to rain and to rain and, be redtom, she was back again at Jarl van

Hoother's in a brace of samers and the jiminy with her in her pinafrond, lace at night, at another time. And where did she come but to the bar of his bristolry. And Jarl von Hoother had his baretholobruised heels drowned in his cellarmalt, shaking warm hands with himself and the jimminy Hilary and the dummy in their first infancy were below on the tearsheet, wringing and coughing, like brodar and histher. And the prankquean nipped a paly one and lit up again and redcocks flew flackering from the hillcombs. And she made her witter before the wicked, saying: Mark the Twy, why do I am alook alike two poss of porterpease? And: Shut! says the wicked, handwording her madesty. So her madesty a forethought set down a jiminy and took up a jiminy and all the lilipath ways to Woeman's Land she rain, rain, rain. And Jarl von Hoother bleethered atter her with a loud finegale: Stop domb stop come back with my earring stop. But the prankquean swaradid: Am liking it. And there was a wild ole grannewwail that laurency night of starshootings somewhere in Erio. And the prankquean went for her forty years' walk in Turnlemeem and she punched the curses of cromcruwell with the nail of a top into the jiminy and she had her four larksical monitrix to touch him his tears and she provorted him to the onecertain allsecure and he became a tristian. So then she started raining, raining, and in a pair of changers, be dom ter, she was back again at Jarl von Hoother's and the Larryhill with her under her abromette. And why would she halt at all if not by the ward of his mansionhome of another nice lace for the third charm? And Jarl von Hoother had his hurricane hips up to his pantrybox, ruminating in his holdfour stomachs (Dare! O dare!), and the jiminy Toughertrees and the dummy were belove on the watercloth, kissing and spitting, and roguing and poghuing, like knavepaltry and naivebride and in their second infancy. And the prankquean picked a blank and lit out and the valleys lay twinkling. And she made her wittest in front of the arkway of trihump, asking: Mark the Tris, why do I am alook alike three poss of porter pease? But that was how the skirtmishes endupped. For like the campbells acoming with a fork lance of lightning, Jarl von Hoother Boanerges himself, the old terror of the dames, came hip hop handihap out through the pikeopened arkway of his three shuttoned castles, in his broadginger hat and his civic chollar and his allabuff hemmed and his bullbraggin soxangloves and his ladbroke breeks and his cattegut bandolair and his furframed panuncular cumbottes like a rudd yellan gruebleen orangeman in his violet indigonation, to the whole length of the strongth of his bowman's bill. And he clopped his rude hand to his eacy hitch and he ordurd and his thick spch spck for her to shut up shop, dappy. And the duppy shot the shutter clup (Perkodhuskurunbarggruauyagokgorlayorgromgremmitghu ndhurthrumathunaradidillifaititillibumullunukkunun!) And they all drank free. For one man in his armour was a fat match always for any girls under shurts. And that was the first peace of illiterative porthery in all the flamend floody flatuous world. How kirssy the tiler made a sweet unclose to the Narwhealian captol. Saw fore shalt thou sea. Betoun ye and be. The prankquean was to hold her dummyship and the jimminies was to keep the peacewave and van Hoother was to git the wind up. Thus the hearsomeness of the burger felicitates the whole of the polis.

Hosty's rann

A nd around the lawn the rann it rann and this is the rann that Hosty made. Spoken. Boyles and Cahills, Skerretts and Pritchards, viersified and piersified may the treeth we tale of live in stoney. Here line the refrains of. Some vote him Vike, some mote him Mike, some dub him Llyn and Phin while others hail him Lug Bug Dan Lop, Lex, Lax, Gunne or Guinn. Some apt him Arth, some bapt him Barth, Coll, Noll, Soll, Will, Weel, Wall but I parse him Persse O'Reilly else he's called no name at all. Together. Arrah, leave it to Hosty, frosty Hosty, leave it to Hosty for he's the mann to rhyme the rann,

the rann, the rann, the king of all ranns. Have you here?
(Some ha) Have we where? (Some hant) Have you hered?
(Others do) Have we whered? (Others dont) It's cumming,
it's brumming! The clip, the clop! (All cla) Glass crash. The
(klikkaklakkaklaskaklopatzklatschabattacreppycrottygradd-
aghsemmihsammihnouithappluddyappladdypkonpkot!).

{ *Ardite, arditi!*
{ Music cue.

'THE BALLAD OF PERSSE O'REILLY.'

Have you heard of one Humpty Dumpty
How he fell with a roll and a rumble
And curled up like Lord Olofa Crumple
By the butt of the Magazine Wall,
    (Chorus) Of the Magazine Wall,
             Hump, helmet and all?

He was one time our King of the Castle
Now he's kicked about like a rotten old parsnip.
And from Green street he'll be sent by order of His Worship
To the penal jail of Mountjoy
    (Chorus) To the jail of Mountjoy!
             Jail him and joy.

He was fafafather of all schemes for to bother us
Slow coaches and immaculate contraceptives for the populace,
Mare's milk for the sick, seven dry Sundays a week,
Openair love and religion's reform,
    (Chorus) And religious reform,
             Hideous in form.

Arrah, why, says you, couldn't he manage it?
I'll go bail, my fine dairyman darling,
Like the bumping bull of the Cassidys
All your butter is in your horns.
    (Chorus) His butter is in his horns.
             Butter his horns!

(Repeat) Hurrah there, Hosty, frosty Hosty, change that shirt
   on ye,
Rhyme the rann, the king of all ranns!

             Balbaccio, balbuccio!
We had chaw chaw chops, chairs, chewing gum, the chicken-
   pox and china chambers
Universally provided by this soffsoaping salesman.
Small wonder He'll Cheat E'erawan our local lads nicknamed
   him
When Chimpden first took the floor
    (Chorus) With his bucketshop store
             Down Bargainweg, Lower.

So snug he was in his hotel premises sumptuous
But soon we'll bonfire all his trash, tricks and trumpery
And 'tis short till sheriff Clancy'll be winding up his unlimited
   company
With the bailiff's bom at the door,
    (Chorus) Bimbam at the door.
             Then he'll bum no more.

Sweet bad luck on the waves washed to our island
The hooker of that hammerfast viking
And Gall's curse on the day when Eblana bay
Saw his black and tan man-o'-war.
> (Chorus) Saw his man-o'-war.
> On the harbour bar.

Where from? roars Poolbeg. Cookingha'pence, he bawls
  Donnez-moi scampitle, wick an wipin'fampiny
Fingal Mac Oscar Onesine Bargearse Boniface
Thok's min gammelhole Norveegickers moniker
Og as ay are at gammelhore Norveegickers cod.
> (Chorus) A Norwegian camel old cod.
> He is, begod.

Lift it, Hosty, lift it, ye devil ye! up with the rann, the rhyming
  rann!

It was during some fresh water garden pumping
Or, according to the *Nursing Mirror*, while admiring the
  monkeys
That our heavyweight heathen Humpharey
Made bold a maid to woo
> (Chorus) Woohoo, what'll she doo!
> The general lost her maidenloo!

He ought to blush for himself, the old hayheaded philosopher,
For to go and shove himself that way on top of her.
Begob, he's the crux of the catalogue
Of our antediluvial zoo,
> (Chorus) Messrs. Billing and Coo.
> Noah's larks, good as noo.

He was joulting by Wellinton's monument
Our rotorious hippopopotamuns
When some bugger let down the backtrap of the omnibus
And he caught his death of fusiliers,
    (Chorus) With his rent in his rears.
           Give him six years.

'Tis sore pity for his innocent poor children
But look out for his missus legitimate!
When that frew gets a grip of old Earwicker
Won't there be earwigs on the green?
    (Chorus) Big earwigs on the green,
           The largest ever you seen.

     Suffoclose! Shikespower! Seudodanto! Anonymoses!

Then we'll have a free trade Gaels' band and mass meeting
For to sod the brave son of Scandiknavery.
And we'll bury him down in Oxmanstown
Along with the devil and Danes,
    (Chorus) With the deaf and dumb Danes,
           And all their remains.

And not all the king's men nor his horses
Will resurrect his corpus
For there's no true spell in Connacht or hell
    (bis) That's able to raise a Cain.

Attabom

Wery weeny wight, plead for Morandmor! *Notre Dame de la Ville*, mercy of thy balmheartzyheat! Ogrowdnyk's beyond herbata tay, wort of the drogist. Bulk him no bulkis. And let him rest, thou wayfarre, and take no gravespoil from him! Neither mar his mound! The bane of Tut is on it.

Ware! But there's a little lady waiting and her name is A.L.P.
And you'll agree. She must be she. For her holden heirheaps
hanging down her back. He spenth his strenth amok
haremscarems. Poppy Narancy, Giallia, Chlora, Marinka,
Anileen, Parme. And ilk a those dames had her rainbow
huemoures yet for whilko her whims but he coined a cure.
Tifftiff today, kissykissy tonay and agelong pine tomauranna.
Then who but Crippled-with-Children would speak up for
Dropping-with-Sweat?

> *Sold him her lease of nineninenimetee,*
> *Tresses undresses so dyedyedaintee,*
> *Goo, the groot gudgeon, gulped it all.*
> *Hoo was the C. O. D.?*
>
> Bum!

> *At Island Bridge she met her tide.*
> *Attabom, attabom, attabombomboom!*
> *The Fin had a flux and his Ebba a ride.*
> *Attabom, attabom, attabombomboom!*
> *We're all up to the years in hues and cribies.*
> *That's what she's done for wee!*
>
> Woe!

Nomad may roam with Nabuch but let naaman laugh at
Jordan! For we, we have taken our sheet upon her stones
where we have hanged our hearts in her trees; and we list, as
she bibs us, by the waters of babalong.

The Mookse he had reason

Gentes and laitymen, fullstoppers and semicolonials,
hybreds and lubberds!

Eins within a space and a wearywide space it wast ere
wohned a Mookse. The onesomeness wast alltolonely,

archunsitslike, broady oval, and a Mookse he would a walking go (My hood! cries Antony Romeo), so one grandsumer evening, after a great morning and his good supper of gammon and spittish, having flabelled his eyes, pilleoled his nostrils, vacticanated his ears and palliumed his throats, he put on his impermeable, seized his impugnable, harped on his crown and stepped out of his immobile *De Rure Albo* (socolled becauld it was chalkfull of masterplasters and had borgeously letout gardens strown with cascades, pintacoste-cas, horthoducts and currycombs) and set off from Ludstown *a spasso* to see how badness was badness in the weirdest of all pensible ways.

As he set off with his father's sword, his *lancia spezzata*, he was girded on, and with that between his legs and his tarkeels, our once in only Bragspear, he clanked, to my clinking, from veetoes to threetop, every inch of an immortal.

He had not walked over a pentiadpair of parsecs from his azylium when at the turning of the Shinshone Lanteran near Saint Bowery's-without-his-Walls he came (secunding to the one one oneth of the propecies, *Amnis Limina Permanent*) upon the most unconsciously boggylooking stream he ever locked his eyes with. Out of the colliens it took a rise by daubing itself Ninon. It looked little and it smelt of brown and it thought in narrows and it talked showshallow. And as it rinn it dribbled like any lively purliteasy: *My, my my! Me and me! Little down dream don't I love thee!*

And, I declare, what was there on the yonder bank of the stream that would be a river, parched on a limb of the olum, bolt downright, but the Gripes? And no doubt he was fit to be dried for why had he not been having the juice of his times?

His pips had been neatly all drowned on him; his polps were charging odours every older minute; he was quickly for getting the dresser's desdaign on the flyleaf of his frons; and he was quietly for giving the bailiff's distrain on to the bulkside of his *cul de Pompe*. In all his specious heavings, as be lived by Optimus Maximus, the Mookse had never seen his Dubville brooder on-low so nigh to a pickle.

Adrian (that was the Mookse now's assumptinome) stuccstill phiz-à-phiz to the Gripes in an accessit of aurignacian. But Allmookse must to Moodend much as Allrouts, austereways or wastersways, in roaming run through Room. Hic sor a stone, singularly illud, and on hoc stone Seter satt huc sate which it filled quite poposterously and by acclammitation to its fullest justotoryum and whereopum with his unfallable encyclicling upom his alloilable, diupetriark of the wouest, and the athemystsprinkled pederect he always walked with, *Deusdedit*, cheek by jowel with his frisherman's blague, *Bellua Triumphanes*, his everyway addedto wallat's collectium, for yea longer he lieved yea broader he betaught of it, the fetter, the summe and the haul it cost, he looked the first and last micahlike laicness of Quartus the Fifth and Quintus the Sixth and Sixtus the Seventh giving allnight sitting to Lio the Faultyfindth.

– Good appetite us, sir Mookse! How do you do it? cheeped the Gripes in a wherry whiggy maudelenian woice and the jackasses all within bawl laughed and brayed for his intentions for they knew their sly toad lowry now. I am rarumominum blessed to see you, my dear mouster. Will you not perhopes tell me everything if you are pleased, sanity? All about aulne and lithial and allsall allinall about awn and liseias? Ney?

Think of it! O miserendissimest retempter! A Gripes!

– Rats! bullowed the Mookse most telesphorously, the concionator, and the sissymusses and the zozzymusses in their robenhauses quailed to hear his tardeynois at all for you cannot wake a silken nouse out of a hoarse oar. Blast yourself and your anathomy infairioriboos! No, hang you for an animal rurale! I am superbly in my supremest poncif! Abase you, baldyqueens! Gather behind me, satraps! Rots!

– I am till infinity obliged with you, bowed the Gripes, his whine having gone to his palpruy head. I am still always having a wish on all my extremities. By the watch, what is the time, pace?

Figure it! The pining peever! To a Mookse!

– Ask my index, mund my achilles, swell my obolum,

woshup my nase serene, answered the Mookse, rapidly by turning clement, urban, eugenious and celestian in the formose of good grogory humours. Quote awhore? That is quite about what I came on *my* missions with *my* intentions *laudibiliter* to settle with *you*, barbarousse. Let thor be orlog. Let Pauline be Irene. Let you be Beeton. And let me be Los Angeles. Now measure your length. Now estimate my capacity. Well, sour? Is this space of our couple of hours too dimensional for you, temporiser? Will you give you up? *Como? Fuert it?*

Sancta Patientia! You should have heard the voice that answered him! *Culla vosellina.*

– I was just thinking upon that, swees Mooksey, but, for all the rime on my raisins, if I connow make my submission, I cannos give you up, the Gripes whimpered from nethermost of his wanhope. Ishallassoboundbewilsothoutoosezit. My tumble, loudy bullocker, is my own. My velicity is too fit in one stockend. And my spetial inexshellsis the belowing things ab ove. But I will never be abler to tell Your Honoriousness (here he near lost his limb) though my corked father was bott a pseudowaiter, whose o'cloak you ware.

Incredible! Well, hear the inevitable.

– *Your* temple, *sus in cribro!* Semperexcommunicambiambisumers. Tugurios-in-Newrobe or Tukurias-in-Ashies. Novarome, my creature, blievend bleives. My building space in lyonine city is always to let to leonlike Men, the Mookse in a most consistorous allocution pompifically with immediate jurisdiction constantinently concludded (what a crammer for the shapewrucked Gripes!). And I regret to proclaim that it is out of my temporal to help you from being killed by inchies, (what a thrust!), as we first met each other newwhere so airly. (Poor little sowsieved subsquashed Gripes! I begin to feel contemption for him!). My side, thank decretals, is as safe as motherour's houses, he continued, and I can seen from my holeydome what it is to be wholly sane. Unionjok and be joined to yok! Parysis, *tu sais*, crucycrooks, belongs to him who parises himself. And there I must leave you subject for the pressing. I can prove that against you, weight a momentum, mein goot enemy! or Cospol's not our star. I bet you this dozen odd. This foluminous dozen odd. *Quas primas* – but 'tis bitter to compote my knowledge's fructos of. Tomes.

Elevating, to give peint to his blick, his jewelled pederect to the allmysty cielung, he luckystruck blueild out of a few shouldbe santillants, a cloister of starabouts over Maples, a lucciolys in Teresa street and a stopsign before Sophy Barratt's, he gaddered togodder the odds docence of his vellumes, gresk, letton and russicruxian, onto the lapse of his prolegs, into umfullth onescuppered, and sat about his widerproof. He proved it well whoonearth dry and drysick times, and *vremiament, tu cesses*, to the extinction of Niklaus altogether (Niklaus Alopysius having been the once Gripes's popwilled nimbum) by Neuclidius and Inexagoras and Mumfsen and Thumpsem, by Orasmus and by Amenius, by Anacletus the Jew and by Malachy the Augurer and by the Cappon's collection and after that, with Cheekee's gelatine and Alldaybrandy's formolon, he reproved it ehrltogether when not in that order sundering in some different order, alter three thirty and a hundred times by the binomial dioram and the penic walls and the ind, the Inklespill legends and the rure, the rule of the hoop and the blessons of expedience and the jus, the jugicants of Pontius Pilax and all the mummy-scrips in Sick Bokes' Juncroom and the Chapters for the Cunning of the Chapters of the Conning Fox by Tail.

While that Mooksius with preprocession and with pro-precession, duplicitly and diplussedly, was promulgating ipsofacts and sadcontras this raskolly Gripos he had allbust seceded in monophysicking his illsobordunates. But asawfulas he had caught his base semenoyous sarchnaktiers to combuc-cinate upon the silipses of his aspillouts and the acheporeoozers of his haggyown pneumax to synerethetise with the breadchestviousness of his sweeatovular ducose sofarfully the loggerthuds of his sakellaries were fond at variance with the synodals of his somepooliom and his babskissed nepogreasy-most got the hoof from his philioquus.

– Efter thousand yaws, O Gripes con my sheepskins, yow will be belined to the world, enscayed Mookse the pius.

– Ofter thousand yores, amsered Gripes the gregary, be the goat of MacHammud's, yours may be still, O Mookse, more botheared.

– Us shall be chosen as the first of the last by the electress of Vale Hollow, obselved the Mookse nobily, for par the unicum of Elelijiacks, Us am in Our stabulary and that is what Ruby and Roby fall for, blissim.

The Pills, the Nasal Wash (Yardly's), the Army Man Cut, as british as bondstrict and as straightcut as when that brokenarched traveller from Nuzuland . . .

– Wee, cumfused the Gripes limply, shall not even be the last of the first, wee hope, when oust are visitated by the Veiled Horror. And, he added: Mee are relying entirely, see the fortethurd of Elissabed, on the weightiness of mear's breath. Puffut!

Unsightbared embouscher, relentless foe to social and business succes! (Hourihaleine) It might have been a happy evening but . . .

And they viterberated each other, *canis et coluber* with the wildest ever wielded since Tarriestinus lashed Pissasphaltium.

– Unuchorn!

– Ungulant!

– Uvuloid!

– Uskybeak!

And bullfolly answered volleyball.

Nuvoletta in her lightdress, spunn of sisteen shimmers, was looking down on them, leaning over the bannistars and listening all she childishly could. How she was brightened when Shouldrups in his glaubering hochskied his welkinstuck and how she was overclused when Kneesknobs on his zwivvel was makeacting such a paulse of himshelp! She was alone. All her nubied companions were asleeping with the squirrels. Their mivver, Mrs Moonan, was off in the Fuerst quarter scrubbing the backsteps of Number 28. Fuvver, that Skand, he was up in Norwood's sokaparlour, eating oceans of Voking's Blemish. Nuvoletta listened as she reflected herself, though the heavenly one with his constellatria and his emanations stood between, and she tried all she tried to make the Mookse look up at her (but *he* was fore too adiaptotously farseeing) and to make the Gripes hear how coy she could be (though he was much too schystimatically auricular about *his ens* to heed her) but it was all mild's vapour moist. Not even her feignt reflection, Nuvoluccia, could they toke their gnoses off for their minds with intrepifide fate and bungless curiasity, were conclaved with Heliogobbleus and Commodus and Enobarbarus and whatever the co-ordinal dickens they did as their damprauch of papyrs and buchstubs said. As if that was their spiration! As if theirs could duiparate her queendim! As if she would be third perty to search on search proceedings! She tried all the winsome wonsome ways her four winds had taught her. She tossed her sfumastelliacinous hair like *la princesse de la Petite Bretagne* and she rounded her mignons arms like Mrs Cornwallis-West and she smiled over herself like the beauty of the image of the pose of the daughter of the queen of the Emperour of Irelande and she sighed after herself as were she born to bride with Tristis Tristior Tristissimus. But, sweet madonine, she might fair as well have carried her daisy's worth to Florida. For the Mookse, a dogmad Accanite, were not amoosed and the Gripes, a dubliboused Catalick, wis pinefully obliviscent.

– I see, she sighed. There are menner.

The siss of the whisp of the sigh of the softzing at the stir of the ver grose O arundo of a long one in midias reeds: and shades began to glidder along the banks, greepsing, greepsing, duusk unto duusk, and it was as glooming as gloaming could be in the waste of all peacable worlds. Metamnisia was allsoonome coloroform brune; citherior spiane an eaulande, innemorous and unnumerose. The Mookse had a sound eyes right but he could not all hear. The Gripes had light ears left yet he could but ill see. He ceased. And he ceased, tung and trit, and it was neversoever so dusk of both of them. But still Moo

thought on the deeps of the undths he would profoundth
come the morrokse and still Gri feeled of the scripes he would
escipe if by grice he had luck enoupes.

Oh, how it was duusk! From Vallee Maraia to Grasyaplaina,
dormimust echo! Ah dew! Ah dew! It was so duusk that the
tears of night began to fall, first by ones and twos, then by
threes and fours, at last by fives and sixes of sevens, for the
tired ones were wecking, as we weep now with them. *O! O! O!
Par la pluie!*

Then there came down to the thither bank a woman of no
appearance (I believe she was a Black with chills at her feet)
and she gathered up his hoariness the Mookse motamourfully
where he was spread and carried him away to her invisible
dwelling, thats hights, *Aquila Rapax,* for he was the holy
sacred solem and poshup spit of her boshop's apron. So you
see the Mookse he had reason as I knew and you knew and he
knew all along. And there came down to the hither bank a
woman to all important (though they say that she was comely,
spite the cold in her heed) and, for he was as like it as blow it
to a hawker's hank, she plucked down the Gripes, torn
panicky autotone, in angeu from his limb and cariad away its
beotitubes with her to her unseen shieling, it is, *De Rore Coeli.*
And so the poor Gripes got wrong; for that is always how a
Gripes is, always was and always will be. And it was never so
thoughtful of either of them. And there were left now an only
elmtree and but a stone. Polled with pietrous, Sierre but saule.
O! Yes! And Nuvoletta, a lass.

Then Nuvoletta reflected for the last time in her little long
life and she made up all her myriads of drifting minds in one.
She cancelled all her engauzements. She climbed over the
bannistars; she gave a childy cloudy cry: *Nuée! Nuée!* A
lightdress fluttered. She was gone. And into the river that had
been a stream (for a thousand tears had gone eon her and
come on her and she was stout and struck on dancing and her
muddied name was Missisliffi) there fell a tear, a singult tear,
the loveliest of all tears (I mean for those crylove fables fans
who are 'keen' on the prettypretty commonface sort of thing

you meet by hopeharrods) for it was a leaptear. But the river tripped on her by and by, lapping as though her heart was brook: *Why, why, why! Weh, O weh! I'se so silly to be flowing but I no canna stay!*

Departure: the stages of life

O ne hailcannon night (for his departure was attended by a heavy downpour) as very recently as some thousand rains ago he was therefore treated with what closely resembled parsonal violence, being soggert all unsuspectingly through the deserted village of Tumblin-on-the-Leafy from Mr Vanhomrigh's house at 81 *bis* Mabbot's Mall as far as Green Patch beyond the brickfields of Salmon Pool by rival teams of slowspiers counter quicklimers who finally, as rahilly they had been deteened out rawther laetich, thought, busnis hits busnis, they had better be streaking for home after their Auborne-to-Auborne, with thanks for the pleasant evening, one and all disgustedly, instead of ruggering him back, and awake, reconciled (though they were as jealous as could be cullions about all the truffles they had brought on him) to a friendship, fast and furious, which merely arose out of the noxious pervert's perfect lowness. Again there was a hope that people, looking on him with the contemp of the contempibles, after first gaving him a roll in the dirt, might pity and forgive him, if properly deloused, but the pleb was born a Quicklow and sank alowing till he stank out of sight.

All Saints beat Belial! Mickil Goals to Nichil! Notpossible! Already?

In Nowhere has yet the Whole World taken part of himself for his Wife;

By Nowhere have Poorparents been sentenced to Worms, Blood and Thunder for Life

Not yet has the Emp from Corpsica forced the Arth out of Engleterre;

Not yet have the Sachsen and Judder on the Mound of a Word
    made Warre;
Not yet Witchywithcy of Wench struck Fire of his Heath
    from on Hoath;
Not yet his Arcobaleine forespoken Peacepeace upon Oath;
Cleftfoot from Hempal must tumpel, Blamefool Gardener's
    bound to fall;
Broken Eggs will poursuive bitten Apples for where theirs is
    Will there's his Wall;
But the Mountstill frowns on the Millstream while their
    Madsons leap his Bier
And her Rillstrill liffs to His Murkesty all her daft Daughters
    laff in her Ear.
Till the four Shores of deff Tory Island let the douze dumm
    Eirewhiggs raille!
Hirp! Hirp! for their Missed Understandings! chirps the
    Ballat of Perce-Oreille.

Anna Livia Plurabelle

O
tell me all about
Anna Livia! I want to hear all
about Anna Livia. Well, you know Anna Livia? Yes, of course,
we all know Anna Livia. Tell me all. Tell me now. You'll die
when you hear. Well, you know, when the old cheb went futt
and did what you know. Yes, I know, go on. Wash quit and
don't be dabbling. Tuck up your sleeves and loosen your
talktapes. And don't butt me – hike! – when you bend. Or
whatever it was they threed to make out he thried to two in
the Fiendish park. He's an awful old reppe. Look at the shirt
of him! Look at the dirt of it! He has all my water black on me.
And it steeping and stuping since this time last wik. How
many goes is it I wonder I washed it? I know by heart the
places he likes to saale, duddurty devil! Scorching my hand and

starving my famine to make his private linen public. Wallop
it well with your battle and clean it. My wrists are wrusty
rubbing the mouldaw stains. And the dneepers of wet and the
gangres of sin in it! What was it he did a tail at all on Animal
Sendai? And how long was he under loch and neagh? It was
put in the newses what he did, nicies and priers, the King
fierceas Humphrey, with illysus distilling, exploits and all. But
toms will till. I know he well. Temp untamed will hist for no
man. As you spring so shall you neap. O, the roughty old
rappe! Minxing marrage and making loof. Reeve Gootch was
right and Reeve Drughad was sinistrous! And the cut of him!
And the strut of him! How he used to hold his head as high
as a howeth, the famous eld duke alien, with a hump of
grandeur on him like a walking wiesel rat. And his derry's
own drawl and his corksown blather and his doubling stutter
and his gullaway swank. Ask Lictor Hackett or Lector Reade
of Garda Growley or the Boy with the Billyclub. How elster is
he a called at all? Qu'appelle? Huges Caput Earlyfouler. Or
where was he born or how was he found? Urgothland,
Tvistown on the Kattekat? New Hunshire, Concord on the
Merrimake? Who blocksmitt her saft anvil or yelled lep to her
pail? Was her banns never loosened in Adam and Eve's or
were him and her but captain spliced? For mine ether duck I
thee drake. And by my wildgaze I thee gander. Flowey and
Mount on the brink of time makes wishes and fears for a
happy isthmass. She can show all her lines, with love, license
to play. And if they don't remarry that hook and eye may! O,
passmore that and oxus another! Don Dom Dombdomb and
his wee follyo! Was his help inshored in the Stork and Pelican
against bungelars, flu and third risk parties? I heard he dug
good tin with his doll, delvan first and duvlin after, when he
raped her home, Sabrine asthore, in a parakeet's cage, by
dredgerous lands and devious delts, playing catched and
mythed with the gleam of her shadda, (if a flic had been there
to pop up and pepper him!) past auld min's manse and
Maisons Allfou and the rest of incurables and the last of
immurables, the quaggy waag for stumbling. Who sold you

that jackalantern's tale? Pemmican's pasty pie! Not a grass-
hoop to ring her, not an antsgrain of ore. In a gabbard he
barqued it, the boat of life, from the harbourless Ivernikan
Okean, till he spied the loom of his landfall and he loosed two
croakers from under his tilt, the gran Phenician rover. By the
smell of her kelp they made the pigeonhouse. Like fun they
did! But where was Himself, the timoneer? That marchant-
man he suivied their scutties right over the wash, his
cameleer's burnous breezing up on him, till with his runagate
bowmpriss he roade and borst her bar. Pilcomayo! Such-
caughtawan! And the whale's away with the grayling! Tune
your pipes and fall ahumming, you born ijypt, and you're
nothing short of one! Well, ptellomey soon and curb your
escumo. When they saw him shoot swift up her sheba sheath,
like any gay lord salomon, her bulls they were ruhring, surfed
with spree. Boyarka buah! Boyana bueh! He erned his lille
Bunbath hard, our staly bred, the trader. He did. Look at here.
In this wet of his prow. Don't you know he was kaldt a bairn
of the brine, Wasserbourne and waterbaby? Havemmarea, so
he was! H.C.E. has a codfisck ee. Shyr she's nearly as badher as
him herself. Who? Anna Livia? Ay, Anna Livia. Do you know
she was calling bakvandets sals from all around, nyumba noo,
chamba choo, to go in till him, her erring cheef, and tickle the
pontiff aisy-oisy? She was? Gota pot! Yssel that the limmat?
As El Negro winced when he wonced in La Plate. O, tell me
all I want to hear, how loft she was lift a laddery dextro! A
coneywink after the bunting fell. Letting on she didn't care,
sina feza, me absantee, him man in passession, the proxenete!
Proxenete and phwhat is phthat? Emme for your reussischer
Honddu jarkon! Tell us in franca langua. And call a spate a
spate. Did they never sharee you ebro at skol, you antiabece-
darian? It's just the same as if I was to go par examplum now
in conservancy's cause out of telekinesis and proxenete you.
For coxyt sake and is that what she is? Botlettle I thought
she'd act that loa. Didn't you spot her in her windaug,
wubbling up on an osiery chair, with a meusic before her all
cunniform letters, pretending to ribble a reedy derg on a fiddle

she bogans without a band on? Sure she can't fiddan a dee, with bow or abandon! Sure, she can't! Tista suck. Well, I never now heard the like of that! Tell me moher. Tell me moatst. Well, old Humber was as glommen as grampus, with the tares at his thor and the buboes for ages and neither bowman nor shot abroad and bales allbrant on the crests of rockies and nera lamp in kitchen or church and giant's holes in Grafton's causeway and deathcap mushrooms round Funglus grave and the great tribune's barrow all darnels occumule, sittang sambre on his sett, drammen and drommen, usking queasy quizzers of his ruful continence, his childlinen scarf to encourage his obsequies where he'd check their debths in that mormon's thames, be questing and handsetl, hop, step and a deepend, with his berths in their toiling moil, his swallower open from swolf to fore and the snipes of the gutter pecking his crocs, hungerstriking all alone and holding doomsdag over hunselv, dreeing his weird, with his dander up, and his fringe combed over his eygs and droming on loft till the sight of the sternes, after zwarthy kowse and weedy broeks and the tits of buddy and the loits of pest and to peer was Parish worth thette mess. You'd think all was dodo belonging to him how he durmed adranse in durance vaal. He had been belching for severn years. And there she was, Anna Livia, she darent catch a winkle of sleep, purling around like a chit of a child, Wendawanda, a fingerthick, in a Lapsummer skirt and damazon cheeks, for to ishim bonzour to her dear dubber Dan. With neuphraties and sault from his maggias. And an odd time she'd cook him up blooms of fisk and lay to his heartsfoot her meddery eygs, yayis, and staynish beacons on toasc and a cupenhave so weeshywashy of Greenland's tay or a dzoupgan of Kaffue mokau an sable or Sikiang sukry or his ale of ferns in trueart pewter and a shinkobread (hamjambo, bana?) for to plaise that man hog stay his stomicker till her pyrraknees shrunk to nutmeg graters while her togglejoints shuck with goyt and as rash as she'd russ with her peakload of vivers up on her sieve (metauwero rage it swales and rieses) my hardey Hek he'd kast them frome him, with a stour of scorn, as much as to say you sow and you sozh, and if he didn't peg the platteau on her tawe, believe you me, she was safe enough. And then she'd esk to vistule a hymn, *The Heart Bowed Down* or *The Rakes of Mallow* or Chelli Michele's *La Calumnia è un Vermicelli* or a balfy bit ov *old Jo Robidson*. Sucho fuffing a fifeing 'twould cut you in two! She'd bate the hen that crowed on the turrace of Babbel. What harm if she knew how to cockle her mouth! And not a mag out of Hum no more than out of the mangle weight. Is that a faith? That's the fact. Then riding the ricka and roya romanche, Annona, gebroren aroostokrat Nivia, dochter of Sense and Art, with Sparks' pirryphlickathims funkling her fan, anner frostivying tresses dasht with virevlies – while the prom beauties sreeked nith their bearers' skins! – in a period gown of changeable jade that would robe the wood of two cardinals' chairs and crush poor Cullen and smother MacCabe. O blazerskate! Theirs porpor patches! And brahming to him down the feedchute, with her femtyfyx kinds of fondling endings, the poother rambling off her nose: *Vuggybarney, Wickerymandy! Hello, ducky, please don't die!* Do you know what she started cheeping after, with a choicey voicey like waterglucks or Madame Delba to Romeoreszk? You'll never guess. Tell me. Tell me. *Phoebe, dearest, tell, O tell me* and *I loved you better nor you knew*. And letting on hoon var daft about the warbly sangs from over holmen: *High hellskirt saw ladies hensmoker lilyhung pigger:* and soay and soan and so firth and so forth in a tone sonora and Oom Bothar below like Bheri-Bheri in his sandy cloak, so umvolosy, as deaf as a yawn, the stult! Go away! Poor deef old deary! Yare only teasing! Anna Liv? As chalk is my judge! And didn't she up in sorgues and go and trot doon and stand in her douro, puffing her old dudheen, and every shirvant siligirl or wensum farmerette walking the pilend roads, Sawy, Fundally, Daery or Maery, Milucre, Awny or Graw, usedn't she make her a simp or sign to slip inside by the sullyport? You don't say, the sillypost? Bedouix but I do! Calling them in, one by one (To Blockbeddum here! Here the Shoebenacaddie!) and legging a jig or so on the sihl to show

them how to shake their benders and the dainty how to bring
to mind the gladdest garments out of sight and all the way of
a maid with a man and making a sort of a cackling noise like
two and a penny or half a crown and holding up a silliver
shiner. Lordy, lordy, did she so? Well, of all the ones ever I
heard! Throwing all the neiss little whores in the world at
him! To inny captured wench you wish of no matter what sex
of pleissful ways two adda tammar a lizzy a lossie to hug and
hab haven in Humpy's apron!

And what was the wyerye rima she made! Odet! Odet! Tell
me the trent of it while I'm lathering hail out of Denis
Florence MacCarthy's combies. Rise it, flut ye, pian piena! I'm
dying down off my iodine feet until I lerryn Anna Livia's
cushingloo, that was writ by one and rede by two and trouved
by a poule in the parco! I can see that, I see you are. How does
it tummel? Listen now. Are you listening? Yes, yes! Idneed I
am! Tarn your ore ouse! Essonne inne!

*By earth and the cloudy but I badly want a brandnew
bankside, bedamp and I do, and a plumper at that!*

*For the putty affair I have is wore out, so it is, sitting, yaping
and waiting for my old Dane hodder dodderer, my life in death
companion, my frugal key of our larder, my much-altered
camel's hump, my jointspoiler, my maymoon's honey, my fool
to the last Decemberer, to wake himself out of his winter's
doze and bore me down like he used to.*

*Is there irwell a lord of the manor or a knight of the shire
at strike, I wonder, that'd dip me a dace or two in cash for
washing and darning his worshipful socks for him now we're
run out of horse-brose and milk?*

*Only for my short Brittas bed made's as snug as it smells it's
out I'd lep and off with me to the slobs della Tolka or the plage
au Clontarf to feale the gay aire of my salt troublin bay and the
race of the saywint up me ambushure.*

Onon! Onon! tell me more. Tell me every tiny teign. I want
to know every single ingul. Down to what made the potters fly
into jagsthole. And why were the vesles vet. That homa
fever's winning me wome. If a mahun of the horse but hard

me! We'd be bundukiboi meet askarigal. Well, now comes the
hazelhatchery part. After Clondalkin the Kings's Inns. We'll
soon be there with the freshet. How many aleveens had she in
tool? I can't rightly rede you that. Close only knows. Some say
she had three figures to fill and confined herself to a hundred
eleven, wan bywan bywan, making meanacuminamoyas.
Olaph lamm et, all that pack? We won't have room in the
kirkeyaard. She can't remember half of the cradlenames she
smacked on them by the grace of her boxing bishop's infallible
slipper, the cane for Kund and abbles for Eyolf and ayther
nayther for Yakov Yea. A hundred and how? They did well to
re-christien her Pluhurabelle. O loreley! What a loddon lodes!
Heigh ho! But it's quite on the cards she'll shed more and
merrier, twills and trills, sparefours and spoilfives, nordsihkes
and sudsevers and ayes and neins to a litter. Grandfarthring
nap and Messamisery and the knave of all knaves and the
joker. Heehaw! She must have been a gadabount in her day, so
she must, more than most. Shoal she was, gidgad. She had a
flewmen of her owen. Then a toss nare scared that lass, so
aimai moe, that's agapo! Tell me, tell me, how cam she camlin
through all her fellows, the neckar she was, the diveline?
Casting her perils before our swains from Fonte-in-Monte to
Tidingtown and from Tidingtown tilhavet. Linking one and
knocking the next, tapting a flank and tipting a jutty and
palling in and pietaring out and clyding by on her eastway.
Waiwhou was the first thurever burst? Someone he was,
whuebra they were, in a tactic attack or in single combat.
Tinker, tilar, souldrer, salor, Pieman Peace or Polistaman.
That's the thing I'm elwys on edge to esk. Push up and push
vardar and come to uphill headquarters! Was it waterlows
year, after Grattan or Flood, or when maids were in Arc or
when three stood hosting? Fidaris will find where the Doubt
arises like Nieman from Nirgends found the Nihil. Worry
you sighin foh, Albern, O Anser? Untie the gemman's
fistiknots, Qvic and Nuancee! She can't put her hand on him
for the moment. Tez thelon langlo, walking weary! Such a
loon waybashwards to row! She sid herself she hardly knows

whuon the annals her graveller was, a dynast of Leinster, a wolf of the sea, or what he did or how blyth she played or how, when, why, where and who offon he jumpnad her and how it was gave her away. She was just a young thin pale soft shy slim slip of a thing then, sauntering, by silvamoonlake and he was a heavy trudging lurching lieabroad of a Curraghman, making his hay for whose sun to shine on, as tough as the oaktrees (peats be with them!) used to rustle that time down by the dykes of killing Kildare, for forstfellfoss with a plash across her. She thought she's sankh neathe the ground with nymphant shame when he gave her the tigris eye! O happy fault! Me wish it was he! You're wrong there, corribly wrong! Tisn't only tonight you're anacheronistic! It was ages behind that when nullahs were nowhere, in county Wickenlow, garden of Erin, before she ever dreamt she'd lave Kilbride and go foaming under Horsepass bridge, with the great souther-western windstorming her traces and the midland's grain-waster asarch for her track, to wend her ways byandby, robecca or worse, to spin and to grind, to swab and to thrash, for all her golden lifey in the barleyfields and pennylotts of Humphrey's fordofhurdlestown and lie with a landleaper, wellingtonorseher. Alesse, the lagos of girly days! For the dove of the dunas! Wasut? Izod? Are you sarthin suir? Not where the Finn fits into the Mourne, not where the Nore takes lieve of Blœm, not where the Braye divarts the Farer, not where the Moy changez her minds twixt Cullin and Conn tween Cunn and Collin? Or where Neptune sculled and Tritonville rowed and leandros three bumped heroines two? Neya, narev, nen, nonni, nos! Then whereabouts in Ow and Ovoca? Was it yst with wyst or Lucan Yokan or where the hand of man has never set foot? Dell me where, the fairy ferse time! I will if you listen. You know the dinkel dale of Luggelaw? Well, there once dwelt a local heremite, Michael Arklow was his riverend name, (with many a sigh I aspersed his lavabibs!) and one venersderg in junojuly, oso sweet and so cool and so limber she looked, Nance the Nixie, Nanon L'Escaut, in the silence, of the sycomores, all listening, the

kindling curves you simply can't stop feeling, he plunged both
of his newly anointed hands, the core of his cushlas, in
her singimari saffron strumans of hair, parting them and
soothing her and mingling it, that was deep dark and ample
like this red bog at sundown. By that Vale Vowclose's lucydlac,
the reignbeau's heavenarches arronged orranged her. Afroth-
dizzying galbs, her enamelled eyes indergoading him on to the
vierge violetian. Wish a wish! Why a why? Mavro! Letty
Lerck's lafing light throw those laurals now on her daphdaph
teasesong petrock. Maass! But the majik wavus has elfun anon
meshes. And Simba the Slayer of his Oga is slewd. He cuddle
not help himself, thurso that hot on him, he had to forget the
monk in the man so, rubbing her up and smoothing her down,
he baised his lippes in smiling mood, kiss akiss after
kisokushk (as he warned her niver to, niver to, nevar) on
Anna-na-Poghue's of the freckled forehead. While you'd
parse secheressa she hielt her souff'. But she ruz two feet hire
in her aisne aestumation. And steppes on stilts ever since.
That was kissuahealing with bantur for balm! O, wasn't he the
bold priest? And wasn't she the naughty Livvy? Nautic
Naama's now her navn. Two lads in scoutsch breeches went
through her before that, Barefoot Burn and Wallowme Wade,
Lugnaquillia's noblesse pickts, before she had a hint of a hair
at her fanny to hide or a bossom to tempt a birch canoedler not
to mention a bulgic porterhouse barge. And ere that again,
leada, laida, all unraidy, too faint to buoy the fairiest rider, too
frail to flirt with a cygnet's plume, she was licked by a hound,
Chirripa-Chirruta, while poing her pee, pure and simple, on
the spur of the hill in old Kippure, in birdsong and
shearingtime, but first of all, worst of all, the wiggly livvly, she
sideslipped out by a gap in the Devil's glen while Sally her
nurse was sound asleep in a sloot and, feefee fiefie, fell over a
spillway before she found her stride and lay and wriggled in all
the stagnant black pools of rainy under a fallow coo and she
laughted innocefree with her limbs aloft and a whole drove of
maiden hawthorns blushing and looking askance upon her.

Drop me the sound of the findhorn's name. Mtu or Mti,

somebogger was wisness. And drip me why in the flenders
was she frickled. And trickle me through was she marcelle-
waved or was it weirdly a wig she wore. And whitside did they
droop their glows in their florry, aback to wist or affront to
sea? In fear to hear the dear so near or longing loth and
loathing longing? Are you in the swim or are you out? O go
in, go on, go an! I mean about what you know. I know right
well what you mean. Rother! You'd like the coifs and
guimpes, snouty, and me to do the greasy jub on old
Veronica's wipers. What am I rancing now and I'll thank you?
Is it a pinny or is it a surplice? Arran, where's your nose? And
where's the starch? That's not the vesdre benediction smell. I
can tell from here by their *eau de Colo* and the scent of her
oder they're Mrs Magrath's. And you ought to have aird them.
They've moist come off her. Creases in silk they are, not
crampton lawn. Baptiste me, father, for she has sinned!
Through her catchment ring she freed them easy, with her
hips' hurrahs for her knees' dontelleries. The only parr with
frills in old the plain. So they are, I declare! Welland well! If
tomorrow keeps fine who'll come tripping to sightsee?
How'll? Ask me next what I haven't got! The Belvedarean
exhibitioners. In their cruisery caps and oarsclub colours.
What hoo, they band! And what hoa, they buck! And here is
her nubilee letters too. Ellis on quay in scarlet thread. Linked
for the world on a flushcaloured field. Annan exe after to
show they're not Laura Keown's. O, may the diabolo twisk
your seifety pin! You child of Mammon, Kinsella's Lilith!
Now who has been tearing the leg of her drawers on her?
Which leg is it? The one with the bells on it. Rinse them out
and aston along with you! Where did I stop? Never stop!
Continuarration! You're not there yet. I amstel waiting.
Garonne, garonne!

Well, after it was put in the Mercy Cordial Mendicants'
Sitterdag–Zindeh–Munaday Wakeschrift (for once they sul-
lied their white kidloves, chewing cuds after their dinners of
cheeckin and beggin, with their show us it here and their mind
out of that and their when you're quite finished with the

reading matarial), even the snee that snowdon his hoaring
hair had a skunner against him. Thaw, thaw, sava, savuto!
Score Her Chuff Exsquire! Everywhere erriff you went and
every bung you arver dropped into, in cit or suburb or in
addled areas, the Rose and Bottle or Phoenix Tavern or
Power's Inn or Jude's Hotel or wherever you scoured the
countryside from Nannywater to Vartryville or from Porta
Lateen to the lootin quarter you found his ikom etsched
tipside down or the cornerboys cammocking his guy and
Morris the Man, with the role of a royss in his turgos the
turrible, (Evropeahahn cheic house, unskimmed sooit and
yahoort, hamman now cheekmee, Ahdahm this way make,
Fatima, half turn!) reeling and railing round the local as the
peihos piped und ubanjees twanged, with oddfellow's triple
tiara busby rotundarinking round his scalp. Like Pate-by-the-
Neva or Pete-over-Meer. This is the Hausman all paven and
stoned, that cribbed the Cabin that never was owned that
cocked his leg and hennad his Egg. And the mauldrin rabble
around him in areopage, fracassing a great bingkan cagnan
with their timpan crowders. Mind your Grimmfather! Think
of your Ma! Hing the Hong is his jove's hangnomen! Lilt a
bolero, bulling a law! She swore on croststyx nyne wyndabouts
she's be level with all the snags of them yet. Par the
Vulnerable Virgin's Mary del Dame! So she said to herself
she'd frame a plan to fake a shine, the mischiefmaker, the like
of it you niever heard. What plan? Tell me quick and dongu so
crould! What the meurther did she mague? Well, she
bergened a zakbag, a shammy mailsack, with the lend of a loan
of the light of his lampion, off one of her swapsons, Shaun the
Post, and then she went and consulted her chapboucqs, old
Mot Moore, Casey's Euclid and the Fashion Display and made
herself tidal to join in the mascarete. O gig goggle of gigguels.
I can't tell you how! It's too screaming to rizo, rabbit it all!
Minneha, minnehi, minaaehe, minneho! O but you must, you
must really! Make my hear it gurgle gurgle, like the farest
gargle gargle in the dusky dirgle dargle! By the holy well of
Mulhuddart I swear I'd pledge my chanza getting to heaven

through Tirry and Killy's mount of impiety to hear it all, aviary word! O, leave me my faculties, woman, a while! If you don't like my story get out of the punt. Well, have it your own way, so. Here, sit down and do as you're bid. Take my stroke and bend to your bow. Forward in and pull your overthepoise! Lisp it slaney and crisp it quiet. Deel me longsome. Tongue your time now. Breathe thet deep. Thouat's the fairway. Hurry slow and scheldt you go. Lynd us your blessed ashes here till I scrub the canon's underpants. Flow now. Ower more. And pooleypooley.

First she let her hair fal and down it flussed to her feet its teviots winding coils. Then, mothernaked, she sampood herself with galawater and fraguant pistania mud, wupper and lauar, from crown to sole. Next she greesed the groove of her keel, warthes and wears and mole and itcher, with antifouling butterscatch and turfentide and serpenthyme and with leafmould she ushered round prunella isles and eslats dun, quincecunct, allover her little mary. Peeld gold of waxwork her jelly-belly and her grains of incense anguille bronze. And after that she wove a garland for her hair. She pleated it. She plaited it. Of meadowgrass and riverflags, the bulrush and waterweed, and of fallen griefs of weeping willow. Then she made her bracelets and her anklets and her armlets and a jetty amulet for necklace of clicking cobbles and pattering pebbles and rumbledown rubble, richmond and rehr, of Irish rhunerhinerstones and shellmarble bangles. That done, a dawk of smut to her airy ey, Annushka Lutetiavitch Pufflovah, and the lellipos cream to her lippe-leens and the pick of the paintbox for her pommettes, from strawbirry reds to extra violates, and she sendred her boudeloire maids to His Affluence, Ciliegia Grande and Kirschie Real, the two chirsines, with respecks from his missus, seepy and sewery, and a request might she passe of him for a minnikin. A call to pay and light a taper, in Brie-on-Arrosa, back in a sprizzling. The cock striking mine, the stalls bridely sign, there's Zambosy waiting for Me! She said she wouldn't be half her length away. Then, then, as soon as the lump his back was turned, with her mealiebag slang over her shulder, Anna Livia, oysterface, forth of her bassein came.

Describe her! Hustle along, why can't you? Spitz on the iern while it's hot. I wouldn't miss her for irthing on nerthe. Not for the lucre of lomba strait. Oceans of Gaud, I mosel hear that! Ogowe presta! Leste, before Julia sees her! Ishekarry and washemeskad, the carishy caratimaney? Whole lady fair? Duodecimoroon? Bon a ventura? Malagassy? What had she on, the liddel oud oddity? How much did she scallop, harness and weights? Here she is, Amnisty Ann! Call her calamity electrifies man.

No electress at all but old Moppa Necessity, angin mother of injons. I'll tell you a test. But you must sit still. Will you hold your peace and listen well to what I am going to say now? It might have been ten or twenty to one of the night of Allclose or the next of April when the flip of her hoogly igloo flappered and out toetippit a bushman woman, the dearest little moma ever you saw, nodding around her, all smiles, with ems of embarras and aues to awe, between two ages, a judyqueen, not up to your elb. Quick, look at her cute and saise her quirk for the bicker she lives the slicker she grows. Save us and tagus! No more? Werra where in ourthe did you ever pick a Lambay chop as big as a battering ram? Ay, you're right. I'm epte to forgetting, Like Liviam Liddle did Loveme Long. The linth of my hough, I say! She wore a ploughboy's nailstudded clogs, a pair of ploughfields in themselves: a sugarloaf hat with a gaudyquiviry peak and a band of gorse for an arnoment and a hundred streamers dancing off it and a guildered pin to pierce it: owlglassy bicycles boggled her eyes: and a fish-netzeveil for the sun not to spoil the wrinklings of her hydeaspects: potatorings boucled the loose laubes of her laudsnarers: her nude cuba stockings were salmospot-speckled: she sported a galligo shimmy of hazevaipar tinto that never was fast till it ran in the washing: stout stays, the rivals, lined her length: her bloodorange bockknickers, a two in one garment, showed natural nigger boggers, fancyfas-tened, free to undo: her blackstripe tan joseph was sequan-

sewn and teddybearlined, with wavy rushgreen epaulettes and
a leadown here and there of royal swansruff: a brace of
gaspers stuck in her hayrope garters: her civvy codroy coat
with alpheubett buttons was boundaried round with a twobar
tunnel belt: a fourpenny bit in each pocketside weighed her
safe from the blowaway windrush; she had a clothespeg tight
astride on her joki's nose and she kep on grinding a
sommething quaint in her fiumy mouth and the rrreke of the
fluve of the tail of the gawan of her snuffdrab siouler's skirt
trailed ffiffty odd Irish miles behind her lungarhodes.

Hellsbells, I'm sorry I missed her! Sweet gumptyum and
nobody fainted! But in whelk of her mouths? Was her naze
alight? Everyone that saw her said the dowce little delia
looked a bit queer. Lotsy trotsy, mind the poddle! Missus, be
good and don't fol in the say! Fenny poor hex she must have
charred. Kickhams a frumpier ever you saw! Making mush
mullet's eyes at her boys dobelon. And they crowned her their
chariton queen, all the maids. Of the may? You don't say! Well
for her she couldn't see herself. I recknitz wharfore the darling
murrayed her mirror. She did? Mersey me! There was a koros
of drouthdropping surfacemen, boomslanging and plugchew-
ing, fruiteyeing and flowerfeeding, in contemplation of the
fluctuation and the undification of her filimentation, lolling
and leasing on North Lazers' Waal all eelfare week by the
Jukar Yoick's and as soon as they saw her meander by that
marritime way in her grasswinter's weeds and twigged who
was under her archdeaconess bonnet, Avondale's fish and
Clarence's poison, sedges an to aneber, Wit-upon-Crutches to
Master Bates: *Between our two southsates and the granite
they're warming, or her face has been lifted or Alp has doped!*

But what was the game in her mixed baggyrhatty? Just the
tembo in her tumbo or pilipili from her pepperpot? Saas and
taas and specis bizaas. And where in thunder did she plunder?
Fore the battle or efter the ball? I want to get it frisk from the
soorce. I aubette my bearb it's worth while poaching on! Shake
it up, do, do! That's a good old son of a ditch! I promise I'll

make it worth your while. And I don't mean maybe. Nor yet with a goodfor. Spey me pruth and I'll tale you true.

Well, arundgirond in a waveney lyne aringarouma she pattered and swung and sidled, dribbling her boulder through narrowa mosses, the diliskydrear on our drier side and the vilde vetchvine agin us, curara here, careero there, not knowing which medway or weser to strike it, edereider, making chattahoochee all to her ain chichiu, like Santa Claus at the cree of the pale and puny, nistling to hear for their tiny hearties, her arms encircling Isolabella, then running with reconciled Romas and Reims, on like a lech to be off like a dart, then bathing Dirty Hans' spatters with spittle, with a Christmas box apiece for aisch and iveryone of her childer, the birthday gifts they dreamt they gabe her, the spoiled she fleetly laid at our door! On the matt, by the pourch and inunder the cellar. The rivulets ran aflod to see, the glashaboys, the pollynooties. Out of the paunschaup on to the pyre. And they all about her, juvenile leads and ingenuinas, from the slime of their slums and artesaned wellings, rickets and riots, like the Smyly boys at their vicereine's levee. Vivi vienne, little Annchen! Vielo Anna, high life! Sing us a sula, O, susuria! Ausone sidulcis! Hasn't she tambre! Chipping her and raising a bit of a chir or a jary every dive she'd neb in her culdee sacco of wabbash she raabed and reach out her maundy meerschaundize, poor souvenir as per ricorder and all for sore aringarung, stinkers and heelers, laggards and primelads, her furzeborn sons and dribblederry daughters, a thousand and one of them, and wickerpotluck for each of them. For evil and ever. And kiks the buch. A tinker's bann and a barrow to boil his billy for Gipsy Lee; a cartridge of cockaleekie soup for Chummy the Guardsman; for sulky Pender's acid nephew deltoïd drops, curiously strong; a cough and a rattle and wildrose cheeks for poor Piccolina Petite MacFarlane; a jigsaw puzzle of needles and pins and blankets and shins between them for Isabel, Jezebel and Llewelyn Mmarriage; a brazen nose and pigiron mittens for Johnny Walker Beg; a papar flag of the saints and stripes for Kevineen O'Dea;

a puffpuff for Pudge Craig and a nightmarching hare for
Techertim Tombigby; waterleg and gumboots each for Bully
Hayes and Hurricane Hartigan; a prodigal heart and fatted
calves for Buck Jones, the pride of Clonliffe; a loaf of bread and
a father's early aim for Val from Skibereen; a jauntingcar for
Larry Doolin, the Ballyclee jackeen; a seasick trip on a
government ship for Teague O'Flanagan; a louse and trap for
Jerry Coyle; slushmincepies for Andy Mackenzie; a hairclip
and clackdish for Penceless Peter; that twelve sounds look for
G. V. Brooke; a drowned doll, to face downwards for modest
Sister Anne Mortimer; altar falls for Blanchisse's bed;
Wildairs' breechettes for Magpeg Woppington; to Sue Dot a
big eye; to Sam Dash a false step; snakes in clover, picked and
scotched, and a vaticanned viper catcher's visa for Patsy
Presbys; a reiz every morning for Standfast Dick and a drop
every minute for Stumblestone Davy; scruboak beads for
beatified Biddy; two appletweed stools for Eva Mobbely; for
Saara Philpot a jordan vale tearorne; a pretty box of Pettyfib's
Powder for Eileen Aruna to whiten her teeth and outflash
Helen Arhone; a whippingtop for Eddy Lawless; for Kitty
Coleraine of Butterman's Lane a penny wise for her foolish
pitcher; a putty shovel for Terry the Puckaun; an apotamus
mask for Promoter Dunne; a niester egg with a twicedated
shell and a dynamight right for Pavl the Curate; a collera
morbous for Mann in the Cloack; a starr and girton for Draper
and Deane; for Will-of-the-Wisp and Barny-the-Bark two
mangolds noble to sweeden their bitters; for Oliver Bound a
way in his frey; for Seumas, thought little, a crown he feels big;
a tibertine's pile with a Congoswood cross on the back for
Sunny Twimjim; a praises be and spare me days for Brian the
Bravo; penteplenty of pity with lubilashings of lust for Olona
Lena Magdalena; for Camilla, Dromilla, Ludmilla, Mamilla, a
bucket, a packet, a book and a pillow; for Nancy Shannon a
Tuami brooch; for Dora Riparia Hopeandwater a cooling
douche and a warmingpan; a pair of Blarney braggs for Wally
Meagher; a hairpin slatepencil for Elsie Oram to scratch her
toby, doing her best with her volgar fractions; an old age

pension for Betty Bellezza; a bag of the blues for Funny Fitz;
a *Missa pro Messa* for Taff de Taff; Jill, the spoon of a girl, for
Jack, the broth of a boy; a Rogerson Crusoe's Friday fast for
Caducus Angelus Rubiconstein; three hundred and sixtysix
poplin tyne for revery warp in the weaver's woof for Victor
Hugonot; a stiff steaded rake and good varians muck for Kate
the Cleaner; a hole in the ballad for Hosty; two dozen of
cradles for J.F.X.P. Coppinger; tenpounten on the pop for the
daulphins born with five spoiled squibs for Infanta; a letter to
last a lifetime for Maggi beyond by the ashpit; the heftiest
frozenmeat woman from Lusk to Livienbad for Felim the
Ferry; spas and speranza and symposium's syrup for decayed
and blind and gouty Gough; a change of naves and joys of ills
for Armoricus Tristram Amoor Saint Lawrence; a guillotine
shirt for Reuben Redbreast and hempen suspendeats for
Brennan on the Moor; an oakanknee for Conditor Sawyer and
musquodoboits for Great Tropical Scott; a C_3 peduncle for
Karmalite Kane; a sunless map of the month, including the
sword and stamps, for Shemus O'Shaun the Post; a jackal with
hide for Browne but Nolan; a stonecold shoulder for Donn Joe
Vance; all lock and no stable for Honorbright Merreytrickx; a
big drum for Billy Dunboyne; a guilty goldeny bellows, below
me blow me, for Ida Ida and a hushaby rocker, Elletrouvetout,
for Who-is-silvier – Where-is-he?; whatever you like to swilly
to swash, Yuinness or Yennessy, Laagen or Niger, for Festus
King and Roaring Peter and Frisky Shorty and Treacle Tom
and O. B. Behan and Sully the Thug and Master Magrath and
Peter Cloran and O'Delawarr Rossa and Nerone MacPacem
and whoever you chance to meet knocking around; and a pig's
bladder balloon for Selina Susquehanna Stakelum. But what
did she give to Pruda Ward and Katty Kanel and Peggy Quilty
and Briery Brosna and Teasy Kieran and Ena Lappin and
Muriel Maassy and Zusan Camac and Melissa Bradogue and
Flora Ferns and Fauna Fox-Goodman and Grettna Greaney
and Penelope Inglesante and Lezba Licking like Leytha Liane
and Roxana Rohan with Simpatica Sohan and Una Bina
Laterza and Trina La Mesme and Philomena O'Farrell and

Irmak Elly and Josephine Foyle and Snakeshead Lily and
Fountainoy Laura and Marie Xavier Agnes Daisy Frances de
Sales Macleay? She gave them ilcka madre's daughter a
moonflower and a bloodvein; but the grapes that ripe before
reason to them that devide the vinedress. So on Izzy, her
shamemaid, love shone befond her tears as from Shem, her
penmight, life past befoul his prime.

My colonial, wardha bagful! A bakereen's dusind with tithe
tillies to boot. That's what you may call a tale of a tub! And
Hibernonian market! All that and more under one crinoline
envelope if you dare to break the porkbarrel seal. No wonder
they'd run from her pison plague. Throw us your hudson soap
for the honour of Clane! The wee taste the water left. I'll raft
it back, first thing in the marne. Merced mulde! Ay, and don't
forget the reckitts I lohaned you. You've all the swirls your
side of the current. Well, am I to blame for that if I have? Who
said you're to blame for that if you have? You're a bit on the
sharp side. I'm on the wide. Only snuffers' cornets drifts my
way that the cracka dvine chucks out of his cassock, with her
estheryear's marsh narcissus to make him recant his vanitty
fair. Foul strips of his chinook's bible I do be reading, dodwell
disgustered but chickled with chuckles at the tittles is drawn
on the tattlepage. *Senior ga dito: Faciasi Omo! E omo fu fò.*
Ho! Ho! *Senior ga dito: Faciasi Hidamo! Hidamo se ga facessà.*
Ha! Ha! And *Die Windermere Dichter* and Lefanu (Sheri-
dan's) old *House by the Coachyard* and Mill (J.) *On Woman*
with *Ditto on the Floss*. Ja, a swamp for Altmuehler and a
stone for his flossies! I know how racy they move his wheel.
My hands are blawcauld between isker and suda like that piece
of pattern chayney there, lying below. Or where is it? Lying
beside the sedge I saw it. Hoangho, my sorrow, I've lost it!
Aimihi! With that turbary water who could see? So near and
yet so far! But O, gihon! I lovat a gabber. I could listen to maure
and moravar again. Regn onder river. Flies do your float.
Thick is the life for mere.

Well, you know or don't you kennet or haven't I told you
every telling has a taling and that's the he and the she of it.

Look, look, the dusk is growing! My branches lofty are taking root. And my cold cher's gone ashley. Fieluhr? Filou! What age is at? It saon is late. 'Tis endless now senne eye or erewone last saw Waterhouse's clogh. They took it asunder, I hurd thum sigh. When will they reassemble it? O, my back, my back, my bach! I'd want to go to Aches-les-Pains. Pingpong! There's the Belle for Sexaloitez! And Concepta de Send-us-pray! Pang! Wring out the clothes! Wring in the dew! Godavari, vert the showers! And grant thaya grace! Aman. Will we spread them here now? Ay, we will. Flip! Spread on your bank and I'll spread mine on mine. Flep! It's what I'm doing. Spread! It's churning chill. Der went is rising. I'll lay a few stones on the hostel sheets. A man and his bride embraced between them. Else I'd have sprinkled and folded them only. And I'll tie my butcher's apron here. It's suety yet. The strollers will pass it by. Six shifts, ten kerchiefs, nine to hold to the fire and this for the code, the convent napkins, twelve, one baby's shawl. Good mother Jossiph knows, she said. Whose head? Mutter snores? Deataceas! Wharnow are alle her childer, say? In kingdome gone or power to come or gloria be to them farther? Allalivial, allalluvial! Some here, more no more, more again lost alla stranger. I've heard tell that same brooch of the Shannons was married into a family in Spain. And all the Dunders de Dunnes in Markland's Vineland beyond Brendan's herring pool takes number nine in yang-see's hats. And one of Biddy's beads went bobbing till she rounded up lost histereve with a marigold and a cobbler's candle in a side strain of a main drain of a manzinahurries off Bachelor's Walk. But all that's left to the last of the Meaghers in the loup of the years prefixed and between is one kneebuckle and two hooks in the front. Do you tell me that now? I do in troth. Orara por Orbe and poor Las Animas! Ussa, Ulla, we're umbas all! Mezha, didn't you hear it a deluge of times, ufer and ufer, respund to spond? You deed, you deed! I need, I need! It's that irrawaddyng I've stoke in my aars. It all but husheth the lethest zswound. Oronoko! What's your trouble? Is that the great Finnleader himself in his joakimono

on his statue riding the high horse there forehengist? Father
of Otters, it is himself! Yonne there! Isset that? On Fallareen
Common? You're thinking of Astley's Amphitheayter where
the bobby restrained you making sugarstuck pouts to the
ghostwhite horse of the Peppers. Throw the cobwebs from
your eyes, woman, and spread your washing proper! It's well
I know your sort of slop. Flap! Ireland sober is Ireland stiff.
Lord help you, Maria, full of grease, the load is with me! Your
prayers. I sonht zo! Madammangut! Were you lifting your
elbow, tell us, glazy cheeks, on Conway's Carrigacurra
canteen? Was I what, hobbledyhips? Flop! Your rere gait's
creakorheuman bitts your butts disagrees. Amn't I up since
the damp dawn, marthared mary allacook, with Corrigan's
pulse and varicoarse veins, my pramaxle smashed, Alice Jane
in decline and my oneeyed mongrel twice run over, soaking
and bleaching boiler rags, and sweating cold, a widow like me,
for to deck my tennis champion son, the laundryman with the
lavandier flannels? You won your limpopo limp from the
husky hussars when Collars and Cuffs was heir to the town
and your slur gave the stink to Carlow. Holy Scamander, I sar
it again! Near the golden falls. Icis on us! Seints of light!
Zezere! Subdue your noise, you hamble creature! What is it
but a blackburry growth or the dwyergray ass them four old
codgers owns. Are you meanam Tarpey and Lyons and
Gregory? I meyne now, thank all, the four of them, and the
roar of them, that draves that stray in the mist and old Johnny
MacDougal along with them. Is that the Poolbeg flasher
beyant, pharphar, or a fireboat coasting nyar the Kishtna or a
glow I behold within a hedge or my Garry come back from the
Indes? Wait till the honeying of the lune, love! Die eve, little
eve, die! We see that wonder in your eye. We'll meet again,
we'll part once more. The spot I'll seek if the hour you'll find.
My chart shines high where the blue milk's upset. Forgiveme-
quick, I'm going! Bubye! And you, pluck your watch, forgetme-
not. Your evenlode. So save to jurna's end! My sights are
swimming thicker on me by the shadows to this place. I sow

home slowly now by own way, moyvalley way. Towy I too, rathmine.

Ah, but she was the queer old skeowsha anyhow, Anna Livia, trinkettoes! And sure he was the quare old buntz too, Dear Dirty Dumpling, foostherfather of fingalls and dotthergills. Gammer and gaffer we're all their gangsters. Hadn't he seven dams to wive him? And every dam had her seven crutches. And every crutch had its seven hues. And each hue had a differing cry. Sudds for me and supper for you and the doctor's bill for Joe John. Befor! Bifur! He married his markets, cheap by foul, I know, like any Etrurian Catholic Heathen, in their pinky limony creamy birnies and their turkiss indienne mauves. But at milkidmass who was the spouse? Then all that was was fair. Tys Elvenland! Teems of times and happy returns. The seim anew. Ordovico or viricordo. Anna was, Livia is, Plurabelle's to be. Northmen's thing made southfolk's place but howmulty plurators made eachone in person? Latin me that, my trinity scholard, out of eure sanscreed into oure eryan! *Hircus Civis Eblanensis!* He had buckgoat paps on him, soft ones for orphans. Ho, Lord! Twins of his bosom. Lord save us! And ho! Hey? What all men. Hot? His tittering daughters of. Whawk?

Can't hear with the waters of. The chittering waters of. Flittering bats, fieldmice bawk talk. Ho! Are you not gone ahome? What Thom Malone? Can't hear with bawk of bats, all thim liffeying waters of. Ho, talk save us! My foos won't moos. I feel as old as yonder elm. A tale told of Shaun or Shem? All Livia's daughtersons. Dark hawks hear us. Night! Night! My ho head halls. I feel as heavy as yonder stone. Tell me of John or Shaun? Who were Shem and Shaun the living sons or daughters of? Night now! Tell me, tell me, tell me, elm! Night night! Telmetale of stem or stone. Beside the rivering waters of, hitherandthithering waters of. Night!

Tristram's triangle

- Three quarks for Muster Mark!
Sure he hasn't got much of a bark
And sure any he has it's all beside the mark.
But O, Wreneagle Almighty, wouldn't un be a sky of a lark
To see that old buzzard whooping about for uns shirt in the
dark
And he hunting round for uns speckled trousers around by
Palmerstown Park?
Hohohoho, moulty Mark!
You're the rummest old rooster ever flopped out of a Noah's
ark
And you think you're cock of the wark.
Fowls, up! Tristy's the spry young spark
That'll tread her and wed her and bed her and red her
Without ever winking the tail of a feather
And that's how that chap's going to make his money and
mark!

Overhoved, shrillgleescreaming. That song sang seaswans.
The winging ones. Seahawk, seagull, curlew and plover,
kestrel and capercallzie. All the birds of the sea they trolled out
rightbold when they smacked the big kuss of Trustan with
Usolde.

The old men appeal to the woman

Hear, O hear, Iseult la belle! Tristan, sad hero, hear! The
Lambeg drum, the Lombog reed, the Lumbag fiferer,
the Limibig brazenaze.

Anno Domini nostri sancti Jesu Christi
Nine hundred and ninetynine million pound sterling in the
blueblack bowels of the bank of Ulster.

*Braw bawbees and good gold pounds, galore, my girleen, a
    Sunday'll prank thee finely.*
*And no damn loutll come courting thee or by the mother of the
    Holy Ghost there'll be murder!*

*O, come all ye sweet nymphs of Dingle beach to cheer
    Brinabride queen from Sybil surfriding*
*In her curragh of shells of daughter of pearl and her
    silverymonnblue mantle round her.*
*Crown of the waters, brine on her brow, she'll dance them a jig
    and jilt them fairly.*
*Yerra, why would she bide with Sig Sloomysides or the grogram
    grey barnacle gander?*

*You won't need be lonesome, Lizzy my love, when your beau
    gets his glut of cold meat and hot soldiering*
*Nor wake in winter, window machree, but snore sung in my
    old Balbriggan surtout.*
*Wisha, won't you agree now to take me from the middle, say,
    of next week on, for the balance of my days, for nothing
    (what?) as your own nursetender?*
*A power of highsteppers died game right enough – but who,
    acushla, 'll beg coppers for you?*

I tossed that one long before anyone.
*It was of a wet good Friday too she was ironing and, as I'm given
    now to understand, she was always mad gone on me.*
*Grand goosegreasing we had entirely with an allnight eiderdown
    bed picnic to follow.*
*By the cross of Cong, says she, rising up Saturday in the twilight
    from under me, Mick, Nick the Maggot or whatever your
    name is, you're the mose likable lad that's come my ways
    yet from the barony of Bohermore.*

Mattheehew, Markeehew, Lukeehew, Johnheehewwheehew!
Haw!
And still a light moves long the river. And stiller the mermen
    ply their keg.

Its pith is full. The way is free. Their lot is cast.
So, to john for a john, johnajeams, led it be!

Shaun's song of the Ondt
and the Gracehoper

Quoniam, I am as plain as portable enveloped, inhow-
much, you will now parably receive, care of one of
Mooseyeare Goonness's registered andouterthus barrels.
Quick take um whiffat andrainit. Now!

– So vi et! we responded. Song! Shaun, song! Have mood!
Hold forth!

– I apologuise, Shaun began, but I would rather spinooze
you one from the grimm gests of Jacko and Esaup, fable one,
feeble too. Let us here consider the casus, my dear little cousis
(husstenhasstencaffincoffintussemtossemdamandamnacosa-
ghcusaghhobixhatouxpeswchbechoscashlcarcarcaract) of the
Ondt and the Gracehoper.

The Gracehoper was always jigging ajog, hoppy on akkant
of his joyicity, (he had a partner pair of findlestilts to supplant
him), or, if not, he was always making ungraceful overtures to
Floh and Luse and Bienie and Vespatilla to play pupa-pupa
and pulicy-pulicy and langtennas and pushpygyddyum and to
commence insects with him, there mouthparts to his orefice
and his gambills to there airy processes, even if only in chaste,
ameng the everlistings, behold a waspering pot. He would of
curse melissciously, by his fore feelhers, flexors, contractors,
depressors and extensors, lamely, harry me, marry me, bury
me, bind me, till she was puce for shame and allso fourmish
her in Spinner's housery at the earthsbest schoppinhour so
summery as his cottage, which was cald fourmillierly Ting-
somingenting, groped up. Or, if he was always striking up
funny funereels with Besterfarther Zeuts, the Aged One, with
all his wigeared corollas, albedinous and oldbuoyant, inscythe

his elytrical wormcasket and Dehlia and Peonia, his druping
nympths, bewheedling him, compound eyes on hornitose-
head, and Auld Letty Plussiboots to scratch his cacumen and
cackle his tramsitus, diva deborah (seven bolls of sapo, a lick
of lime, two spurts of fussfor, threefurts of sulph, a shake
o'shouker, doze grains of migniss and a mesfull of midcap
pitchies. The whool of the whaal in the wheel of the whorl of
the Boubou from Bourneum has thus come to taon!), and with
tambarins and cantoridettes soturning around his eggshill
rockcoach their dance McCaper in retrophoebia, beck from
bulk, like fantastic disossed and jenny aprils, to the ra, the ra,
the ra, the ra, langsome heels and langsome toesis, attended to
by a mutter and doffer duffmatt baxingmotch and a myrmid-
ins of pszozlers pszinging *Satyr's Caudledayed Nice* and
Hombly, Dombly Sod We Awhile but *Ho, Time Timeagen,
Wake!* For if sciencium (what's what) can mute uns nought, 'a
thought, abought the Great Sommboddy within the Omni-
boss, perhops an artsaccord (hoot's hoot) might sing ums
tumtim abutt the Little Newbuddies that ring his panch. A
high old tide for the barheated publics and the whole day as
gratiis! Fudder and lighting for ally looty, any filly in a fog, for
O'Cronione lags acrumbling in his sands but his sunsunsuns
still tumble on. Erething above ground, as his Book of
Breathings bed him, so as everwhy, sham or shunner,
zeemliangly to kick time.

Grouscious me and scarab my sahul! What a bagateller it is!
Libelulous! Inzanzarity! Pou! Pschla! Ptuh! What a zeit for the
goths! vented the Ondt, who, not being a sommerfool, was
thothfolly making chilly spaces at hisphex affront of the
icinglass of his windhame, which was cold antitopically
Nixnixundnix. We shall not come to party at that lopp's, he
decided possibly, for he is not on our social list. Nor to Ba's
berial nether, thon sloghard, this oldeborre's yaar ablong as
there's a khul on a khat. Nefersenless, when he had safely
looked up his ovipository, he loftet hails and prayed: May he
me no voida water! Seekit Hatup! May no he me tile pig shed
on! Suckit Hotup! As broad as Beppy's realm shall flourish my

reign shall flourish! As high as Heppy's hevn shall flurrish my haine shall hurrish! Shall grow, shall flourish! Shall hurrish! Hummum.

The Ondt was a weltall fellow, raumybult and abelboobied, bynear saw altitudinous wee a schelling in kopfers. He was sair sair sullemn and chairmanlooking when he was not making spaces in his psyche, but, laus! when he wore making spaces on his ikey, he ware mouche mothst secred and muravyingly wisechairmanlooking. Now whim the sillybilly of a Gracehoper had jingled through a jungle of love and debts and jangled through a jumble of life in doubts afterworse, wetting with the bimblebeaks, drikking with nautonects, bilking with durrydunglecks and horing after ladybirdies (*ichnehmon diagelegenaitoikon*) he fell joust as sieck as a sexton and tantoo pooveroo quant a churchprince, and wheer the midges to wend hemsylph or vosch to sirch for grub for his corapusse or to find a hospes, alick, he wist gnit! Bruko dryl fuko spint! Sultamont osa bare! And volomundo osi videvide! Nichtsnichtsundnichts! Not one pickopeck of muscow-money to bag a tittlebits of beebread! Iomio! Iomio! Crick's corbicule, which a plight! O moy Bog, he contrited with melanctholy. Meblizzered, him sluggered! I am heartily hungry!

He had eaten all the whilepaper, swallowed the lustres, devoured forty flights of styearcases, chewed up all the mensas and seccles, ronged the records, made mundballs of the ephemerids and vorasioused most glutinously with the very timeplace in the ternitary – not too dusty a cicada of neutriment for a chittinous chip so mitey. But when Chrysal-mas was on the bare branches, off he went from Tingsoming-enting. He took a round stroll and he took a stroll round and he took a round strollagain till the grillies in his head and the leivnits in his hair made him thought he had the Tossmania. Had he twicycled the sees of the deed and trestraversed their revermer? Was he come to hevre with his engiles or gone to hull with the poop? The June snows was flocking in thuckflues on the hegelstomes, millipeeds of it and myriopoods, and a lugly whizzling tournedos, the Boraborayellers, blohablasting tegolhuts up to tetties and ruching sleets off the coppeehouses, playing ragnowrock rignewreck, with an irritant, penetrant, siphonopterous spuk. Grausssssss! Opr! Grausssssss! Opr!

The Gracehoper who, though blind as batflea, yet knew, not a leetle beetle, his good smetterling of entymology asped nissunitimost lous nor liceens but promptly tossed himself in the vico, phthin and phthir, on top of his buzzer, tezzily wondering wheer would his aluck alight or boss of both appease and the next time he makes the aquinatance of the Ondt after this they have met themselves, these mouschical umsummables, it shall be motylucky if he will beheld not a world of differents. Behailed His Gross the Ondt, prostrandvorous upon his dhrone, in his Papylonian babooshkees, smolking a spatial brunt of Hosana cigals, with unshrinkables farfalling from his unthinkables, swarming of himself in his sunnyroom, sated before his comfortumble phullupsuppy of a plate o'monkynous and a confucion of minthe (for he was a conformed aceticist and aristotaller), as appi as a oneysucker or a baskerboy on the Libido, with Floh biting his leg thigh and Luse lugging his luff leg and Bieni bussing him under his bonnet and Vespatilla blowing cosy fond tutties up the allabroad length of the large of his smalls. As entomate as intimate could pinchably be. Emmet and demmet and be jiltses crazed and be jadeses whipt! schneezed the Gracehoper, aguepe with ptchjelasys and at his wittol's indts, what have eyeforsight!

The Ondt, that true and perfect host, a spiter aspinne, was making the greatest spass a body could with his queens laceswinging for he was spizzing all over him like thingsumanything in formicolation, boundlessly blissfilled in an allallahbath of houris. He was ameising himself hugely at crabround and marypose, chasing Floh out of charity and tickling Luse, I hope too, and tackling Bienie, faith, as well, and jucking Vespatilla jukely by the chimiche. Never did Dorsan from Dunshanagan dance it with more devilry! The veripa-

tetic imago of the impossible Gracehoper on his odderkop in
the myre, after his thrice ephemeral journeeys, sans mantis
ne shooshooe, featherweighed animule, actually and pre-
sumptuably sinctifying chronic's despair, was sufficiently and
probably coocoo much for his chorus of gravitates. Let him be
Artalone the Weeps with his parisites peeling off him I'll be
Highfee the Crackasider. Flunkey Footle furloughed foul,
writing off his phoney, but Conte Carme makes the melody
that mints the money. *Ad majorem l.s.d.! Divi gloriam.* A
darkener of the threshold. Haru? Orimis, capsizer of his
antboat, sekketh rede from Evil-it-is, lord of loaves in
Amongded. Be it! So be it! Thou-who-thou-art, the fleet-as-
spindhrift, impfang thee of mine wideheight. Haru!

The thing pleased him andt, and andt,

He larved ond he larved on he merd such a nauses
The Gracehoper feared he would mixplace his fauces.
I forgive you, grondt Ondt, said the Gracehoper, weeping,
For their sukes of the sakes you are safe in whose keeping.
Teach Floh and Luse polkas, show Bienie where's sweet
And be sure Vespatilla fines fat ones to heat.
As I once played the piper I must now pay the count
So saida to Moyhammlet and marhaba to your Mount!
Let who likes lump above so what flies be a full 'un;
I could not feel moregruggy if this was prompollen.
I pick up your reproof, the horsegift of a friend,
For the prize of your save is the price of my spend.
Can castwhores pulladeftkiss if oldpollocks forsake 'em
Or Culex feel etchy if Pulex don't wake him?
A locus to loue, a term it t'embarass,
These twain are the twins that tick Homo Vularis.
Has Aquileone nort winged to go syf
Since the Gwyfyn we were in his farrest drewbryf
And that Accident Man not beseeked where his story ends
Since longsephyring sighs sought heartseast for their orience?
We are Wastenot with Want, precondamned, two and true,
Till Nolans go volants and Bruneyes come blue.

Ere those gidflirts now gadding you quit your mocks for my
*   gropes*
An extense must impull, an elapse must elopes,
Of my tectucs takestock, tinktact, and ail's weal;
As I view by your farlook hale yourself to my heal.
Partiprise my thinwhins whiles my blink points unbroken on
Your whole's whercabroads with Tout's trightyright token on.
My in risible universe youdly haud find
Sulch oxtrabeeforeness meat soveal behind.
Your feats end enormous, your volumes immense,
(May the Graces I hoped for sing your Ondtship song sense!),
Your genus its worldwide, your spacest sublime!
But, Holy Saltmartin, why can't you beat time?

In the name of the former and of the latter and of their holocaust. Allmen.

In my end is my beginning

For I feel I could near to faint away. Into the deeps. Annamores leep. Let me lean, just a lea, if you le, bowldstrong big-tider. Allgearls is wea. At times. So. While you're adamant evar. Wrhps, that wind as if out of norewere! As on the night of the Apophanypes. Jumpst shootst throbbst into me mouth like a bogue and arrohs! Ludegude of the Lashlanns, how he whips me cheeks! Sea, sea! Here, weir, reach, island, bridge. Where you meet I. The day. Remember! Why there that moment and us two only? I was but teen, a tiler's dot. The swankysuits was boosting always, sure him, he was like to me fad. But the swaggerest swell off Shackvulle Strutt. And the fiercest freaky ever followed a pining child round the sluppery table with a forkful of fat. But a king of whistlers. Scieoula! When he'd prop me atlas against his goose and light our two candles for our singers duohs on the sewingmachine. I'm sure he squirted juice in his eyes to make

them flash for flightening me. Still and all he was awful fond
to me. Who'll search for *Find Me Colours* now on the hilly-
droops of Vikloefells? But I read in Tobecontinued's tale that
while blubles blows there'll still be sealskers. There'll be
others but non so for me. Yed he never knew we seen us
before. Night after night. So that I longed to go to. And still
with all. One time you'd stand fornenst me, fairly laughing, in
your bark and tan billows of branches for to fan me coolly.
And I'd lie as quiet as a moss. And one time you'd rush upon
me, darkly roaring, like a great black shadow with a sheeny
stare to perce me rawly. And I'd frozen up and pray for thawe.
Three times in all. I was the pet of everyone then. A
princeable girl. And you were the pantymammy's Vulking
Corsergoth. The invision of Indelond. And, by Thorror, you
looked it! My lips went livid for from the joy of fear. Like
almost now. How? How you said how you'd give me the keys
of me heart. And we'd be married till delth to uspart. And
though dev do espart. O mine! Only, no, now it's me who's got
to give. As duv herself div. Inn this linn. And can it be it's
nnow fforvell? Illas! I wisht I had better glances to peer to you
through this baylight's growing. But you're changing, acool-
sha, you're changing from me, I can feel. Or is it me is? I'm
getting mixed. Brightening up and tightening down. Yes,
you're changing, sonhusband, and you're turning, I can feel
you, for a daughterwife from the hills again. Imlamaya. And
she is coming. Swimming in my hindmoist. Diveltaking on
me tail. Just a whisk brisk sly spry spink spank sprint of a
thing theresomere, saultering. Saltarella come to her own. I
pity your oldself I was used to. Now a younger's there. Try not
to part! Be happy, dear ones! May I be wrong! For she'll be
sweet for you as I was sweet when I came down out of me
mother. My great blue bedroom, the air so quiet, scarce a
cloud. In peace and silence. I could have stayed up there for
always only. It's something fails us. First we feel. Then we fall.
And let her rain now if she likes. Gently or strongly as she
likes. Anyway let her rain for my time is come. I done me best
when I was let. Thinking always if I go all goes. A hundred

cares, a tithe of troubles and is there one who understands
me? One in a thousand of years of the nights? All me life I
have been lived among them but now they are becoming
lothed to me. And I am lothing their little warm tricks. And
lothing their mean cosy turns. And all the greedy gushes out
through their small souls. And all the lazy leaks down over
their brash bodies. How small it's all! And me letting on to
meself always. And lilting on all the time. I thought you were
all glittering with the noblest of carriage. You're only a
bumpkin. I thought you the great in all things, in guilt and in
glory. You're but a puny. Home! My people were not their
sort out beyond there so far as I can. For all the bold and bad
and bleary they are blamed, the seahags. No! Not for all our
wild dances in all their wild din. I can see meself among them,
allaniuvia pulchrabelled. How she was handsome, the wild
Amazia, when she would seize to my other breast! And what
is she weird, haughty Niluna, that she will snatch from my
ownest hair. For 'tis they are the stormies. Ho hang! Hang ho!
And the clash of our cries till we spring to be free. Auravoles,
they says, never heed of your name! But I'm loothing them
that's here and all I lothe. Loonely in me loneness. For all their
faults, I am passing out. O bitter ending! I'll slip away before
they're up. They'll never see. Nor know. Nor miss me. And
it's old and old it's sad and old it's sad and weary I go back to
you, my cold father, my cold mad father, my cold mad feary
father, till the near sight of the mere size of him, the moyles
and moyles of it, moananoaning, makes me seasilt saltsick and
I rush, my only, into your arms. I see them rising! Save me
from those therrble prongs! Two more. Onetwo moremens
more. So. Avelaval. My leaves have drifted from me. All. But
one clings still. I'll bear it on me. To remind me of. Lff! So soft
this morning, ours. Yes. Carry me along, taddy, like you done
through the toy fair! If I seen him bearing down on me now
under whitespread wings like he'd come from Arkangels, I
sink I'd die down over his feet, humbly dumbly, only to
washup. Yes, tid. There's where. First. We pass through grass
behush the bush to. Whish! A gull. Gulls. Far calls. Coming,

far! End here. Us then. Finn, again! Take. Bussoftlhee,
mememormee! Till thousandsthee. Lps. The keys to. Given!
A way a lone a last a loved a long the

riverrun, past Eve and Adam's, from swerve of shore to
bend of bay, brings us by a commodius vicus of recirculation
back to Howth Castle and Environs.

Sir Tristram, violer d'amores, fr'over the short sea, had
passencore rearrived from North Armorica on this side the
scraggy isthmus of Europe Minor to wielderfight his peniso-
late war: nor had topsawyer's rocks by the stream Oconee
exaggerated themselse to Laurens County's gorgios while they
went doublin their mumper all the time: nor avoice from afire
bellowsed mishe mishe to tauftauf thuartpeatrick: not yet,
though venissoon after, had a kidscad buttended a bland old
isaac: not yet, though all's fair in vanessy, were sosie sesthers
wroth with twone nathandjoe. Rot a peck of pa's malt had
Jhem or Shen brewed by arclight and rory end to the
regginbrow was to be seen ringsome on the aquaface.

The fall (bababadalgharaghtakamminarronnkonnbronn-
tonnerronntuonnthunntrovarrhounawnskawntoohoohoor-
denenthurnuk!) of a once wallstrait oldparr is retaled early in
bed and later on life down through all christian minstrelsy.
The great fall of the offwall entailed at such short notice the
pftjschute of Finnegan, erse solid man, that the humpty-
hillhead of humself prumptly sends an unquiring one well to
the west in quest of his tumptytumtoes: and their upturnpike-
pointandplace is at the knock out in the park where oranges
have been laid to rust upon the green since devlinsfirst loved
livvy.

What clashes here of wills gen wonts, oystrygods gaggin
fishygods! Brékkek Kékkek Kékkek Kekkék! Kóax Kóax
Kóax! Uálu Ualu Ualu! Quaouauh! Where the Baddelaries
partisans are still out to mathmaster Malachus Micgranes and
the Verdons catapelting the camibalistics out of the Whoyte-
boyce of Hoodie Head. Assiegates and boomeringstroms.
Sod's brood, be me fear! Sanglorians, save! Arms apeal with
larms, appalling. Killykillkilly: a toll, a toll. What chance

cuddleys, what cashels aired and ventilated! What bidimeto-
loves sinduced by what tegotetabsolvers! What true feeling
for their's hayair with what strawng voice of false jiccup! O
here here how both sprowled met the duskt the father of
fornicationists but, (O my shining stars and body!) how hath
fanespanned most high heaven the skysign of soft advertise-
ment! But waz iz? Iseut? Ere were sewers? The oaks of ald
now they lie in peat yet elms leap where askes lay. Phall if you
but will, rise you must: and none so soon either shall the
pharce for the nunce come to a setdown secular phoenish.

Bygmester Finnegan, of the Stuttering Hand, freemen's
maurer, lived in the broadest way immarginable in his rushlit
toofarback for messuages before joshuan judges had given us
numbers or Helviticus committed deuteronomy (one yeasty-
day he sternely struxk his tete in a tub for to watsch the future
of his fates but ere he swiftly stook it out again, by the might
of moses, the very water was eviparated and all the guenneses
had met their exodus so that ought to show you what a
pentschanjeuchy chap he was!) and during mighty odd years
this man of hod, cement and edifices in Toper's Thorp piled
buildung supra buildung pon the banks for the livers by the
Soangso. He addle liddle phifie Annie ugged the little
craythur. Wither hayre in honds tuck up your part inher.
Oftwhile balbulous, mithre ahead, with goodly trowel in grasp
and ivoroiled overalls which he habitacularly fondseed, like
Haroun Childeric Eggeberth he would caligulate by multipli-
cables the alltitude and malltitude until he seesaw by neatlight
of the liquor wheretwin 'twas born, his roundhead staple of
other days to rise in undress maisonry upstanded (joygran-
tit!), a waalworth of a skyerscape of most eyeful hoyth
entowerly, erigenating from next to nothing and celescalating
the himals and all, hierarchitectitiptitoploftical, with a burn-
ing bush abob off its baubletop and with larrons o'toolers
clittering up and tombles a'buckets clottering down.

Of the first was he to bare arms and a name: Wassaily
Booslaeugh of Riesengeborg. His crest of huroldry, in vert
with ancillars, troublant, argent, a hegoak, poursuivant,

horrid, horned. His scutschum fessed, with archers strung, helio, of the second. Hootch is for husbandman handling his hoe. Hohohoho, Mister Finn, you're going to be Mister Finnagain! Comeday morm and, O, you're vine! Sendday's eve and, ah, you're vinegar! Hahahaha, Mister Funn, you're going to be fined again!

AFTERWORD

Joyce's life

James Joyce, born in Dublin on 2 February 1882, was the second-born child, the eldest son of a family of thirteen children, of whom ten survived. His father, John Joyce, had inherited some property in Cork and became a Collector of Rates in Dublin; he was, however, incapable of living within his means, and when he was made redundant as a result of civic reorganisation he was left with a quarter of his former salary as pension – he had mortgaged all his properties and finally disposed of them by 1894. The family moved from Rathgar in Dublin to Bray, a seaside resort some thirteen miles south of Dublin, when James was five, and lived there for five years. After a year at Blackrock, on the sea coast five miles south of Dublin, increasing poverty forced Joyce's father to move the family into the city where rented accommodation succeeded rented accommodation as rents were dodged, often by midnight flitting.

There was enough money, however, for John Joyce to send his eldest son, at the age of six, to a well-known Jesuit boarding school, Clongowes Wood College in County Kildare. But in 1891 lack of money meant that the boy was withdrawn. He stayed at home for some time, then went to a Christian Brothers School for a few months before it was arranged that he should attend Belvedere College, a Jesuit day-school, without payment of fees. He left this school in the summer of 1898 and entered University College, Dublin, where he studied English, French and Italian until he took his BA in 1902. He then went to Paris with the idea of studying medicine there. He stayed till April 1903, writing poems and prose, beginning to formulate his aesthetic theories.

Joyce then returned to Dublin because his mother was fatally ill; she died in August 1903. He left the family home, staying, among other places, in the Martello tower (one of many built as coastal defences in the period of the Napoleonic War) which his friend Oliver St John Gogarty, then a medical student, rented at Sandycove, south of Dublin. Joyce met Nora Barnacle, a Galway girl who was working in Finn's Hotel in Dublin, and fell in love with her, their first evening walk taking place on 16 June 1904, the day on which the events in his novel *Ulysses* take place. In October he and Nora left Ireland, his plan being to make a living by teaching English on the Continent. They lived in Pola (now in Croatia) for some months, then moved in March 1905 to Trieste where Joyce taught in the Berlitz School. They lived there until June 1915, apart from spending seven months in Rome in 1906. Joyce made three trips back to Ireland. He stayed in Dublin and Galway, by himself, in 1909. He returned in 1910 and, with Nora, again visited Dublin and Galway in 1912. They had two children, a son Giorgio, born in 1905, and a daughter, Lucia, born in 1907.

Joyce's first book, the poems of *Chamber Music*, was published in 1907; it was followed by the short stories of *Dubliners* in 1914. Because of Italy's entry into the 1914–18 war the Joyces moved to Zurich in Switzerland where they stayed until 1919, when the family returned briefly to Trieste. While in Zurich Joyce published his novel *A Portrait of the Artist as a Young Man* in 1916, and his play *Exiles* in 1918.

In 1920 he decided to move to Paris; like his father he was improvident and extravagant, and, like him, he often drank heavily, but from 1917 on he was fortunate in receiving regular financial assistance from Harriet Shaw Weaver (who had published *A Portrait of the Artist* serially from 1914–15 in *The Egoist*, a review she and Dora Marsden nominally edited). Her support enabled Joyce to concentrate on writing *Ulysses*, on which he had been working since 1914. Episodes were published from March 1918 in the *Little Review*, and the complete book appeared, on Joyce's birthday, in Paris in 1922 and won him international repute from responsible critics. Publicly, however, *Ulysses* had a stormy reception. After it was published copies of the first English edition were burned by post office authorities in New York, while in England the book was banned for obscenity, the Customs in Folkestone seizing the second edition in 1923. Later editions appeared abroad, but it was not until 1933 that Judge Woolsey pronounced in the United States District Court that the book was not obscene. The first English edition appeared in 1936, the first unlimited edition in America and England in 1937.

In 1922 Joyce began work on *Finnegans Wake*, the first fragment of which, *Work in Progress*, appeared in *Transatlantic Review*, Paris, in 1924. He completed it in 1939 and it was published that year.

In the 1930s Joyce's eyesight gave him much trouble. His father died in 1931, and Joyce regretted he had not seen more of him. In 1931, too, Joyce and Nora visited London and were married there. From 1932 on (when she suffered her first breakdown from schizophrenia) Joyce was deeply anxious about his daughter's deteriorating mental condition. In the 1939–45 war the family moved to unoccupied France, and then got permission to return to Zurich in December 1940. After an operation for a duodenal ulcer, Joyce died there, on 13 January 1941. He was buried in Zurich, as was Nora, who died ten years later.

Joyce's writings in *Joycechoyce*

We have included all the poems in *Chamber Music*, a volume first published in 1907, many of the poems in which had been written before Joyce left Ireland in 1904. The title was owed to a woman who had relieved herself behind a screen, interrupting the poet's reading of the poems. They have been frequently set to music, as have the poems of Joyce's other volume of verse, *Pomes Penyeach*, published in 1937, all of which are included here. This book cost a shilling, so that we might have expected from its title a dozen poems, but Joyce followed an Irish custom in adding a 'tilly' (from Irish *tuilleadh*, an added measure), a thirteenth poem, the first poem in the book being titled 'Tilly'. He probably had in mind the custom of Dublin milkmen and milkwomen of pouring an extra amount of milk into the purchaser's receptacle from the small, usually pint-sized, tilly can that accompanied a larger can or churn. The composers who have set *Pomes Penyeach* to music include Georges Anthiel, Arnold Bax, Arthur Bliss (Joyce particularly liked his setting of 'Simples'), Herbert Havells, Herbert Hughes, John Ireland, E. J. Morran, C. W. Orr, Albert Roussel, Roger Sessions and Bernard Van Dieren.

'The Holy Office' (p. 42) is a poem Joyce wrote at the age of twenty-two (his earliest effort was 'Et Tu. Healy', written at the age of nine, which praised Parnell and attacked Timothy Healy, Parnell's chief enemy), a savaging of the 'mumming company' of the Celtic Twilight writers, for whom he, 'Unfellowed, friendless and alone', saw himself performing the office of purgation. It is a proclamation of his independence, for while they may spurn him from their door his soul 'shall spurn them evermore'. 'Gas from a Burner' (p. 44), a broadside published in 1912, provided an angry reaction to the behaviour of the Dublin printer who had broken up the type of *Dubliners* in disgust, while 'Ecce Puer' (p. 47), written in 1932, was prompted by the birth of Joyce's grandson Stephen and by the death of his father.

Three of the fifteen short stories of *Dubliners* first appeared in the *Irish Homestead*, edited by A. E. (George Russell), who had suggested that Joyce should write a story for the journal. The result was 'The Sisters', included in the issue of 13 August 1904, and followed in September by 'Eveline' and in December by 'After the Race'. The other stories were mainly written in 1905, 'The Dead' being added in 1907. Joyce sent the collection to the English publisher Grant Richards, who became nervous when the printers objected to some of its language. (He asked Joyce to amend a passage about Edward VII being kept out of the throne till he was grey by 'his old mother'. Joyce's response was to alter 'his old mother' to 'his bloody old bitch of a mother'). The newly established Dublin publishing firm of Maunsel and Co. then got as far as sending the book to a printer but, after some shilly-shallying, postponed publication in 1910, and the printer broke up the type in 1912. Joyce's letters revealed the anxiety and tension this situation created. Eventually, in 1914, Grant Richards did publish the book.

Stephen Hero, an autobiographical novel, was begun in February 1904. Joyce wrote several hundred pages of it in the following months. By 1906 he had completed half the book he planned; it ran to some 900 pages. He then stopped work, later categorising the novel as a 'schoolboy's production'. But though it lacks the architectonic control, the effective economy of its successor, *A Portrait of the Artist as a Young Man*, it is a novel rich in detail and background with many enlightening episodes and crucial conversations which occur in the life of Stephen Daedalus, a fictionalised picture of James Joyce as heroic martyr. Stephen, prophetic, ahead of his time, is condemned by the institutions which have shaped him; he finds them oppressive. The novel gives us in a relatively conventional format a direct and explicit narrative of Stephen's life at home, of his clashes with his orthodoxly religious mother, of his impulsive and frustrating relationship with Emma Cleary, of his intellectual development, and of his rebellion against the Catholic Church. Most of the novel was lost; the posthumous publication of 1944 begins in the middle of chapter XV, at p. 519.

Out of *Stephen Hero* grew *A Portrait of the Artist as a Young Man*, published in book form by Huebsch in New York in 1916. In this novel Stephen Dedalus (the alteration from the spelling Daedalus is significant; the novel is being distanced even from its symbolic reference to the myth of Daedalus, the Athenian craftsman who built the labyrinth at Crete, and, imprisoned in it, escaped with his son Icarus on wings made of wax and feathers) is given more universal treatment. He is an idealist cast not only in the mould of the artificer Daedalus but in that of St Stephen, the first Christian martyr, stoned to death for his boldness in proclaiming his views before the Sanhedrin. In this novel Stephen grows up from infancy to young manhood; indeed it is a novel about growing up, a kind of *Bildungsroman*, one in which the rebellious hero gains our sympathy for his struggle towards independence but is also shown ironically as having a considerable capacity for pretentiousness and posturing.

Joyce is developing new techniques in *A Portrait of the Artist as a Young Man*: he compresses and selects; he refrains from authorial comment; he gives us his hero's thoughts in appropriate styles to suit his different ages. There is great variety of presentation, the progress of the book carefully constructed by a shaping power, which concentrates on moments of crisis in Stephen's life in which he behaves with varying degrees of success or failure. The fourth of the novel's five chapters, for instance, provides the hero's rejections of the priesthood; his vision of the girls wading on the strand symbolises a new development in his life, another kind of vocation, the service of life and beauty. All these crises have their effect upon his development into the artist who rejects his church and country and goes out 'to encounter for the millionth time the reality of experience and to forge in the smithy of my soul the uncreated conscience of my race'. He has finally chosen the only arms he allows himself – 'silence, exile and cunning'.

Ulysses is a novel on a vast scale. It deals with events taking place during one day in Dublin, 16 June 1904. It has three main characters: Leopold Bloom, a Jewish advertisement agent, his wife Molly, and Stephen Dedalus, whom we know from *A Portrait of the Artist as a Young Man*. The plot follows the wanderings of Leopold and Stephen through Dublin and their eventual meeting: it is roughly parallel to the episodes of Homer's *Odyssey*, Bloom representing Odysseus, Stephen Telemachus, the son of Odysseus, and Molly Penelope his wife. There are differences: this is no heroic story in the epic style, it is a retelling of it in the form of a novel about twentieth-century bourgeois life. Odysseus, separated from his chaste wife Penelope, who rejects the advances of the suitors who surround her, spends ten years on his wanderings before he returns from Troy to Ithaca, kills the wooers and is reunited with Penelope and Telemachus, who has gone to search for news of him. Bloom's wanderings are in Dublin; he has to conduct his business affairs there; he lives there. His wife, no chaste Penelope, entertains her lover at home, while Stephen, like Telemachus, is in search of a father.

The novel is large in scope and long: it is aimed at achieving at least the dimensions of classical epic. It imposes structure upon its material by matching its events to those of the *Odyssey*; the pattern is more than a merely convenient ordering of structure, however, for it goes beyond Homer for its parallels, to Dante, to Shakespeare, to Milton … Dublin's life and locale are detailed, and this is done with impressive accuracy. Only recently, for instance, has a copy of the Dublin *Telegraph* for 16 June 1904 come to light (it has been reproduced as *The Ulysses Telegraph* (Split Pea Press, Edinburgh, 1990) and much of the material in it demonstrates the faithfulness of the detail in *Ulysses*. The characters' thoughts and actions are conveyed with skill. Here is the stream of consciousness, the interior monologue, carefully delineated for each of the main characters, but the lack of order of human thought and non-verbal thought, of sensation and response, has to be brought within an ordering, within an artistic vision of life. Thus Joyce divided the material of *Ulysses* into three books and eighteen episodes: these are not titled in the novel but the three books cover the Search, the Wanderings and the Homecoming, the first book having three episodes largely concentrated upon Stephen, the second having twelve largely centred upon Bloom, and the third having three in which Stephen and Bloom come together at Bloom's home. This third book echoes the Eumaeus episode in the *Odyssey* in its sixteenth episode, the meeting of Bloom and Stephen, where the one comments on social conditions and politics while the other displays his intellectual interests. In the seventeenth a series of questions and answers clears up many matters, apparently fusing the different natures of Bloom and Stephen, their pragmatism and idealism; and the eighteenth episode reveals the nature of Molly's mind, the prose unpunctuated, flowing onward in a great affirmation of life. Ultimately, *Ulysses* celebrates humanity.

We have included a few of Joyce's letters; they convey a good deal of his complex personality. His precision emerges in the details given to his brother Stanislaus (p. 196) of one's day's eating and drinking. His capacity for self-mockery is there in a limerick contained in a letter to Ezra Pound (p. 196) about his three-act play *Exiles*, a play about presumed betrayal and infidelity, set in Dublin in 1912 and published in 1918. It was probably founded upon Joyce's supposed friend Cosgrave telling him in 1909 that he had been meeting Nora secretly in 1904 when he had actually been rebuffed by her – many of Joyce's letters to Nora were agonised before another friend, Byrne, cleared up the matter; Joyce then wrote letters to her describing himself as unworthy of her. In other letters, notably to Harriet Shaw Weaver (p. 197), he indulged his wry sense of humour, setting out to be entertaining and succeeding. That humour erupted benignly in his two advertisements, for *Anna Livia Plurabelle* (p. 198) and *Haveth Childers Everywhere* (p. 199). The letter to James Stephens (p. 199) shows his technical capacity to translate poetry into several languages, while his ever-present penchant for parody emerges in a letter to his son Giorgio and his wife Helen (p. 201).

In *Finnegans Wake* Joyce allowed his erudition its head; his scope was vast, and so was his experimentation. In this book time, place, identity are fluid. It is a book about everybody and everything. Everywhere is Dublin; the book a blend of Irish balladry (the ballad about Tim Finnegan, a building worker, who falls from a ladder – he has drunk too much – and breaks his skull, ends with his wake turning into a waking-up of the corpse, revived by a noggin of whiskey thrown over him in a quarrel at the wake) and Italian philosophy (Joyce was interested in the theories of the Italian philosopher Giambattista Vico, who developed a cyclical theory of history, as well as those of Giordano Bruno, another Italian thinker who developed a theory of dualism, of opposites). This book is a series of repetitions; a book of dream life set in Dublin, time and creativity flowing through it in the Liffey's run to the sea in Dublin Bay. Joyce uses Tim Finnegan's story to convey human history, then, for his Finnegan is HCE, Humphrey Chimpden Earwicker, the keeper of a pub in Chapelizod, Dublin. His wife is ALP, Anna Livia Plurabelle. They have three children, Shem and Shaun and a daughter Isabel. The initials of the pub keeper can stand for Here Comes Everybody, Haveth Childers Everywhere, and Howth Castle and Envisions; those of his wife, the mother and housewife, can stand for the female river, the Liffey. Shem and Shaun are rivals, and Isabel, the beloved, is Isolde or Iseult (for Chapelizod is the Chapel of Isolde, whence Tristram fetched Iseult). The children contain all rivalry, all love; with their father and mother they are human history. No wonder the book's end is also its beginning.

Some suggestions for further reading

Some books which may prove helpful are Anthony Burgess, *Here Comes Everybody: An Introduction to James Joyce for the Ordinary Reader* (1965); Harry Blamires, *The Bloomsday Book: A Guide through Joyce's Ulysses* (1966); Matthew Hodgart, *James Joyce: A Student's Guide* (1978); Charles Peake, *James Joyce, the Citizen and the Artist* (1980); Patrick Parrinder, *James Joyce* (1984); and Harry Blamires, *Studying James Joyce* (1987). There is a short life by Peter Costello, *James Joyce* (1980), and a full-scale biography by Richard Ellmann, *James Joyce* (1966; rev. edn, 1982). Peter Costello has supplied new information and insights in *James Joyce: The Years of Growth* (1992). Joyce's letters have been published in three volumes, Vol. I edited by Stuart Gilbert (1957; rev. edn, 1966) and Vols II and III by Richard Ellmann (1966).